Keeping the Baby in Mind

Keeping the Baby in Mind builds on the expanding evidence pointing to the crucial importance of parents in facilitating their baby's development, and brings together expert contributors to examine a range of innovative psychological and psychotherapeutic interventions that are currently being used to support parents and their infants. It not only provides an overview of the many projects that are now available but also makes recommendations for future practice and the way in which children's services are organised.

The book brings together interventions and ways of working that can be used both universally to support parents during the transition to parenthood, and with high-risk groups of parents where for example there may be child protection concerns or parents experience severe mental health problems. Each chapter describes the evidence supporting the need for such interventions and the approach being developed, and concludes with a description of its evaluation.

Keeping the Baby in Mind marks a new and exciting phase in the development of interventions to support infant mental health and will be of interest across a wide range of disciplines from primary and community care to early years and Children's Centre settings.

Jane Barlow is Professor of Public Health in the Early Years at Warwick Medical School, University of Warwick.

P. O. Svanberg, OBE is a Consultant Clinical Psychologist, and was previously Project lead for the Sunderland Infant Programme. He is currently working in the FNP and CHPP Implementation, Department of Health.

Keeping the Baby in Mind

Infant Mental Health in Practice

Edited by Jane Barlow and P. O. Svanberg

Routledge
Taylor & Francis Group

LONDON AND NEW YORK

First published 2009 by Routledge
27 Church Road, Hove, East Sussex BN3 2FA

Simultaneously published in the USA and Canada
by Routledge
270 Madison Avenue, New York NY10016

Reprinted 2010

*Routledge is an imprint of the Taylor & Francis Group,
an Informa business*

Typeset in Times by The Manila Typesetting Company, Philippines
Printed and bound in Great Britain by TJ International Ltd, Padstow
Paperback cover design by Sandra Heath

This publication has been produced with paper manufactured to strict
environmental standards and with pulp derived
from sustainable forests.

British Library Cataloguing in Publication Data
A catalogue record for this book is available
from the British Library

Library of Congress Cataloging-in-Publication Data

Keeping the baby in mind : infant mental health in practice / edited by
Jane Barlow & P.O. Svanberg. – 1st ed.
    p. ; cm.
Includes bibliographical references.
ISBN 978-0-415-44297-8 (hardback) – ISBN 978-0-415-44298-5 (pbk.)
1. Infant psychiatry–Great Britain. 2. Infants–Mental health services–
Great Britain. I. Barlow, Jane, 1962– II. Svanberg, P. O., 1948–
[DNLM: 1. Infant. 2. Parent-Child Relations. 3. Early Intervention
(Education) 4. Family Health. 5. Parenting. WS 105.5.F2 K26 2009]
RJ502.5.K44 2009
618.92'89–dc22
                              2008028913

ISBN: 978-0-415-44297-8 (hbk)
ISBN: 978-0-415-44298-5 (pbk)

Contents

Contributors   ix

Foreword   xv
  DILYS DAWS

1 Keeping the baby in mind   1
   JANE BARLOW AND P. O. SVANBERG

PART I
Universal approaches

2 The power of touch – exploring infant massage   17
   ANGELA UNDERDOWN

3 The Solihull Approach: an integrative model across agencies   29
   HAZEL DOUGLAS AND MARY RHEESTON

4 Promoting development of the early parent–infant relationship
   using the Neonatal Behavioural Assessment Scale   39
   JOANNA HAWTHORNE

5 'First Steps in Parenting': developing nurturing parenting skills
   in mothers and fathers in pregnancy and the postnatal period   52
   MEL PARR, IN COLLABORATION WITH CATHERINE JOYCE

6 The Family Partnership Model: understanding the processes
   of prevention and early intervention   63
   HILTON DAVIS

7 The importance of the parental couple in parent–infant
   psychotherapy   77
   PAUL BARROWS

PART II
Targeted approaches

8   Empowering parents through 'Learning Together':
    the PEEP model   89
    ALISON STREET

9   Promoting a secure attachment through early screening
    and interventions: a partnership approach   100
    P. O. SVANBERG

10 Perinatal home visiting: implementing the nurse–family
    partnership in England   115
    ANN ROWE

11 Working with parents from black and minority ethnic
    backgrounds in Children's Centres   128
    LUCY MARKS, SANDY HADLEY, ANTONIA REAY, TAMARA GELMAN
    AND ANNE MCKAY

PART III
Indicated approaches

12 Working with the hidden obstacles in parent–infant relating:
    two parent–infant psychotherapy projects   141
    TESSA BARADON, SUE GERHARDT AND JOANNA TUCKER

13 Mellow Babies: Mellow Parenting with parents of infants   155
    CHRISTINE PUCKERING

14 Enhancing the relationship between mothers with severe
    mental illness and their infants   164
    SUSAN PAWLBY AND CHARLES FERNYHOUGH

15 'Parenting with support': supporting parents with
    learning difficulties to parent   173
    BETH TARLETON

PART IV
Postscript

16 Developing infant-centred services: the way forward   185
     P. O. SVANBERG AND JANE BARLOW

Index   199

Contributors

Tessa Baradon (MA Public Health) is a child and adolescent psychotherapist, and a member of the Association for Child Psychotherapy and the Association of Child Psychoanalysis. Tessa developed and manages the Parent Infant Project at the Anna Freud Centre, integrating training in child psychotherapy and psychoanalysis with a background in public health. She is a practising child psychotherapist and supervisor, and writes and lectures on applied psychoanalysis and parent–infant psychotherapy.

Jane Barlow (DPhil, FFPH Hon) is Professor of Public Health in the Early Years at the University of Warwick. Jane's main research interest is in the field of public mental health, in particular the effectiveness of early interventions aimed at improving parenting practices and evaluating their role in the primary prevention of mental health problems and the reduction of inequalities in health. Her programme of research focuses on interventions that are provided around infancy, and she is currently setting up the Warwick Infant and Family Wellbeing Unit, which will provide training and research in innovative evidence-based methods of supporting parenting during pregnancy and the early years, for a wide range of early years and primary care practitioners. She is a committee member of the Association of Infant Mental Health (UK), and a member of an expert group making revisions to the Child Health Promotion Programme (0–3 years).

Paul Barrows (PhD) is a consultant child and adult psychotherapist working for the United Bristol Healthcare Trust. He was until recently editor of the World Association for Infant Mental Health newsletter and editor of the *Journal of Child Psychotherapy*. He is also the former chair of the UK Association for Infant Mental Health.

Hilton Davis (BA, DipClinPsych, CPsychol, FBPsS, PhD) is Emeritus Professor of Child Health Psychology, King's College London, and recently retired as Head of the Centre for Parent and Child Support, South London and Maudsley NHS Foundation Trust. Hilton is particularly concerned with the design and evaluation of services to support families and to prevent psychosocial problems and has been developing a model of process (i.e. the

Family Partnership Model) to underpin and guide this work (see www.cpcs.
org.uk).

Hazel Douglas (BSc, MPsychol, MBA, AFBPS, MA, MPsych, PsychD Psycho-
analytical Psychotherapy) is a clinical psychologist and child psychotherapist,
and has always been interested in prevention and early intervention. She began
her clinical career working with adults but has subsequently slowly worked
her way down the age range. She is Strategic Lead for Solihull Child and Adolescent Mental Health Service and leads on the development of the Solihull
Approach.

Charles Fernyhough (MA, PhD) is a developmental psychologist at Durham
University. He has been involved in the conduct of several longitudinal studies
of children's socio-emotional development, and has recently been pursuing an
interest in developmental approaches to psychosis.

Tamara Gelman (MA, ClinPsych) is a clinical psychologist working in the
Tower Hamlets Primary Care Trust. She works across two Children's Centres in Tower Hamlets, and focuses on the treatment of perinatal distress in
parents.

Sue Gerhardt (BA Hons, MA) is a psychoanalytic psychotherapist (UKCP Registered). After training in baby observation and studying child development,
she became passionate about early intervention and co-founded the Oxford
Parent Infant Project (OXPIP). She has worked part-time for OXPIP as a par-
ent/infant psychotherapist for ten years, and combines this with a private psychotherapy practice, and lecturing and writing. She is the author of *Why Love
Matters: How Affection Shapes a Baby's Brain* (2004).

Sandy Hadley (BA, BSc Hons, RMN, Certificate in Systemic Family Therapy,
DClinPsy) is a clinical psychologist working full-time for the Psychology and
Counselling Team, Tower Hamlets Primary Care Trust. She currently divides
her work between four GP surgeries and two Children's Centres, treating adults
and parents with a range of psychological difficulties.

Joanna Hawthorne (PhD) is a psychologist and senior research associate at the
Centre for Family Research, University of Cambridge, and director and NBAS
trainer at the Brazelton Centre in Great Britain, c/o Addenbrookes Hospital,
Cambridge. Joanna trains health professionals and those who work with newborns nationally and internationally in the NBAS. She is on the committee of
the Association for Infant Mental Health (UK), and council member of the
Maternity and Newborn Forum, Royal Society of Medicine. Her research and
clinical work includes work with parents and babies in neonatal units, and
evaluating the use of the NBAS in early intervention.

Catherine Joyce (Fellow Chartered Institute of Personnel and Development,
Member of the European Coaching Institute, Master Practitioner Neuro Lin-
guistic Programming, Independent member of Parenting UK and WAVE) is

founder of BlueQuay Consulting and works as an organisation change consultant and business coach with individuals, teams and work groups who are undergoing major change. She has a wealth of experience in the private, public and voluntary sectors, consulting at all levels. Catherine was Assistant Director, Projects and Training PIPPIN (2000–2003), and Director, Projects and Training (2003–2005).

Anne Mckay (MClinPsych, Masters in Consulting to Organisations, Dip Forensic Psychotherapeutic Studies, DipEd) is a chartered clinical psychologist (BPS) with the Children's Centres Adult Psychology Team, Tower Hamlets Primary Care Trust.

Lucy Marks (MClinPsych) is a consultant clinical psychologist, joint team leader of the Primary Care Psychology and Counselling Service in Tower Hamlets, and co-chair of Tower Hamlets Professional Executive Committee (PEC), Tower Hamlets Primary Care Trust. Lucy has a special interest in primary care mental health services and particularly services for parents of under-fives, and set up and developed the Sure Start Children's Centres Adult Psychology Service. She is also interested in ensuring there is strong clinical leadership in the process of commissioning health services, and she works alongside the management team of Tower Hamlets Primary Care Trust in her capacity as co-chair of PEC with this remit.

Mel Parr (PhD) is a chartered counselling psychologist and adult psychotherapist (UKCP) who also has over fourteen years' experience in the NHS in adult mental health, and is an Honorary Fellow at the University of Hertfordshire. Mel has over thirty years' experience working with parents through the voluntary sector and was the founding director of 'Parents In Partnership–Parent Infant Network' (PIPPIN) (1993-2004). She is the named leading contributor to parent and infant mental health for the UKCP Tenth Anniversary Lecture Series. She currently works with Hertfordshire Partnership NHS Foundation Trust in secondary/continuing care and is the clinical lead for perinatal mental health for the Enhanced Primary Care Mental Health Service as part of the Department of Health 'Improving Access to Psychological Therapies'/Perinatal Mental Health pilot. She trains and supervises nurses, midwives, health visitors, social workers, psychologists and medical doctors. Mel is also a co-tutor on the MSc in Family Health at the University of Hertfordshire, and an independent consultant working on the development of a university qualification template for training trainers of parenting practitioners to work with parents of children aged 0-3 years with Parenting UK/National Academy Parenting Practitioners 'Early Learning Partnership'. She is a committee member of the Association of Infant Mental Health UK, WAVE Trust, and a member of the international advisory board for the journal *Attachment and Human Development*.

Susan Pawlby (BSc, MA, PhD) is a chartered psychologist (British Psychological Society) in the section of Perinatal Psychiatry, Institute of Psychiatry, King's

College London and Channi Kumar Mother and Baby Unit, Bethlem Royal Hospital, South London and Maudsley NHS Trust. Susan is a developmental psychologist with a specific research interest in infancy and the developing relationship between a mother and her baby. Her research work has pioneered the use of video feedback techniques in supporting the developing relationship between mothers with severe mental illness and their infants during their admission to a specialist mother and baby unit.

Christine Puckering (BSc, MPhil, PhD) is a chartered clinical psychologist, a chartered forensic psychologist, a full practitioner of the Neuropsychological Division, and Consultant Clinical Psychologist and Research Fellow at the Royal Hospital for Sick Children, Glasgow; Honorary Senior Research Fellow at the University of Glasgow; and Honorary Lecturer in Forensic Psychology at Glasgow Caledonian University. Christine is a clinical psychologist and research fellow with a specific research interest in measuring and helping parents to change their relationship with their child. She is co-author of the Mellow Parenting programme and has developed and researched the core under-fives programme and Mellow Babies which was developed to meet the needs of under-one-year-olds and their parents. Mellow Parenting is now an independent charity. In 2006, she chaired a short-life expert group on infant mental health for the Scottish Executive which made policy and practice development proposals for supporting all infants and protecting those who are particularly vulnerable.

Antonia Reay (BA, MSc) is a chartered counselling psychologist at Tower Hamlets Primary Care Trust, Lincoln and Burdett Children's Centre and Bromley by Bow Children's Centre. Antonia works in primary care and in Children's Centres with parents of young children, and is currently training as a cognitive analytic therapy practitioner. She previously worked at Henderson Hospital and with the Crisis Counselling Service at Holloway Prison.

Mary Rheeston coordinates the Solihull Approach and has been involved in developing their training, parenting group and resources. She is also a Solihull Approach trainer, a health visitor, and an infant massage teacher.

Ann Rowe (BA, MMedSci, RGN, RHV) works independently and is currently contracted to act as Implementation Lead for the Health Led Parenting Programme for the Department of Children, Schools and Families. In this role she has been responsible for the training and implementation of the Nurse Family Partnership programme. During a career in nursing, health visiting and practice development roles, Ann has led a teenage parenting project, developed and delivered learning programmes, designed and run change programmes and acted as an external organisational consultant to a variety of organisations. More recently Ann has worked as a research and development facilitator at the University of Sheffield, and as a Nurse Advisor to the Department of Health in the Long Term Conditions team.

Alison Street (PhD) is an early years music specialist at Roehampton University. Alison devised and compiled the musical materials and piloted the group work with parents in the PEEP project from 1995 to 2000. Her doctoral research (2006) explored the role of singing in mother–infant interactions and its influence on engagement patterns. As a trustee of PEEP, she contributes to training and development, and lectures at Roehampton in music education.

P. O. Svanberg (BSc, MSc, Dip Psychotherapy, PhD, AFBPSs) is a chartered clinical psychologist. He originally trained in Sweden and has lived and worked in the northeast of England since 1979 following early work at Dingleton Hospital in the Scottish Borders and in Yorkshire. He worked as an adult psychotherapist for many years and, following his doctorate in the late 1980s, became very interested in adult attachment. Having trained in the Adult Attachment Interview he became passionate about primary prevention and early intervention, an area of interest he has pursued since 1997, resulting in the development and evaluation of the Sunderland Infant Programme. He currently works at the FNP and CHPP Implementation Team at the Department of Health.

Beth Tarleton (BSc, PGCE, MPhil) is a Research Fellow at the Norah Fry Research Centre, University of Bristol. Beth has carried out research in a wide variety of areas, including housing, short breaks, and most recently around the support available to parents with learning difficulties, all of which relate to her central interest in learning disability and empowerment. Beth currently coordinates the Working Together with Parents Network which aims to improve policy and practice in supporting parents with learning difficulties (www.rightsupport.org.uk).

Joanna Tucker (BA Hons, MA, CQSW, UKCP) is a registered psychotherapist. Joanna trained first as a social worker, and then as an adult psychotherapist with the Jungian training of the West Midlands Institute of Psychotherapy. She currently divides her time between private practice, working as a therapist and trainer for the Oxford Parent Infant Project, and teaching infant observation.

Angela Underdown (MSc, HV, RGN, BEd Hons, PGCert in Applied Systemic Theory) was previously Associate Professor of Early Childhood at the University of Warwick, and has recently taken up a post as Public Health Advisor to the NSPCC. She originally trained as a health visitor and has a longstanding interest in supporting infant mental health within family relationships. Angela has been researching infant massage interventions in the UK and has recently completed a Cochrane Systematic Review exploring the effects of infant massage on the mental and physical health of infants under 6 months of age.

Foreword

Dilys Daws

William Blake wrote, 'He who would do good to another must do it in Minute Particulars: general Good is the plea of the scoundrel, hypocrite, and flatterer, for Art and Science cannot exist but in minutely organized particulars' (Blake, 1804: ch. 3, line 60). Harsh words for those of us optimistically engaged in grand general policies aimed at reform and development, but perhaps there is some truth in what he says when it comes to thinking about what to do for the good of babies.

This excellent book starts with an overview of recent developments within the field of infant mental health, spanning the decades of research about infant attachment and maternal sensitivity, and more recent theories about the importance of helping parents to keep the baby's mind, in mind. We now know that the transition to parenthood is challenging for both men and women and that services to support them during this period need to focus on the emotional preparation of parents for parenthood, as couples negotiate their new relationships with their infant and each other. All infant mental health provision needs to be underpinned by a universally available service comprising practitioners with the necessary knowledge, skills and capacity to build a trusting relationship. In the UK we are fortunate to have a dedicated group of professionals (i.e. health visitors) who perform this function. The knowledge for every new mother that a 'someone' exists, who has her and her baby in mind, and whom she has a right to contact, can help many parents through the often lonely and confused weeks of early infancy. A sensitive response by the health visitor can help a seriously distressed mother to begin responding to her baby. It is so simple when it exists and so unattainable when it does not. Many of the chapters in this book describe interventions delivered by health visitors and other professionals who are working in new and innovative ways to support parents to provide the sort of parenting that recent research suggests to be important if we are to help every infant to achieve their full potential. What all of these ways of working have in common is a shared recognition of the importance of helping parents to be sensitively attuned to the communications of their infant, and of promoting the parent–infant relationship.

The core of the work being explored in this book is as such with parents and their infants, and clinical anecdotes give us 'minute particular' glimpses of real parents and babies. All of the interventions described have in common the crucial role of the relationship between professionals and families, with professionals first needing to understand parents, so that the parents can understand their baby. When attachment between parents and their baby has faltered, this crucial relationship with the professional can symbolically provide an experience which can be a model for a new beginning. Parenting takes time. The minute repeated details of feeding, changing, playing and putting a baby to bed are the foundations of attachment and family life. Professionals who do the valuable work of supporting parents during this period need to be able to take the necessary time to reflect on the experience of the families they are working with, and for their relationship to model the type of reciprocal and containing relationship that will optimally exist between the parent and their baby.

The recent UK government initiatives to combat social exclusion and reach out into the community, particularly to young families at risk, provide the necessary backdrop against which infant mental health can be promoted. What is of course revealed by such initiatives is that those families who have been excluded, or who have excluded themselves, often endure a considerable degree of deprivation and disturbance, especially emotional distress. The professionals and volunteers who work with these families may in turn be distressed by what they encounter and need consistent and sensitive supervision that contains and helps them to understand their own feelings and reactions. They also need, of course, support from their organisations and a management hierarchy that appreciates the emotional investment that they are making.

It is striking that many of the projects described in this book have grown in similar ways in different parts of the country. Some have sprung up independently, while others have cross-fertilised each other. New ideas are often created spontaneously more than once when their time has come. I am proud that many of the contributors are active members of AIMH-UK (i.e. the Association for Infant Mental Health – UK), which is affiliated to the World Association of Infant Mental Health. I founded AIMH-UK in 1997 after visiting Australia to speak to the Australian sister organisation - AAIMH. At the time I was impressed by the way clinicians there got together with primary care workers to discuss clinical work and research, and the provision of infant mental health services. On the long plane journey back to the UK I thought, 'We in the UK could do that', and the AIMH which emerged has been a fruitful place for all of us interested in infancy to meet and share ideas, and may have contributed to at least some of the ideas and programmes described in this book.

There has been a lack of a clear, conceptual framework in the UK concerning the processes involved in helping families, particularly during the transition to parenthood and the first few years of life. This coherently edited book adds to the development of such a framework, as well as providing stimulating examples of how it can be realised in practice. However, such a framework must not become rigid. Parent–infant work is by its nature chaotic. As Picasso said, 'If you know exactly what you are going to do, what is the point of doing it?' The parent–infant worker needs to go into a visit with a family open to the emotions that will greet him or her. In home visits this is often expressed in visible chaos with nowhere apparent for the visitor to sit down. Alternatively, there may be conspicuous over-tidiness, as though the feelings stirred up by having a baby must be organised out-of-sight. Whatever the setting, professionals need the skills to recognise and support parents who may be struggling with the intense emotions that are evoked at this time.

Why do we do this work? I can only answer for myself, having worked for over thirty years as a child psychotherapist in the baby clinic of the James Wigg General Practice in London and for many years in the Under Fives Service of the Tavistock Clinic. There is the pleasure of helping families make a relationship with their baby, and of getting in early and perhaps repairing something after generations of deprivation and despair. There is also the unexpectedness of the work, of coming into contact with raw emotions, of making yourself vulnerable and rising to the occasion. Trying to contain the feelings of parents, who may never have felt properly understood before, can sometimes lead to the humility of discovering that their problems mirror those of our own. There is also the satisfaction of working with 'ordinary' families who have become temporarily stuck with the impact of the 'life and death emotions' that new babies elicit. These families may need only a little help in re-connecting with their capacities as parents. Professionals working with parents during this period have the deep pleasure of seeing mothers, fathers, and babies in the reciprocal interactions of a healthy relationship as it grows and develops. I believe that there is an emotionally integrative effect for the worker in going through such a process with parents and their baby, which is deeply satisfying. So, while working this way is often painful it is also often very enjoyable. It can bring out the creativity in workers, and also their playfulness. New populations of patients also bring out new ways of working, and the human propensity for risk-taking and innovation can lead to the development of new projects and clinical approaches, as is so aptly illustrated in this timely book.

Reference

Blake, W. (1804). *Jerusalem.*

1 Keeping the baby in mind

Jane Barlow and P. O. Svanberg

It is not easy being a baby in the hurried, post-industrial world of twenty-first-century Britain. Although their chances of survival are much higher than in the past, babies are not naturally designed for a noisy, fast and over-stimulating environment. The task of parenting has also been made much harder by the wide-ranging social changes that have taken place in the family, and a falling-off in the level of support that has been available during pregnancy and the postnatal period to date. There is, in addition, a general lack of understanding in the UK about how to intervene effectively to support parenting and the parent–infant relationship during the perinatal period, and a paucity of primary preventive, early intervention and infant mental health services.

The aim of this book is to try to address some of these challenges by bringing together significant early interventions that are being used in the UK, and which have as their focus the aim of improving the social and emotional well-being of infants and toddlers. The interventions that are reviewed in this volume are based on evidence concerning the benefits of intervening early, alongside recent research pointing to the importance of the first two years of life for later development.

This chapter will provide a brief review of the policy context for recent developments in Britain, alongside an examination of the development of the discipline of 'infant mental health' internationally. We review recent developments in the field of attachment and beyond, before providing a summary of some of the new methods of working to promote infant mental health.

The policy context

The current UK government has been the first to prioritise the promotion of health and well-being in the early years. The Sure Start initiative in England and Wales (DfES, 1999), partly modelled on Early Head Start in the US, reflected the government's views expressed in the Consultation Paper *Supporting Families* (in addition to other documents published since then including *Every Child Matters* (DfES, 2003), *The National Service Framework for Children, Young People and Maternity Services* (DH 2004), and the public health White Paper *Choosing Health* (DH 2004), about the importance of the family environment, and parenting in particular, in determining key outcomes for children.

The emphasis in Sure Start on local autonomy and empowering the local community through the use of a 'bottom up' approach to service provision, alongside a reluctance to prescribe models or protocols, gave rise for the first time to the development of a range of innovative parent–infant programmes. However, these pockets of innovation (which tended to have in common a lead from a psychologist or a child psychotherapist, very close multi-disciplinary work with health visitors and family support workers, and a focus on the parent–infant relationship) have on the whole been masked by a continuity in the standard focus of practitioners working within Sure Start (particularly midwives and health visitors) (Barlow *et al.*, 2007). In addition, the move to Children's Centres has been underpinned by an emphasis on educational outcomes alongside a retreat from prevention and a gradual return of focus to toddlers and young children. Consequently a number of emerging and highly innovative infant mental health programmes and projects across the country have been lost.

Most recently, however, 'Aiming High for Children: Supporting the Family' (HM Treasury, 2007) has emphasised the need to increase the resilience of children by supporting parenting through early intervention. The introduction of home visiting programmes in ten demonstration sites across the UK, beginning during pregnancy and continuing until the child is 2 years of age, has thereby introduced a way of working with families that is evidence-based (Olds *et al.*, 1986, 1999, 2007) and underpinned by attachment theory.

There is, however, still a paucity of innovative infant mental health programmes being used as part of standard practice in the UK, and considerable scope for improvement.

Infant mental health in the twenty-first century

The emergence of innovative infant mental health programmes in some Sure Start centres, and across the UK more generally, was due in part to the rise of a group of practitioners who believed that 'infant mental health' was formative in the later health of children and adults. The discipline of infant mental health began in the US in the immediate post-war years of the last century when Fraiberg (1977) was using her work with congenitally blind babies to understand the needs of 'normal' infants, and the types of developmental deviations and delays that can occur. The 'ghosts in the nursery' (Fraiberg *et al.*, 1980) referred to 'the visitors from the unremembered pasts of the parents' and emphasised the ways in which aspects of the mother's internal world continued to influence the way in which she interacted with and cared for her own baby, and in particular the way in which this could condemn her to 'repeat the tragedy of [her] own childhood with [her] own baby in terrible and exacting detail' (ibid.: 101). The model of intervention developed by Fraiberg involved intensive psychoanalytically informed work with extremely deprived parents and infants, and was eventually to become what we now call parent–infant psychotherapy.

At around the same time in the UK, Esther Bick, a physician and psychoanalyst who had moved to London in 1938, developed a method of infant observation that encouraged observers to watch and listen to babies during the first and second years of life in order to chart the changes taking place. Bick focused attention on the earliest stages of mental development in the infant, and this model of infant observation became the basis for child and infant psychotherapy training in the UK, and eventually served as the basis for early therapeutic intervention.

Alongside Bick at the Tavistock Clinic, John Bowlby was beginning his seminal work on infant attachment. Bowlby was the first person to identify the infant's need for a trusted attachment figure. Attachment theory (Bowlby, 1969), which was developed in the post-war atmosphere of loss and bereavement, emphasised that it was real lived experiences, in terms of the way that parents actually treat their children and the sense that children make of these experiences, that are of key importance in children's development. Following Bick and Bowlby in the 1970s the Tavistock Clinic set up the first 'Under-Fives Counselling Service' in the country, using the skills learned from infant observation (Miller, 1992), and Dilys Daws pioneered child psychotherapy in the baby clinic at the James Wigg General Practice in London (Daws, 1985, 2006).

Two further seminal thinkers emerged in the field of infant mental health – Daniel Stern and Edward Tronick. Building on the work of Trevarthen (1980), these developmental psychologists began to explore the 'protoconversational turn taking' occurring between mother and infant, which is now recognised to be characterised by a 'rhythmical pattern of looking and withdrawal' (Stern, 1985; Tronick and Cohn, 1989). This gave rise to a series of research studies based on videotape films of micro-interactions showing that mother and baby engage in a synchronous dance made up of brief periods of attunement followed by brief periods of disruption. These researchers showed that the baby is able to 'control' this input by looking away, and that 'attuned' mothers are able to engage in this 'dance' by regulating their interaction to meet the baby's needs, and by repairing disruptions. Not all mothers are able to engage in attuned interaction of this nature, however, and women experiencing depression or unresolved loss, for example, can overwhelm the baby with their intrusiveness. As a result, such infants experience extended periods of disruption rather than attunement. Where this disruption is sufficiently chronic, it may eventually be systematised into a defensive 'avoidant' stance, which has been documented as early as 3 months of age. The importance of these findings is that later research has shown that such early disturbances in mother–child interactions are implicated in a range of longer-term adverse child cognitive (Meins, 1997) and emotional outcomes (Caplan *et al.*, 1989; Cogill *et al.*, 1986) including behavioural problems (Murray and Cooper, 1997).

More recently the development of new techniques within the field of neuro-developmental science has facilitated the conduct of research which points to a significant impact of the early caregiving environment (i.e. interactions with key people in the baby's environment) on the developing brain.[1] In conjunction with research from a range of other disciplines, these findings suggest that babies not only build their brains as a result of this early interaction, but that they also build their minds and construct a sense of themselves that will last them a lifetime (for an overview see Schore, 2001 or Gerhardt, 2004).

Together, these early theorists facilitated a new way of viewing babies by drawing attention for the first time to the importance of the baby's 'emotional' well-being, particularly their capacity for emotional regulation, and to the way in which the primary caretaker influences this. This was to become part of a rapidly expanding infant mental health movement, underpinned by a recognition of the 'social baby' (i.e. the way in which babies are born primed to be sociable (Murray and Andrews, 2000)), their sensitivity to the quality of their interactions with other people (Murray and Cooper, 1997), and more recently a recognition that the process of regulation between mother and baby is dynamic and bi-directional – that is, there is considerable co-regulation taking place between them (Beebe *et al.*, 1997) – and of the importance of primary caregivers being able to 'keep the baby in mind' (Fonagy *et al.*, 1991a).

Attachment and beyond

Bowlby (1969) described how attachment in evolutionary terms increases the likelihood of the infant's survival. More recently, researchers have begun to recognise that attachment has more far-reaching functions in terms of the way in which the proximity of the mother helps the infant to modulate or regulate an aroused emotional state, until they are able to do this for themselves.[2] Securely attached infants[3] seek comfort when distressed and recover from an aroused, disorganised state to a calm, organised state when comforted. Insecurely attached infants, however, are unable to use the caregiver to modulate their aroused state. They may over-regulate,[4] under-regulate,[5] or show evidence of both, reflecting conflicting emotions.[6]

Ainsworth and her colleagues (1978) showed that these insecure attachment behaviours are help-seeking strategies that have been 'moulded' by the caregiver's inability to provide 'sensitive-enough' caregiving. Avoidant (Type A) infants learn to 'down-regulate', to inhibit expression of affect - in particular distress–whilst Ambivalent (Type C) infants are unable to predict or anticipate continuity and proximity of the caregiver and consequently become highly vigilant, guarding against anticipated abandonment/separation, usually with great displays of affect, i.e. they learn to 'up-regulate'. Main and her colleagues have argued that there is an additional category of Disorganised/Disorientated (Type D) infants (Main and Solomon, 1986, 1990) who have experienced caregiving from mothers who were either frightened or frightening and who as a consequence are unable to sustain a coherent attachment strategy, i.e. they are disorganised. However, Crittenden (2000b, 2002) has argued that these attachment behaviours are in fact highly organised in response to threatening or dangerous environments, which can be highly contingent and/or highly unpredictable. She has identified a number of Compulsive (Type A+) infants, Coy/Coercive (Type C+) infants, and a group of infants who show a combination of strategies (Type A/C).

Attachment is important because it provides the infant with a 'secure base' from which to begin to explore the world, and because it acts as a prototype for later relations (Bowlby, 1988). Thus, infants' early attachment interactions are eventually internalised, becoming an 'internal working model' that enables them to know what to expect in terms of their interactions with other people (Bowlby, 1969, 1989). This 'representational model' provides children with a very early set of expectations in relation to 'self' and 'self with others' that will continue with them throughout their life (see, for example, Prior and Glaser, 2006). While internal working models may be modified through experience, they mainly function outside of awareness and are therefore resistant to change (Crittenden, 1990). Insecurely attached children range from expecting others to be unresponsive, unavailable and unwilling to meet their needs, to being threatening, abusive and/or endangering.

The availability of the Strange Situation and additional methods of assessing the attachment of older children led to a formidable explosion of research which has not yet abated (Belsky, 1999). A number of longitudinal studies following children for up to twenty years (e.g. Sroufe *et al.*, 2005) have also attested to the great vulnerability of insecurely attached children in terms of their high risk of developing psychological and psychiatric disorders.

Researchers have also begun to disentangle the intergenerational continuities in attachment patterns and have identified a significant association between a parent's security of attachment (internal working model) and the likelihood that their baby will be securely attached (Fonagy *et al.*, 1991b). This suggests that insecurely attached adults are more likely to have insecurely attached babies.

The most crucial indication of a parent's attachment status is the way in which a parent thinks about the early care that they received, which can be measured using the Adult Attachment Interview (Main and Goldwyn, 1984). Attachment is thus thought to pass from one generation to another because the parents' attachment security influences the way in which they parent their baby.

Mentalisation and 'keeping the baby in mind'

It is now reasonably well established that sensitive attunement, warmth, synchrony and the reparation of 'ruptures' in the very early interactions with the baby are associated with later secure attachment of the child (De Wolff and Van IJzendoorn, 1997; Braungart-Rieker *et al.*, 2001). Recent research has also highlighted the importance of the parents' capacity for 'mind-mindedness'. A study of 200 mothers (half of whom had left school at 16) and their infants found that in the first two years of life the most important factor in a child's development was how well the mother was able to interpret her baby's feelings (Meins, 2004). This study suggested that the ability of the mother to understand the child using video footage predicted the baby's language and play skills at 8, 14 and 24 months of age, and showed that 'mind-mindedness' was a better predictor of child development rates than background, income or socioeconomic status. The better a mother interpreted her child's intentions and mood, the faster he developed the ability to represent his thoughts and feelings through language and play, i.e. acquired a representational system.

This research builds on the work of Peter Fonagy and his colleagues (1991a, 2004), who describe such mind-mindedness as 'mentalisation'. This refers to the capacity of the parents to experience the baby as an 'intentional' being rather than simply viewing him or her in terms of physical characteristics or behaviour. Fonagy *et al.* (2004) suggest that it is the child's experiences of being treated as an intentional being that help the child to develop an understanding of mental states in other people and to regulate their own internal experiences.

Intervening to promote infant mental health: new approaches

The implications of the infant mental health movement and the research that has been associated with it (both within developmental psychology and within psychoanalysis) are that infant developmental or behavioural disturbances have been reconceptualised as arising from disturbances in the parent–infant relationship. This has led to an increase in interventions that are focused on the parent–infant relationship as opposed to the mother or baby alone. This in turn has led to recognition that there are possibilities for intervening not only at a behavioural level, but also in terms of changes that might be made to the internal world of the mother, the baby, and/or the family system. This book summarises a number of approaches that endeavour to do just that.

What this book is about

The aim of this book is to make a strong case for supportive early interventions and primary/secondary prevention. Using a public health framework, the book is divided into three parts, according to the focus of the intervention: universal, targeted, and indicated.

Universal programmes

The first part starts with interventions that can be provided on a universal basis (i.e. that are in principle available to everyone). The focus of such programmes is primarily on *promoting* infant mental health. In Chapter 2, Angela Underdown examines the rationale behind, and use of, infant massage in community-based settings with healthy mother–infant dyads to promote mother–infant interaction. She describes the history of infant massage globally, including an exploration of the context for the increasing interest in western countries. She provides a description of infant massage programmes being used in the UK, prior to examining the evidence from a recent systematic review of their effectiveness in 'low risk' mother–infant dyads.

The Solihull Approach to early intervention and prevention is a unique model of working with families which is being used by different professional groups across the UK to promote infant mental health. In Chapter 3 Hazel Douglas and Mary Rheeston describe how this model of working with young families is underpinned by three key concepts: 'containment' and a recognition of the need to help parents to contain their anxieties; the promotion of 'reciprocity' both between mother and baby and between mother and helper; and 'behaviour management' which is aimed at providing parents with the tools to promote positive interactions. Douglas and Rheeston describe how these concepts are being used by a range of professionals across a number of early years settings.

The Neonatal Behavioural Assessment scale (NBAS) is used with parents of newborn babies to enhance the mother–infant relationship by focusing on reciprocity, maternal representations and intersubjectivity. In Chapter 4 Joanna Hawthorne describes the development and use of NBAS and how it can be used to produce a behavioural 'portrait' of the infant in order to enhance the earliest relationship between babies and parents, by describing the individual baby's strengths, adaptive responses and possible vulnerabilities.

'First Steps in Parenting' is a psychologically informed and preventive parent–infant programme for the antenatal and postnatal period which focuses on couple and parent–infant relationships, and in Chapter 5 Mel Parr describes the key concepts and methods of working using this approach.

The Family Partnership Model describes the process involved in relating to families, and in Chapter 6, Hilton Davis points to the need for services to be underpinned by such a model of working. He describes a universal and targeted promotional service called the European Early Promotion Project (EEPP), which is underpinned by the Family Partnership Model of working. This involves the use of promotional interviewing immediately before and after all new births to promote positive interaction between parent and baby as a key element of healthy psychosocial development during infancy and childhood, and to facilitate the transition to parenthood. The chapter also describes how such a programme can be used to identify families at risk of developing child mental health problems and what might be done about this. The chapter concludes with an examination of some of the evidence about the effectiveness of this service. This part concludes with Chapter 7 highlighting the importance of attempting, wherever possible, to include fathers in work with parents and infants. Paul Barrows argues that it is the parents' relationship that sets the emotional atmosphere in which the infant develops, and that this has major implications for their infant's long-term mental health.

Targeted programmes

The second part of the book focuses on programmes that are provided on a targeted basis to families at increased risk of poor outcomes due to a range of psychological or social factors.

The Peers Early Education Programme (PEEP) aims to promote learning and cognitive development during the first few years of a child's life, and is based on the growing body of evidence that links the early development of language, literacy, and personal and social development with outcomes relating to higher educational attainment, improved behaviour, and crime prevention. In Chapter 8, Alison Street describes the development of PEEP from its earliest starting point through its expansion into a nation-wide intervention whose curriculum and principles have been adopted in many Children's Centres throughout the UK.

Reflective video feedback is an innovative way of using technology to support the parent–infant relationship and in Chapter 9 P. O. Svanberg outlines the development and use of a joint programme between health visitors and psychologists which involves the use of video screening and video focused reflective feedback. He describes how this targeted preventive approach can be used to screen for vulnerable parent–infant interactions, also providing a tailor-made intervention. The chapter reports the main findings of a twelve-month evaluation, showing that the model is an effective and cost-effective way of increasing the proportion of children who become securely attached.

Home visiting programmes are widely used now across the world to support parenting during the perinatal period, and in 2007 the UK government began a pilot programme in England of the widely evaluated Nurse–Family Partnership (FNP). In Chapter 10 Ann Rowe describes the implementation of the FNP at ten demonstration sites across the UK.

Involving minority ethnic families and non-English-speaking mothers living in deprived parts of the country is central to the work of many professionals, and in Chapter 11 Lucy Marks and her colleagues examine how the theory and practice of delivering psychological therapies, which has often been based on a white western model, needs to be adapted so that it is accessible and acceptable to black and minority ethnic groups, particularly during the perinatal period. Their chapter discusses a range of adaptations that can be made to standard clinical practice.

Indicated programmes

The third and final part of the book focuses on programmes that are delivered as part of an indicated approach to families and parents with substantial social, psychiatric or psychological problems which overwhelm their capacity to be sensitively attuned, and increase the infant's risk of a range of poor outcomes in later life.

Parent–infant psychotherapy, which evolved in the US during the middle of the last century, is the focus of Chapter 12, which examines two different ways of using a one-to-one intervention to work with mothers and babies. Tessa Baradon describes the work of the Anna Freud Centre for Parents and Infants and their use of a representational and attachment-based model of working with both mother and baby together, and Sue Gerhardt and Joanna Tucker examine the role of an infant-led method of parent–infant psychotherapy which is used by OXPIP (Oxford Parent Infant Programme). This chapter shows the way in which brief (i.e. lasting less than fifteen weeks) therapy, which focuses on the positive transference relationship between therapist and mother, can utilise the infant as a catalyst for change in the emotional functioning of the mother and thereby improve the mother–infant relationship.

Mellow Babies is one of the few indicated interventions that utilise group-based working and in Chapter 13 Christine Puckering examines how a fourteen-week intensive group-based programme can be used in conjunction with personal reflection, video feedback and hands-on parenting sessions to enhance the capacity of mothers with a variety of problems, such as depression or child protection issues, to respond more sensitively to their babies. She describes the theory and method using a number of clinical vignettes, and concludes by examining early evidence about its effectiveness.

As was indicated in Chapter 9, videotape feedback is now being used in a number of ways with mothers and babies, and in Chapter 14, Susan Pawlby and Charles Fernyhough examine the use of videotape feedback of play sessions with mothers who are suffering from a severe mental illness (including psychotic depression, postpartum psychosis, bipolar disorder, and schizophrenia) recorded during their admission to the Mother and Baby Unit (MBU) at the Bethlem Royal Hospital, London. They examine how this method of intervening provides seriously ill mothers with the opportunity to develop their parenting skills and promote their relationships with their babies. They conclude by describing the findings of a study which show that the less optimal quality of mother–infant interaction observed in the acute phase of the mother's illness improves over the period of admission so that at discharge the quality of their interaction is indistinguishable from that of a well group of mothers and babies in the community.

In Chapter 15 Beth Tarleton examines some of the reasons why early intervention with infants of parents with learning disabilities is important, and describes some of the barriers to early intervention, such as the fears and anxieties of many professionals, which it is argued are based on (mis)perceptions about the abilities of these women. This chapter discusses professional values, attitudes and views about what good parenting is, and the role that these play not only in preventing early intervention, but also in precipitating early removal from the home of the children of parents with learning disabilities.

Many of the models of working with parents that have been explored in this volume are exemplary of an infant-centred approach to supporting parenting during the perinatal period. In Chapter 16 we look to the future and examine why an infant-centred approach to the provision of services during this period is now necessary, and what it would involve.

Conclusion

Richard Bowlby has noted that issues related to infant attachment and emotional well-being often stir up emotional and, at times, highly defensive reactions. These issues may resonate on a personal level, triggering 'what must not be thought about or what must not be felt' (Bowlby, 1988), and/or they relate to one's own children and one's own parenting practices, and must therefore be defensively excluded (Bowlby, 1989). This of course also applies to planners and policy makers, who may find it much easier to think about 'them' rather than 'us'.

This book is aimed at everyone involved in working with parents and infants or in setting up services to support the parenting of infants, and presents a veritable 'smorgasbord' of projects, programmes and approaches in the field, in the hope that these will inform policy, practice and the future development of services both in the UK and internationally.

As we noted at the beginning, it is hard being a baby in the post-industrial, post-capitalist twenty-first century. It is also hard being a parent with the responsibility of bringing up a child in an increasingly complex world. It has been suggested that 'the responsibility for the child's well-being go[es] beyond the family to the broader society' (Sroufe *et al.*, 2005: 18), and we very much hope that this book will encourage policy makers and practitioners to recognise this responsibility, and will provide the means to enable them to keep the baby in mind.

Notes

1 It should be noted that much of this research is still limited to animals.
2 Fonagy (2001) has more recently suggested that the evolutionary significance of this is that it brings the baby into closer proximity with another brain (see section below on mentalisation).
3 Categorised as Type B using the Strange Situation which is a laboratory procedure used to assess attachment behaviour in infants aged 12-15 months by focusing on the infant's behaviour *on reunion* following two brief separations (Ainsworth *et al.*, 1978).
4 Categorised as Type A (Avoidant).
5 Categorised as Type C (Ambivalent).
6 Categorised as Type D (Disorganised).

References

Ainsworth, M. D. S., Blehar, M. C., Waters, E. and Wall, S. (1978). *Patterns of Attachment: A Psychological Study of the Strange Situation*. Hillsdale, NJ: Lawrence Erlbaum Associates.

Barlow, J., Kirkpatrick, S., Wood, D., Ball, M. and Stewart-Brown, S. (2007). *Family and Parenting Support in Sure Start Local Programmes*. London: DfES.

Barrett, H. (2006). *Attachment and the Perils of Parenting: A Commentary and a Critique*. London: National Family and Parenting Institute.

Beebe, B., Lachmann, F. and Jaffe, J. (1997). Mother–infant interaction structures and presymbolic self- and object representations. *Psychoanalytic Dialogues*, 2, 133–182.

Belsky, J. (1999). Interactional and contextual determinants of attachment security. In J. Cassidy and P. Shaver (eds), *Handbook of Attachment: Theory, Research and Clinical Applications*. London: Guilford Press.

Bowlby, J. (1969). *Attachment and Loss I: Attachment*. New York: Basic Books.

Bowlby, J. (1988). *A Secure Base*. New York: Basic Books.

Bowlby, J. (1989). The role of attachment in personality development and psychopathology. In G. Pollock (ed.), *The Course of Life, Vol. 1, Infancy* (pp. 229–270). Madison, CT: International Universities Press.

Braungart-Rieker, J. M., Garwood, M. M., Powers, B. P. and Wang, X. Y. (2001). Parental sensitivity, infant affect, and affect regulation: predictors of later attachment. *Child Development*, 72(1), 252–270.

Brazelton, T. B. (1992). *Touchpoints*. New York: Guilford Press.

Caplan, H., Cogill, S., Alexandra, H., Robson, K., Katz, R. and Kumar, R. (1989). Maternal depression and the emotional development of the child. *British Journal of Psychiatry*, 154, 818–823.

Cogill, S. R., Caplan, H. L., Alexandra, H., Robson, K. M., Kumar, R. (1986). Impact of maternal postnatal depression on cognitive development in young children. *British Medical Journal*, 292, 1165–1167.

Conger, R. D., Conger, K., Elder, G., Lorenz, F., Simmons, R. and Whitbeck, L. (1992). A family process model of economic hardship and adjustment of early adolescent boys. *Child Development*, 63, 526–541.

Crittenden, P. M. (1990). Internal representational models of attachment relationships. *Infant Mental Health Journal*, 11, 259–277.

Crittenden, P. M. (2000a). A dynamic-maturational approach to continuity and change in pattern of attachment. In P. M. Crittenden and A. H. Claussen (eds), *The Organisation of Attachment Relationships: Maturation, Culture and Context*. Cambridge: Cambridge University Press.

Crittenden, P. M. (2000b). A dynamic-maturational exploration of the meaning of security and adaptation: empirical, cultural and theoretical considerations. In P. M. Crittenden and A. H. Claussen (eds), *The Organisation of Attachment Relationships: Maturation, Culture and Context*. Cambridge: Cambridge University Press.

Crittenden, P. M. (2002). Modifications and expansions to the Infant Strange Situation. Unpublished manuscript, Miami, FL.

Daws, D. (1985). *Through the Night: Helping Parents and Sleepless Infants*. London: Free Association Books. Reprinted 1993.

Daws, D. (2006). A child psychotherapist in the baby-clinic of a general practice: standing by the weighing scales thirty years on. In J. Launer, S. Blake and D. Daws (eds), *Reflecting on Reality*. London: Karnac Books.

Department for Education and Science (1999). *Making a Difference for Children and Families: Sure Start*. London: Stationery Office.

Desforges, C. (2003). *The Impact of Parental Involvement, Parental Support and Family Education on Pupil Achievement and Adjustment*. London: DfES.

De Wolff, M. S. and Van IJzendoorn, M. H. (1997). Sensitivity and attachment: a meta-analysis on parental antecedents of infant attachment. *Child Development*, 68(4), 571–591.

Egeland, B. E., Carlson, E. and Sroufe, A. (1993). Resilience as process. In *Development and Psychopathology*. Cambridge: Cambridge University Press.

Farrington, D. P. and Welsh, B. C. (2003). Family-based prevention of offending: a meta-analysis. *Australian and New Zealand Journal of Criminology*, 36(2), 127–151.

Felitti, V. J., Anda, R. F., Nordenberg, D., Williamson, D., Spitz, A. M., Edwards, V. *et al.* (1998). Relationship of childhood abuse and household dysfunction to many of the leading causes of death in adults: the Adverse Childhood Experiences (ACE) study. *American Journal of Preventive Medicine,* 14(4), 245–258.

Fonagy, P. (2001). *Attachment Theory and Psychoanalysis.* London: Karnac Books.

Fonagy, P., Steele, M., Steele, H., Moran, G. S. and Higgitt, A. (1991a). The capacity for understanding mental states: the reflective self in parent and child and its significance for security of attachment. *Infant Mental Health Journal,* 12, 201–218.

Fonagy, P., Steele, H. and Steele, M. (1991b). Maternal representations of attachments during pregnancy predict the organisation of infant–mother attachment at one year of age. *Child Development,* 62, 891–905.

Fonagy, P., Gergely, G., Jurist, E. L. and Target, M. (2004). *Affect Regulation, Mentalization, and the Development of the Self.* London: Karnac Books.

Fraiberg, S. (1977). *Insights from the Blind: Comparative Studies of Blind and Sighted Infants.* New York: Basic Books.

Fraiberg, S., Adelson, E. and Shapiro, V. (1980). Ghosts in the nursery: a psychoanalytic approach to the problems of impaired infant–mother relationships. In S. Fraiberg (ed.), *Clinical Studies in Infant Mental Health* (pp. 146–169). New York: Basic Books.

Gergely, G. (2007) The social construction of the subjective self: the role of affect-mirroring, markedness, and ostensive communication in self-development. In L. Mayes, P. Fonagy and M. Target (eds), *Developmental Science and Psychoanalysis: Integration and Innovation.* London: Karnac Books.

Gerhardt, S. (2004). *Why Love Matters: How Affection Shapes a Baby's Brain.* Hove: Brunner-Routledge.

Lieberman, A. F. (1992). Infant–parent psychotherapy with toddlers. *Development and Psychopathology,* 4, 559–574.

McDonough, S. C. (2004). Interaction guidance: promoting and nurturing the caregiving relationship. In A. J. Sameroff, S. C. McDonough and K. L. Rosenblum (eds), *Treating Parent–Infant Relationship Problems.* New York: Guilford Press.

Main, M. and Goldwyn, R. (1984). Predicting rejection of her infant from mother's representation of her own experience: implications for the abused–abusing intergenerational cycle. *Child Abuse and Neglect,* 8, 203–217.

Main, M. and Solomon, J. (1986). Discovery of an insecure disorganized/disoriented attachment pattern: procedures, findings and implications for classification of behaviour. In M. Yogman and T. B. Brazelton (eds), *Affective Development in Infancy* (pp. 95–124). Norwood, NJ: Ablex.

Main, M. and Solomon, J. (1990). Procedures for identifying infants as disorganized/disorientated during the Ainsworth Strange Situation. In M. T. Greenberg, D. Cicchetti and E. M. Cummings (eds), *Attachment in the Pre-school Years: Theory, Research and Innovation* (pp. 121–160). London: University of Chicago Press.

Meins, E. (1997). *Security of Attachment and the Social Development of Cognition.* Hove: Psychology Press.

Meins, E. (2004). Infants' minds, mothers' minds, and other minds: how individual differences in caregivers affect the co-construction of mind. *Behavioral and Brain Sciences*, 27(1), 116.

Miller, L. (1992). The relation of infant observation to clinical practice in an under-fives counselling service. *Journal of Child Psychotherapy*, 18(1), 19–32.

Muir, E., Lojkasek, M. and Cohen, N. (1999). *Watch, Wait and Wonder: A Manual Describing a Dyadic Infant-led Approach to Problems in Infancy and Early Childhood.* Toronto: Hincks-Dellcrest Centre and Institute.

Murray, L. and Andrews, L. (2000). *The Social Baby: Understanding Babies' Communication from Birth.* Richmond, Surrey: CP Publishing.

Murray, L. and Cooper, P. J. (1997). Postpartum depression and child development. *Psychological Medicine*, 27(2), 253–260.

Olds, D. L., Henderson, C. R., Chamberlin, R. and Tatelbaum, R. (1986). Preventing child abuse and neglect: a randomized trial of nurse home visitation. *Pediatrics*, 78(1), 65–78.

Olds, D. L., Henderson, C. R., Kitzman, H. J., Eckenrode, J. J., Cole, R. E. and Tatelbaum, R. C. (1999). Prenatal and infancy home visitation by nurses: recent findings. *Future Child*, 9(1), 44–65.

Olds, D. L., Sadler, L. and Kitzman, H. (2007). Programs for parents of infants and toddlers: recent evidence from randomized trials. *Journal of Child Psychology and Psychiatry,* 48(3-4), 355–391.

Patterson, G. R., DeBaryshe, D. and Ramsey, E. (1989). A developmental perspective on antisocial behavior. *American Psychologist*, 44(2), 329–335.

Perry, B., Pollard, R. A., Blakley, T. L., Baker, W. L. and Vigilante, D. (1995). Childhood trauma, the neurobiology of adaptation, and 'use-dependent' development of the brain: how 'states' become 'traits'. *Infant Mental Health Journal*, 16, 271–291.

Preston, S. D. and deWaal, F. B. M. (2002). Empathy: its ultimate and proximate bases. *Behavioral and Brain Sciences*, 25(1), 1–71.

Prior, V. and Glaser, D. (2006). *Understanding Attachment and Attachment Disorders: Theory, Evidence and Practice.* London: Jessica Kingsley.

Putnam, F. W. (2003). Ten-year research update review: child sexual abuse. *Journal of the American Academy of Child and Adolescent Psychiatry*, 42(3), 269–278.

Putnam, F. W. (2005). The developmental neurobiology of disrupted attachment. In L. Berlin, Y. Ziv, L. Amaya-Jackson and M. T. Greenberg (eds), *Enhancing Early Attachments: Theory, Research, Intervention and Policy.* London: Guilford Press.

Roisman, G. I., Fortuna, K. and Holland, A. (2006). An experimental manipulation of retrospectively defined earned and continuous attachment security. *Child Development*, 77(1), 59–71.

Sameroff, A. J. (2004). Ports of entry and the dynamics of mother–infant interaction. In A. J. Sameroff, S. C. McDonough and K. L. Rosenblum (eds), *Treating Parent–Infant Relationship Problems.* New York: Guilford Press.

Scaramella, L. V., Conger, R. D., Simons, R. L. and Whitbeck, L. B. (1998). Predicting risk for pregnancy by late adolescence: a social contextual perspective. *Developmental Psychology*, 34(6), 1233–1245.

Schore, A. N. (2001). Minds in the making: attachment, the self-organising brain, and developmentally orientated psychoanalytic psychotherapy. *British Journal of Psychotherapy*, 17(3), 299–328.

Sroufe, L. A., Egeland, B., Carlson, E. and Collins, A. W. (2005). *The Development of the Person: The Minnesota Study of Risk and Adaptation from Birth to Adulthood.* New York: Guilford Press.

Stern, D. (1985). *The Interpersonal World of the Infant. A View from Psychoanalysis and Developmental Psychology.* London: Basic Books.

Stewart-Brown, S. and Shaw, R. (2004). The roots of social capital: relationships in the home during childhood and health in later life. In A. Morgan and C. Swann (eds), *Social Capital for Health: Issues of Definition, Measurement and Links to Health.* London: HDA.

Treboux, D., Crowell, J. A. and Waters, E. (2004). When 'new' meets 'old': configurations of adult attachment representations and their implications for marital functioning. *Developmental Psychology*, 40(2), 295–314.

Tremblay, R. E., Masse, L. C., Pagani, L. and Vitaro, F. (1997). From childhood physical aggression to adolescent maladjustment: the Montreal prevention experiment. In R. D. Peters and R. J. McMahon (eds), *Preventing Childhood Disorders, Substance Abuse and Delinquency.* London: Sage.

Trevarthen, C. (1980). The foundations of intersubjectivity: development of interpersonal and cooperative understanding in infants. In D. R. Olson (ed.), *The Social Foundations of Language and Thought: Essays in Honor of Jerome Bruner.* New York: Norton.

Tronick, E. Z. and Cohn, J. F. (1989). Infant–mother face-to-face interactions: age and gender differences in coordination and the occurrence of miscoordination. *Child Development*, 60, 85–92.

Weinfield, N. S., Whaley, G. J. L. and Egeland, B. (2004). Continuity, discontinuity, and coherence in attachment from infancy to late adolescence: sequelae of organization and disorganization. *Attachment and Human Development*, 6(1), 73–97.

White, K. (2004). Developing a secure-enough base: teaching psychotherapists in training the relationship between attachment theory and clinical work. *Attachment and Human Development*, 6(2), 117–130.

Zaslow, M. J., Pedersen, F. A., Suwalsky, J. T. D. *et al.* (1985). The early resumption of employment by mothers: implications for parent–infant interaction. *Journal of Applied Developmental Psychology*, 6, 1–16.

Zeanah, C. H. (2000). Disturbances of attachment in young children adopted from institutions. *Journal of Developmental and Behavioral Pediatrics*, 21(3), 230–236.

Part I
Universal approaches

2 The power of touch – exploring infant massage

Angela Underdown

Touch, which is an intrinsic part of caring for an infant, can establish powerful physical and emotional connections. It is widely claimed that touch in childhood 'is significant for physical growth, health and neurological development' (Blackwell, 2000: 25), and research now shows that infants who are deprived of touch, such as those in orphanages with low infant–adult ratios, do not achieve optimum growth (Kim *et al.*, 2003; Mason and Narad, 2005). The amount of touch thought appropriate between adults and infants, however, varies enormously between cultures, with some babies experiencing close contact with the mother's body during most of the first year, while others are encouraged to be independent early by being put to sleep alone in the nursery. In many areas of the world, especially on the Asian and African continents, in indigenous South Pacific cultures, and in the former Soviet Union, touch, using the medium of infant massage, is a traditional practice (Field, 2000). A recent survey of 332 primary caretakers of neonates in Bangladesh, for example, found that 96 per cent of mothers engaged in massage of the infant's whole body between one and three times daily (Darmstadt *et al.*, 2002). Migration, world travel and the development of global communications have all influenced interest in the practice of infant massage and the techniques are becoming more widely known across the globe.

The popularity of infant massage in western cultures has steadily increased since the founding of the International Association of Infant Massage (IAIM) in the United States by Vimala McClure following her work in an orphanage in India in the 1970s. McClure (1985) became aware of the soothing effects of massage and its role in affectionate non-verbal communication after observing mothers massaging their infants, and older children massaging younger ones in the Indian orphanage. Since the establishment of the IAIM a host of other organisations have developed training programmes to teach the art of infant massage. This chapter starts by reviewing evidence about the importance of sensitivity in interactions and the role of touch for child development. Vignettes from case study material from the author's own observations of infant massage classes are provided to illustrate some emerging themes. The traditional nature of infant massage means that beliefs about the benefits are deeply embedded in cultural folklore and the chapter concludes with a discussion of the evidence about the effectiveness of infant massage from a systematic review of published research from around the world.

Early interactions

Parents play a crucial role in supporting the baby to manage or 'co-regulate' emotional states by sensitively responding so that the infant does not feel over-whelmed. Daniel Stern (1985), an American psychiatrist and psychoanalyst, de-scribed attunement as an empathic responsiveness between two individuals which subtly conveys a shared emotion, and he argues that attuned parents are able to act as sensitive moderators or accelerators of infant emotion. Responses are conveyed by observable characteristics such as eye contact, facial expressions, voice tone and touch, and micro-analysis of video recordings (Beebe and Lachmann, 1988) has enabled identification of matched responses which are so rapid as to suggest a bond of unconscious communication (Schore, 2003). These coping mechanisms are internalized by the infant who forms what Stern refers to as a representation of interaction that is generalized (RIG). The construction of RIGs is not a conscious process, but once these patterns have entered the memory they can be recalled at times of need to help the infant or young child self-soothe and, although RIGs may be adapted and updated, these early experiences with a self-regulating other lay the foundation for later adult capacities (Cole *et al.*, 2004). Other theorists have offered similar accounts about the development of emotional regulation, with Crockenberg and Leerkes (2000) describing how parent–infant interactions that contingently respond and reinforce one another foster emotional regulatory development. Matched emotional states indicate that the main carer is responding to the infant's emotional cues and that regulation is achieved or in the process of being re-established. Mismatches are inevitable and allow an opportunity for the parent to contribute actively to the development of adaptive processes over time. Hopkins (1996) highlights the dangers of 'too good' mothering, arguing that be-ing completely 'tuned in' is not an ideal state, and claims that it is the experience of frustration and conflict, together with their successful repair and resolution, which is optimal for development. The parent's role in moderating and co-regulating the infant's states of arousal is closely linked with the ability to reflect on the baby as an intentional being with thoughts, feelings and desires of his or her own (Fonagy *et al.*, 2004).

Although the majority (60 per cent) (Svanberg, 1998) of parents and infants interact sensitively and form secure attachments, the transition to parenthood is challenging and the tensions of adapting to the new infant leave many parents feeling under-confident and in need of support. The capacity to read infant cues and communications has been clearly linked with the regulation of emotional and bodily functions, and parents who can 'tune in' are less likely to experience sleep-ing and feeding problems with their infants. The foundation for healthy interac-tions is laid early and supporting the establishment of healthy early parent–infant relationships may avoid later difficulties.

Tactile stimulation

For most infants, everyday routines involve many tactile interactions, communicating a range of somatosensory messages including feelings, pressure, temperature, texture, softness or even pain. Touch has been reported as an intrinsic factor in helping to regulate infant behavioural states (Brazelton, 1990), and de Chateau (1976) found that infants who had extra bodily contact after birth smiled more and cried less on observation at 3 months. At birth the primary somatosensory centre, which processes tactile and kinesthetic information in the brain's cerebral hemispheres, is metabolically active (Chugani, 1996). Persistently high levels of stress hormones are known to have damaging effects on the development of neural pathways in the infant brain (Gunnar, 1998). The hypothalamic-pituitary-adrenocorticol (HPA) system produces and regulates the glucocorticoid cortisol in response to stress (Gunnar, 1998) and for the first two months after birth the infant's HPA system is highly labile (Gunnar *et al.*, 1996). However, from the age of about 2 months the infant's stress systems are becoming organised via transactions with sensitive main caregivers who act as a 'buffer' to the reactivity of the HPA system (Nelson and Bosquet, 2000). By 8 weeks the somatosensory connections to the amygdala (the almond-shaped group of neurons located deep within the brain's temporal lobes which have a major role in the processing and memory of emotional reactions) are forming, and Schore (2003) suggests that sufficient levels of tactile stimulation release early pro-attachment behaviour (Bowlby, 1969). Sensitive tactile stimulation during maternal nursing of the infant is thought to play a significant role in the growth of the dendrites that form the crucial neural connections (Greenough and Black, 1992, cited in Schore, 2003), and in primates neurobiological research suggests that 'critical levels of tactile input of specific quality and emotional content [are] important for normal brain maturation' (Martin *et al.*, 1991: 3355). Although most infants will receive adequate sensitive handling, the use of infant massage can offer a medium for promoting sensitive touch during this crucial developmental period.

How is infant massage taught in the UK?

Supporting sensitive early interaction is increasingly being perceived as important for later mental health, and infant massage is seen as a possible means of promoting this. While a few UK parents learn the traditional art from family members, the majority of parents who want to learn how to massage their baby attend a local class. Over the last decade many community infant massage classes have been initiated, both through the National Health Service (NHS) and privately.[1] Generous funding to local Sure Start programmes has ensured a rapid growth in provision, and recent practice guidance to Children's Centres contains a case study entitled 'Baby massage to promote attachment', based on the following justification:

> Baby massage is one way in which children's centres have sought to encourage infant–parent attachment and in turn promote good mental health in both parents

and babies. Instructors ... also include making the baby feel loved, facilitating body awareness, building both parent's and baby's self-esteem, relaxing parents and enabling them to learn about their baby's needs and desires.

(DfES, DH, Sure Start, 2006: 77)

Classes are usually scheduled to last for between one and two hours. Parents sit in a circle on cushions on the floor with their babies on mats in front of them and they are taught a technique for systematically stroking the baby's body using a non-allergenic oil. Sometimes soft music is played to enhance the relaxed atmosphere and parents are encouraged to be 'led' by their baby's needs. The leader models respectful care and attention while demonstrating the massage strokes on a doll. Modelling interaction with the doll has been observed to be more powerful than offering direct advice (Underdown, 2005, unpublished research). The vast majority of classes attract mothers and it is less likely that fathers will attend weekday sessions. However, research (Ballard *et al.*, 1994) indicates that about 9 per cent of fathers suffer depression during the transition to parenthood, and a hidden need may exist to support men as well as women. One Sure Start programme offered a Saturday morning infant massage class for fathers and infants only and, although several fathers indicated that they had been coerced into attending, all mentioned the positive aspects of attending the group:

> 'Well S [his partner] said I was going. So I do as I'm told. And I also do like to be involved where I can be. Although it would have met my expectations if I'd gone to the course and just learnt how to give a baby a massage and then come away. So all the extra discussions with Dads and trying to find out their experiences and finding out that it's not just me. That was just brilliant. That was a nice bonus.'
>
> (Underdown, 2005, unpublished research)

This father valued the opportunity to share experiences with other men who were developing their new roles as fathers, and discussion of this type was not available for him in any other forum within his life. As family mobility increases, parents often do not have adequate support networks and this may increase the risk of depression for men as well as women (Brown and Harris, 1978). Parents who are able to successfully negotiate their new roles as parents are likely to experience less conflict in their relationships and have more emotional 'space' to start engaging with the new family member (Belsky and Kelly, 1994; Cowan and Cowan, 1992).

It could be argued that the parents most likely to attend infant massage classes are the 60 per cent of mothers who are already sensitive and 'tuned in' and that those with more problems are less likely to attend. The National Evaluation of Sure Start indicated that 'harder to reach' families, who were likely to have more social problems, were also the least likely to attend Sure Start groups in general. However, to dismiss infant massage as only supporting those who need it least would be far too simplistic and there is evidence from case studies within practice that some workers are engaging with 'harder to reach' families. Furthermore, the transition to parenthood is complex (Stern, 1998) and men and women who might expect it to be straightforward can find themselves suffering with depression or experience other unexpected difficulties. Each parent–infant dyad negotiates their new relationship in an individual and unique way. The following two case studies describe mother–infant dyads that were experiencing real difficulties with interactions and establishing healthy relationships.

Case study A

Susan never expected to be a mother as she had been told when she was a teenager that she was infertile. She described herself as being in a state of disbelief and said that all her baby did was cry non-stop. Susan said that the crying was really 'getting to her' and she did not know what to do. Susan had also been crying all the time and the doctor had prescribed anti-depressants two weeks previously. The infant was still and unresponsive, and the mother intrusive in her interactions, kissing the baby without waiting for any response, so that the 'timing' was inappropriate. The baby tried to make eye contact with the mother during feeding but the mother had her head turned away and did not engage. Susan said that she wanted to attend infant massage because the health visitor had suggested that it would be good for them to have a break and get out of the flat.

Susan attended every week for a one-hour infant massage class and week by week she began to relax with her baby. During most sessions she sat alongside a mother who interacted joyfully and sensitively with her infant during the class and video footage shows how Susan gradually began to take an interest in her own infant's actions. The class was very accepting and mothers appeared to feel comfortable and valued.

After one class Susan reported that when she massaged her baby he stopped being so miserable, and that since she had been doing it, he had gone to sleep for a lot longer at night, and how this had made her feel much better. She said she used massage any time during the day if her baby was miserable and always before bedtime. Videotape footage of mother and baby at the completion of the course indicated that Susan had shifted from being considerably over-intrusive to having much more sensitive interactions, and that her baby had become very vocal and responsive. It could be argued that time and anti-depressants had caused this positive effect, but infant massage appeared to have improved this mother's sense of self-efficacy, and Susan felt sure that infant massage, which she continued to practise, had played a big part.

Case study B

The health visitor had worked hard to gain Zoe's confidence and had encouraged her to come to an infant massage group. Zoe did not appear to have postnatal depression (the Edinburgh Post Natal Depression Scale (Cox *et al.*, 1987) score was within normal limits) but she was extremely passive with her infant. Videotape footage of mother and infant together showed high levels of passive behaviour with an occasional intrusive 'prodding' of her baby. The baby was described by the mother as sleepy and not doing anything except crying. The mother attended every week with her infant, and again the group was welcoming and supportive. Video footage showed that although Zoe increasingly engaged with her infant, she was jerky and rough in some of her handling.

Each week this group engaged in some singing and on the third week Zoe asked the group leader to write out the words of the song so that she could sing it at home because her infant liked it. This seemed positive but, although weekly observations showed more engagement, a mistiming of interactions and a lack of eye contact and awareness of infant cues were also apparent. The group leader worked hard to promote Zoe's confidence and to tactfully suggest what the baby might be feeling by interpreting cues with the mother. The mother said at the end of the course that she wished it had gone on longer because it was calming for the baby. (The classes should have continued for five weeks but in fact the mother could only go for four as the clinic was closed one week.) Zoe said that she did not massage her infant at home in between groups.

At the end of the course videotape footage[2] showed that Zoe's interactions had changed from being passive with occasional intrusive behaviour to being very intrusive with her infant. Zoe still needed support in helping her to tune in to her baby's cues and signals. The sensitivity of interactions had not improved and almost certainly Zoe and her baby would have benefited from more support than could be offered by learning infant massage in isolation from other services.

This case study suggests that some parents require a higher level of support than can be offered by universal services. The infant massage group had, however, enabled the health visitor to build a trusting relationship with Zoe who felt confident enough to attend other forms of service provision with her infant where there was an opportunity for more intensive support.

Does infant massage work?

Research in western cultures has, to date, tended to focus on investigating infant massage as an intervention for infants in neonatal intensive care units (NICUs) where the environment is stressful and lacking in tactile stimulation. A recent review of the benefits of infant massage for preterm infants found that it improved daily weight gain by 5.1 g and reduced the length of hospital stay by 4.5 days (Vickers *et al.*, 2004). This review also indicated that massage interventions had a small positive effect on weight at 4-6 months. However, serious concerns were raised about the methodological quality of the included studies, and the authors were not able to recommend the widespread use of infant massage for preterm babies.

While there was insufficient evidence to support the introduction of massage in intensive care units to increase infant weight, there was little evidence of adverse effects in medically stable infants who could tolerate handling, and the above review did not focus on possible emotional benefits of parents being involved in massaging their infants. This was a significant omission given that the risks to preterm infants include difficulties with attachment processes, which may be exacerbated by early separation, parental anxiety, and by the fact that immature infants are unable to initiate and sustain interactions in the same way as healthy newborns (Wocadlo and Rieger, 2006; Crnic *et al.*, 1983; Brooten *et al.*, 1988; Corter and Minde, 1987). Evidence of increased behaviour difficulties and poorer social interaction in very low birth-weight infants has been gradually emerging over the last two decades (Hoy *et al.*, 1992; Hack *et al.*, 1994; Szatmari *et al.*, 1993; Rickards *et al.*, 2001; Gardner *et al.*, 2004), and it would therefore seem expedient for more research to consider whether infant massage might contribute to the reduction of stress levels and the establishment of healthy early relationships in high-risk preterm infants.

With regard to other high-risk infants, there is some evidence from single research studies that cocaine-exposed preterm infants had fewer medical complications, less irritability and increased weight gain after being massaged three times a day for a ten-day period (Wheeden *et al.*, 1993). Another single study reported that HIV-exposed infants had greater weight gain, enhanced performance on emotional and social scales, and fewer stress behaviours after their mothers administered infant massage over two weeks, compared to control groups (Scafidi and Field, 1996). Given the importance of promoting positive early infant–parent interactions, this non-invasive treatment could increase parents' involvement and confidence if appropriately implemented in NICUs as an enhancement to care plans. There is an urgent need for more high quality research to document parental views and to measure scientifically a wider range of outcomes in order to assess whether infant massage optimises care for preterm infants and their parents.

Infant massage is increasingly being used in the community with low-risk mother–infant dyads to promote relationships and to improve other outcomes such as improving sleep and reducing colic. The results of a recent systematic review (Underdown *et al.*, 2006) found that infant massage has beneficial effects in terms of reducing and balancing cortisol, epinephrine, and norepinephrine hormones which control stress levels (Field *et al.*, 1996). Persistently high levels of stress hormones are known to have damaging effects on the development of neural pathways in the infant brain (Gunnar, 1998). Evidence from animal studies would suggest that these results are biologically plausible (e.g. tactile stimulation moderates cortisol production and promotes glucocorticoid receptors in the hippocampus (Liu *et al.*, 1997)). Sleep deprivation is a very real problem for many families with a new infant, and one study (Goldstein-Ferber *et al.*, 2002) indicated that massage, given in appropriate amounts and with an appropriate level of pressure, significantly influences melatonin levels which are important in establishing circadian rhythms.

A further study (Onozawa *et al.*, 2001), in which postnatally depressed mothers and their infants attended a seventy-minute infant massage session over five weeks, found a significant increase in the amount of warmth and a reduction in the intrusiveness of maternal interactions (Murray *et al.*, 1996), compared to the control group who did not receive the intervention.

In the absence of evidence of any harm, the findings from this review support the current provision of infant massage in community settings during the postnatal period, particularly in areas where infant care may be deficient. They fall short, however, of providing the evidence necessary to recommend universal provision.

Conclusions

The earliest years are a crucial time for infant development (Bowlby, 1969, 1988; Stern, 1998; Sroufe, 1995; Steele *et al.*, 1996; Schore, 1994, 2001), pointing to the importance of finding acceptable ways of effectively supporting early emotional and social relationships in families with young children. Infant massage appears to be one such method that is suitable with both high- and low-risk groups, and review findings suggest that it is an effective way of reducing stress hormone levels and enhancing interaction when mothers are depressed. Further research is still needed, however, to strengthen the evidence base.

Notes

1 The Guild of Infant and Child Massage (www.gicm.org.uk) is the regulatory body for infant massage teachers and is committed to working towards raising the standards of courses and practice within the UK.
2 The video clips were analysed using Crittenden's (2001) CARE-Index as described in Chapter 9.

References

Ballard, C. G., Davis, R., Cullen, P. C. and Mohan, R. N. (1994). Prevalence of postnatal psychiatric morbidity in mothers and fathers. *British Journal of Psychiatry*, 164(6), 782–788.

Beebe, B. and Lachmann, F. (1988). Mother–infant mutual influence and precursors of psychic structure. In A. Goldberg (ed.), *Progress in Self Psychology*. Hillsdale, NJ: Analytic Press.

Belsky, J. and Kelly, J. (1994). *The Transition to Parenthood: How a First Child Changes a Marriage*. London: Vermilion.

Blackwell, P. (2000). The influence of touch on child development: implications for intervention. *Infants and Young Children*, 13(1), 25–39.

Bowlby, J. (1969). *Attachment and Loss, Vol 1. Attachment*. New York: Basic Books.

Bowlby, J. (1988). *A Secure Base*. London: Routledge.

Brazelton, T. B. (1990). *The Earliest Relationship*. Reading, MA: Addison-Wesley.

Brooten, D., Grennaro, S., Brown, L., Butts, P., Gibbons, A., Bakewill-Sachs, S. and Kumar, S. (1988). Anxiety, depression, and hostility in mothers of preterm infants. *Nursing Research*, 37, 213–216.

Brown, G. and Harris, T. (1978). *The Social Origins of Depression*. London: Tavistock.

Chugani, H. (1996). Neuroimaging of developmental nonlinearity and developmental pathologies. In R. Thatcher, G. Reid Lyon, J. Rumsey and N. Krasnegor (eds), *Developmental Neuro-imagining: Mapping the Development of the Brain and Behavior* (pp. 187–195). San Diego, CA: Academic Press.

Cole, P., Martin, S. and Dennis, T. (2004). Emotion regulation as a scientific construct: methodological challenges and directions for child development research. *Child Development*, 75, 317–333.

Corter, C. and Minde, K. (1987). Impact of infant prematurity on family systems. In M. Wolraich (ed.), *Advances in Developmental Behavioral Pediatrics*, (pp. 1–48). Greenwich, CT: JAI Press.

Cowan, C. and Cowan, P. (1992). *When Partners Become Parents*. New York: Basic Books.

Cox, J., Holden, J. and Sagovsky, R. (1987). Detection of postnatal depression: development of the 10-item Edinburgh Postnatal Depression Scale. *British Journal of Psychiatry*, 150, 782–786.

Crittenden, P. (2001). *CARE-Index Infant and Toddlers. Coding Manual*. Miami, FL: Family Relations Institute.

Crnic, K., Greenberg, M., Ragozin, A., Robinson, N. and Basham, R. (1983). Effects of social support on mothers and premature and full-term infants. *Child Development*, 54, 209–217.

Crockenburg, S. and Leerkes, E. (2000). Infant social and emotional development in family context. In C. H. Zeanah, Jr (ed.), *Handbook of Infant Mental Health*, 2nd edn. New York: Guilford Press.

Darmstadt, G., Samir, K. and Saha, A. (2002). Traditional practice of oil massage of neonates in Bangladesh. *Journal of Health, Population and Nutrition*, 20(2), 184–188.

de Chateau, P. (1976). The influence of early contact on maternal and infant behaviour on primaparae. *Birth and Family Journal*, 3, 149–155.

DfES, DH, Sure Start (2006). *Sure Start Children's Centres: Practice Guidance*. London: DfES, DH, Sure Start.

Field, T. (2000). Infant massage therapy. In C. H. Zeanah, Jr (ed.), *Handbook of Infant Mental Health*, 2nd edn. (pp. 494–500). New York: Guilford Press.

Field, T., Grizzle, N., Scafidi, F., Abrams, S. and Richardson, S. (1996). Massage therapy for infants of depressed mothers. *Infant Behaviour and Development*, 19, 107–112.

Fonagy, P., Gergely, G., Jurist, E. and Target, M. (2004). *Affect Regulation, Mentalization and the Development of the Self*. London: Karnac.

Gardner, F., Johnson, A., Yudkin, P., Bowler, U., Hockley, C., Mutch, L. and Wariyar, U. (2004). Behavioral and emotional adjustment of teenagers in mainstream school who were born before 29 weeks gestation. *Pediatrics*, 114(3), 676–682.

Goldstein-Ferber, S., Laudon, M., Kuint, J., Weller, A. and Zisapel, N. (2002). Massage therapy by mothers enhances the adjustment of circadian rhythms to the nocturnal period in full-term infants. *Developmental and Behavioral Pediatrics*, 23(6), 410–415.

Greenough, W. and Black, J. (1992). Induction of brain structure by experience. Substates for cognitive development. In M. Gunnar and C. Nelson (eds), *Minnesota Symposium on Child Psychology. Vol. 24 Developmental Behavioral Neuroscience* (pp. 155–200). Hillsdale, NJ: Erlbaum.

Gunnar, M. (1998). Quality of early care and buffering of neuroendocrine stress reactions: potential effects on the developing human brain. *Preventive Medicine*, 27, 208–211.

Gunnar, M., Brodersen, L., Krueger, K. and Rigatuso, J. (1996). Dampening of adrenocortical responses during infancy: normative changes and individual differences. *Child Development*, 67, 877–889.

Hack, M., Taylor, H., Klein, N., Eiben, R., Scatschneider, C. and Mercuri-Minich, N. (1994). School-age outcomes in children with birthweights under 750g. *New England Journal of Medicine*, 331(12), 753–759.

Hopkins, J. (1996). The dangers and deprivations of too-good mothering. *Journal of Child Psychotherapy*, 22(3), 407–422.

Hoy, E., Sykes, D., Bill, J., Halliday, H., McClure, B. and Reid, M. (1992). The social competence of very-low-birthweight children: teacher, peer and self-perception. *Journal of Abnormal Child Psychology*, 20(2), 123–150.

Kim, T. I., Shin, Y. H. and White-Traut, A. C. (2003). Multisensory intervention improves physical growth and illness rates in Korean orphaned newborn infants. *Research in Nursing and Health*, 26(6), 424–433.

Liu, D., Diorio, J. and Tannenbaum, B. (1997). Maternal care, hippocampal glucocorticoid receptors and hypothalamic-pituitary-adrenal responses to stress. *Science*, 277, 1659–1662.

McClure, V. (1985). *Infant Massage: A Handbook for Loving Parents*. New York: Bantam Books.

Martin, L., Spicer, D., Lewis, M., Gluck, J. and Cork, L. (1991). Social deprivation of infant rhesus monkeys alters chemoarchitecture of the brain: 1. subcortical regions. *Journal of Neuroscience*, 11(11), 3344–3358.

Mason, P. and Narad, C. (2005). Long-term growth and puberty concerns in international adoptees. *Pediatric Clinics of North America*, 52(5), 1351–1368.

Murray, L., Fiori-Cowley, A., Hooper, R. and Cooper, P. (1996). The impact of postnatal depression and associated adversity on early mother–infant interactions and later infant outcome. *Child Development*, 67, 2512–2526.

Nelson, C. and Bosquet, M. (2000). Neurobiology of fetal and infant development: implications for infant mental health. In C. H. Zeanah, Jr (ed.), *Handbook of Infant Mental Health*, 2nd edn. New York: Guilford Press.

Onozawa, K., Glover, V., Adams, D., Modi, N. and Kumar, C. (2001). Infant massage improves mother–infant interaction for mothers with postnatal depression. *Journal of Affective Disorders*, 63, 201–207.

Rickards, A., Kelly, E., Doyle, L. and Callanan, C. (2001). Cognition, academic progress, behaviour and self-concept at 14 years of very low birthweight children. *Journal of Developmental and Behavioral Pediatrics*, 22(1), 11–18.

Scafidi, F. and Field, T. (1996). Massage therapy improves behaviour in neonates born to HIV positive mothers. *Journal of Pediatric Psychology*, 21, 889–898.

Schore, A. (1994). *After Regulation and the Origin of the Self: The Neurobiology of Emotional Development*. Hillsdale, NJ: Erlbaum.

Schore, A. (2001). The effects of secure attachment relationship on the right brain development, affect regulation and infant mental health. *Infant Mental Health Journal*, 22, 7–66.

Schore, A. (2003). *Affect Dysregulation and Disorders of the Self*. New York: Norton.

Sroufe, L. (1995). *Emotional Development: The Organization of Emotional Life in the Early Years*. Cambridge: Cambridge University Press.

Steele, H., Steele, M. and Fonagy, P. (1996). Associations among attachment classifications of mothers, fathers and their infants. *Child Development*, 67, 541–555.

Stern, D. (1985). *The Interpersonal World of the Infant*. New York: Basic Books.

Stern, D. (1998). *The Motherhood Constellation*. London: Karnac.

Svanberg, P. O. (1998). Attachment, resilience and prevention. *Journal of Mental Health*, 7(6), 543–578.

Szatmari, P., Saigal, S., Rosenbaum, P. and Campbell, D. (1993). Psychopathology and adaptive functioning among extremely low birth weight children at 8 years. *Development and Psychopathology*, 5, 345–357.

Underdown, A., Barlow, J., Chung, V. and Stewart-Brown, S. (2006). Massage intervention for promoting mental and physical health in infants aged under six months. (Cochrane review). In *Cochrane Database of Systematic Reviews*, 4. Chichester: John Wiley and Sons.

Vickers, A., Ohlsson, A., Lacy, J. B. and Horsley, A. (2004). Massage for promoting growth and development of preterm and/or low birth-weight infants. (Cochrane review). In *Cochrane Database of Systematic Reviews*, 4. Chichester: John Wiley and Sons.

Wheeden, A., Scafidi, P., Field, T. and Ironson, G. (1993). Massage effects on cocaine exposed pre-term neonates. *Journal of Developmental and Behavioral Pediatrics*, 14, 318–322.

Wocadlo, C. and Rieger, I. (2006). Social skills and nonverbal decoding of emotions in very preterm infants at school age. *European Journal of Developmental Psychology*, 3(1), 48–70.

3 The Solihull Approach

An integrative model across agencies

Hazel Douglas and Mary Rheeston

Babies have very different experiences at the hands of their carers. Compare, for example, the following two descriptions of mother–baby interaction:

> She then turns and puts him on her knee in the usual way. Freddie arches his back and turns his face towards her. He reaches his little hand up to his mother's cheek and tries for some time to turn her face towards him, but mum seems distracted, first by his brother and sister fighting and squabbling, and then by her own thoughts and she begins to chat distractedly.
>
> (Reid, 1997: 68)

> A few moments later he wakes up. He tries to open his eyes, then closes them again. He repeats this sequence several times. Then his facial expressions become more noticeable, his face puckers, he begins to utter little cries and to wriggle about. He puckers his face even more, his hands twist, his arms begin to flail about, and he starts to cry. Mme Martine arrives with the feeding bottle. She speaks to him reassuringly and lifts him up. Maxime stops crying at once. He immediately relaxes and looks intently at his mother. Mme Martine is still talking to him, telling him how like his father he is - like him, not very lucky as far as hair is concerned! Maxime is very much in contact with his mother; he looks as though he's devouring her with his eyes.
>
> (Besnard *et al.*, 1998: 53)

We know from these two examples that the interaction between Freddie and his mother has not gone well from Freddie's point of view, or indeed from the perspective of his mother enjoying her relationship with her son. We can also tell immediately that Maxime and his mother are both in this moment, and in tune with one another. We know these things intuitively, but the Solihull Approach provides the concepts and the language to describe some of the major aspects of the relationship between babies and their parents. As Wittgenstein said, 'what we cannot speak about we must pass over in silence' (Wittgenstein, 1921: Proposition 7, p. 89). By naming these things it becomes possible to think, discuss and work with them.

In the UK most families with a new baby are in contact with a health visitor, who visits the family soon after birth, and with midwives and the antenatal and birth team throughout pregnancy. The research literature suggests that these professionals are working with families at a time when it is possible to support parents and parenting in a way that will optimise the outcome in terms of the baby's future. The Solihull Approach is aimed at providing this key group of professionals with the skills to do just that.

This chapter describes the research context and the model underpinning the Solihull Approach including the concepts on which it is based. It then provides a description of its application using a number of case studies. The chapter concludes with evidence from a number of studies that have been conducted to evaluate its impact on the relationships between mothers and babies.

The research context

The minutiae of relationships are important because it is within the context of the second-to-second contact with their parent or main carer that babies develop the foundation for everything that follows. Indeed, the development of the baby's brain takes place within the context of a relationship. For example, as a result of the baby's early relationships, connections will be made between the outer cortex, relatively unformed at birth, and the underlying limbic brain, which is the seat of emotion and impulse (Schore, 2001). Within the context of these relationships, the baby will learn to regulate himself, to tolerate the frustration of having to wait, or share, or be said 'no' to (Gianino and Tronick, 1988). He will learn language (Lock, 1978); he will build on his already innate ability to relate to others (Murray and Andrews, 2000; Schore, 2003). He will learn to sit still and concentrate at school (Shonkoff and Phillips, 2000). He will grow into his genetic potential for the number of connections in his brain. Or will he?

Research shows that babies who grow up in poor environments can end up with 25 per cent fewer connections in their brains than they would otherwise have had (Perry, 1995). This reflects the fact that most of the development of the brain occurs in the first three years of life (Perry, 1995). Research has also begun to show exactly what is meant by a 'poor environment' in terms of a baby's early relationships, and one of the most significant findings over the past few decades has been the baby's capacity and need for attuned interaction, and the 'rhythmical pattern of looking and withdrawal' (Tronick, 1989) which characterises the early relationship between primary caregiver and baby. We now know, for example, that the ruptures in Freddie's relationship with his mother would probably have had little negative effect if he had also had the experience of them being repaired. 'Rupture and repair' is a well researched phenomenon, where a mother and baby move in and out of being in tune with one another, as part of their everyday interactions with one another. Tronick (1989) found that mothers and babies are in coordinated interactions about 30 per cent of the time, and that they regularly switch between coordinated and uncoordinated states. This has been hypothesised to be helpful to the baby's development, creating the basis for hope and optimism that things can get better (Tronick, 1989; Beebe and Lachmann, 2002). The experience of events not going right can be tolerated with the hope that they will improve. However, longitudinal observation of Freddie showed that the outcome for him was not good, because he repeatedly had the experience of rupture without repair. Freddie slowly began to give up trying to gain his mother's attention and withdrew into himself. One can imagine that Maxime, on the other hand, would often have had moments of being in tune with his mother and that when their relationship had showed a lack of reciprocity they would soon have been able to get back in step with one another.

The Solihull Approach

The Solihull Approach supports practitioners working with children and their families, especially antenatally and in the early years, to provide the sort of sensitive and attuned parenting that the above research suggests is important in order to optimise the infant's development. It is aimed at practitioners who work with children across agencies, and provides a common language, a shared model, and shared resources for parents. The Solihull Approach helps practitioners to help parents and their infants in several ways. It sets the scene by presenting key messages from research on the maturation of the infant brain and child development, to provide an understanding of how crucial parents are to their children's progress in the early years. It aims to help parents to process emotions and anxieties that are felt to be overwhelming, which in turn both restores the parents' ability to think and enables them to help the baby or child cope with his emotions and anxieties. It helps practitioners and parents to understand how the parents and child interact, which can then provide the basis for feedback in order to facilitate the relationship. It also helps parents work with their child's behaviour.

The Solihull Approach supports practitioners by providing training, and comprehensive resource packs that are underpinned by an integrative theoretical model.

The model

The model underpinning the Solihull Approach emerged over a period of three years. The first two concepts to be used were *containment* (Bion, 1959), from psychoanalytic theory, together with *behaviour management*, from social learning theory (Skinner, 1938). To these was added the concept of *reciprocity* (Brazelton *et al*., 1974), from child development research, to enable practitioners to address the full range of parent–infant relations. These three concepts illuminate many aspects of the world of infants and their parents, and provide a powerful theoretical model for understanding how a family finds itself in its current situation, and which intrinsically supports practitioners to work together in partnership with the family to improve relationships between the parent and child, and to help parents to process indigestible feelings and inform sensitive behaviour management.

Containment (Bion, 1959) refers to a situation in which 'one person receives and understands the emotional communication of another without being over-whelmed by it and communicates this back to the other person', and is aimed at helping practitioners to help parents process emotions and anxieties that are felt to be overwhelming (Douglas, 2004a: 37). This in turn both restores the parents' ability to think and enables them to help the baby or child cope with his emotions and anxieties. Containment contributes to emotional regulation together with reciprocity. Reciprocity (Brazelton *et al.*, 1974) refers to 'the sophisticated interaction between a baby and an adult where both are involved in the initiation, regulation and termination of the interaction' (Douglas, 2004a: 52), and in which the parent is sufficiently attuned to be able to adjust their interaction to meet the baby's emotional needs. It is aimed at helping parents and practitioners to see how a parent and child are interacting. Behaviour management techniques are then used to help parents work with their child's behaviour. The relationship between containment and reciprocity, and their relationship to attachment theory, is explored in greater detail elsewhere (Douglas, 2007).

An antenatal resource pack entitled 'The Journey to Parenthood' is currently being developed by and for practitioners working antenatally and the year after birth, together with a complementary antenatal parenting group manual. Topics include reciprocity *in utero*, prenatal brain development, stress during birth, and developing resilience *in utero*. Each resource pack has been developed by a project group, usually working over at least a two-year period. Eight discussion leaflets for parents, on sleeping, feeding, toileting and behavioural difficulties, have been developed in a range of languages.

The Solihull Approach team has also developed parenting courses (the Solihull Approach Parenting Group - Douglas, 2006), which comprise a structured group-based intervention, based on the application of the above theoretical principles, which includes relationship-enhancing strategies which are provided over the course of ten weeks, in two-hourly sessions. It enables parents to identify their own objectives from session one onwards and the course is then customised around those objectives. Teaching involves the use of role-play, together with homework. The provision of such courses requires practitioners to undergo an additional day of training, and to receive ongoing support and supervision.

Training in the Solihull Approach

The Solihull Approach training courses are structured and designed to be easily transmissible so that they can be 'cascaded' to a wide range of staff. Each training session is supported by a training manual. The Foundation training comprises a two-day programme with an intervening period of two to three weeks between Day 1 and Day 2 to enable the trainee to undertake homework. The course includes theory and brain development on Day 1. The homework in the intervening period requires the practitioner to undertake a number of observations and to begin to apply the theory to practice. Day 2 involves the practitioner using the homework to integrate theory with practice. The training has been designed to have an element of experiential learning – 'learning by doing' (Kolb, 1985) – and can be delivered to uni-professional and multi-professional/multi-agency groups. In some areas of the UK, all child practitioners across agencies are being trained in the application of the model. Where the training is provided to whole centres – e.g. everyone in a Children's Centre – the training can also be split into modules, to enable everyone within the centre to take part, without interfering with service delivery.

The Solihull Approach in practice

Case study

At a routine 8-month assessment with the health visitor Angela's daughter Sophie was shown to have sudden accelerated head growth. While waiting for an appointment with a paediatrician Angela took her daughter to see the health visitor repeatedly to have her head measured. Each time she saw the health visitor she expressed minor worries which included sleep difficulties. The health visitor wondered if Angela's main worries about Sophie's sleep difficulties related to the paediatric referral for her head. She listened to Angela and offered small amounts of behaviour management advice. However, the sleep difficulties worsened and there was increased friction between Angela and her partner.

The health visitor arranged a home visit, during which she listened in more detail to Angela talking about her worries. It became apparent that Angela felt unable to let Sophie cry during the night. When the health visitor asked Angela how she felt when Sophie cried, Angela said that she felt fear. She had worked as a nanny and one of the children had had a febrile fit in the night while asleep in his cot.

As the health visitor listened it also emerged that Angela did not want Sophie to grow up so fast because her partner did not want another child. She therefore tried to monopolise Sophie in order to make the most of the time she had with her, and this excluded her partner.

This was the first time that anyone had helped Angela to think about what was happening and to put her feelings into words. She and the health visitor devised a programme together to work on over the next week. They arranged to meet in ten days, with telephone contact in between if necessary. However, before the appointment Angela telephoned the health visitor and said that she had talked to her partner, who had said how excluded he had felt. Furthermore, Sophie had been sleeping through the night.

This case study may seem straightforward, but it harbours a paradigm shift. Instead of simply providing advice about sleeping difficulties early in the interaction, the health visitor made space to listen. She also made space for emotions, indicating this to the parent by asking about feelings. When they both understood something of 'the story', they jointly created a behavioural programme. Effective behaviour management thus occurred later in the process, was customised, and was worked out jointly with the parent. Containment was thereby used to help develop a narrative and an understanding, which provided a mechanism through which the family could become 'unstuck'.

The Solihull Approach provides a theoretical model to both encourage and support this shift in practice, by giving practitioners knowledge and confidence. While this case study does not demonstrate the use of the concept of reciprocity, this can also be very helpful in enabling the interaction between the parent and child.

An example of this occurred in a postnatal group in a Children's Centre run by a Solihull Approach-trained health visitor. She was explaining the dance of reciprocity using everyday language while the mothers were interacting with their babies. One mother had postnatal depression, which the group had talked about previously. This mother said to the group, 'Oh look, he's looked away now. He doesn't like me.' She said to her baby, 'What? You're bored?' The health visitor explained, 'It's really interesting what happens to babies when they look away. Before they look away they have been having a chat and getting lots of smiles and different experiences. Then their brain wants to save it, so they look away while their brain saves it and then they might think I'd like some more of that and then they turn back.' As if on cue the baby turned back to his mother. She said, 'Oh you do like me, you've come back for a bit more', and they started the dance again. In the discussion afterwards the mother said that she didn't know about babies looking away and thought he didn't like her. Knowing about reciprocity changed her perception of her baby immediately. It was noticeable in the group the following week, when the mothers were discussing weaning, that they were more able to wait for their babies. Knowing about reciprocity is also helpful in infant massage.

Evaluation of the Solihull Approach

Research has shown that the two-day Foundation training has an impact on practice (Douglas and Ginty, 2001), improving both the consistency and the quality of the initial assessment that is made by the health visitor. One health visitor who had been trained in the approach described it as follows:

> 'I used to look at the interaction between mothers and babies and wonder what was going on. Then I learned about containment and reciprocity and it changed the way I look at things.'
>
> (Douglas, 2004a: 13)

This research showed that while the initial assessment with families on the whole took longer than usual, the overall duration of the intervention did not increase because subsequent sessions were shorter, and sometimes only a telephone follow-up was necessary. The confidence of practitioners in their ability to support parents in their parenting also increased as a result of the training, as did job satisfaction.

Lowenhoff (2004) evaluated training in the Solihull Approach in over 100 health and social care professionals in Essex. She found that health visitors who had undertaken the Solihull training during the previous year reported that it had changed their way of thinking about child behaviour. They also reported that in order to understand the problem from both the child's and the parent's perspective, they tended to spend more time undertaking a comprehensive assessment, and that this reaped dividends in the long run in terms of measurable outcomes, and a reduction in the overall time they spent responding to family concerns or crises (Lowenhoff, 2004: 100).

An unpublished study (Lintern, 2005) of eighty-two primary health care professionals (school nurses, nursery nurses, health visitors, psychologists, child protection nurses) similarly found that the majority of respondents who had implemented the approach

> indicated that their practice had improved in terms of an increase in level of skill, particularly in relation to listening and observational skills and also in terms of an increase in understanding of baby brain development and the theoretical basis of the Approach. Improvements were also reported in levels of confidence and in terms of relationships, particularly in relation to *empowering parents*.

(Lintern, 2005: 6)

A further study that was conducted to explore health visitors' perceptions about the changes that had taken place in their practice as a result of the training (Whitehead and Douglas, 2005) found that health visitors perceived themselves to have changed across a range of domains, including their general approach, improved understanding, better structuring of visits, and changes to case and workload. They also identified improvements for the families, improved job satisfaction, and improved relations with other professionals.

The findings from this study also suggested that health visitors perceived the Solihull Approach to have improved their ability to appropriately refer clients to other services, and to have expedited the referral process. These findings were confirmed by an audit, which showed that the quality of referrals from health visitors and school nurses to Solihull Child and Adolescent Mental Health Services (CAMHS) had vastly improved, both in terms of the appropriateness of the referral and the quality of the information given. Furthermore, health visitors were referring much younger infants (i.e. from a few weeks old upwards) to CAMHS, possibly reflecting an increase in their confidence about what they were seeing in terms of the relationship between the mother and baby.

Initial studies to evaluate whether the Solihull Approach improves outcomes for participating families are also encouraging. Douglas and Brennan (2004) found a significant reduction in the severity of the presenting difficulty, and in parental anxiety about the symptom (p<0.001). Parents also showed a significant reduction in their overall anxiety level, which decreased by an average of 66 per cent.

These results were replicated by an independent study (Milford *et al.*, 2006) in another part of the UK, which found some improvements on the Douglas and Brennan study, with a slightly larger sample size, the use of a control group and an increased follow-up period of three months.

Early evaluation of the first seventy-two datasets from parents who had participated in the Solihull Parenting Programme showed statistically significant differences on measures of anxiety (Beck's Anxiety Inventory) and child behaviour (Child Behaviour Checklist and the Strengths and Difficulties Questionnaire), with improvements in parents' anxiety levels being correlated with improvements in children's behaviour.

Early indications are that the Solihull Approach Parenting Group is also effective in improving outcomes for parents and children (Bateson *et al.*, 2008).

Conclusion

Infant mental health strategies should comprise a comprehensive set of services that are underpinned by an integrated theoretical approach such as the one described here, within a broader model of progressive universalism. The Solihull Approach provides an effective way of skilling-up the primary care workforce to enable them to work on a universal basis to support healthy parent–infant relationships. It also provides a system of identifying infants at risk from birth or before, alongside an effective model for generalist health-care practitioners to support the parents of such infants, and to be able to recognise parent–infant dyads who are in need of referral for more specialist support.

References

Bateson, K., Delaney, J. and Pybus, R. (2008) Meeting expectations: the pilot evaluation of the Solihull Approach Parenting Group. *Community Practitioner*, 81, 28–31.

Beebe, B. and Lachmann, F. (2002). *Infant Research and Adult Treatment*. Hillsdale, NJ: Analytic Press.

Besnard, S., Courtois, M., Fayolle, A., Miller, L. and Rustin, M. (1998). Three observations of young infants, with commentary on initial patterns of communication and containment between the babies and their parents. *International Journal of Infant Observation*, 1(2), 51–70.

Bion, W. R. (1959). Attacks on linking. In *Second Thoughts*. London: Karnac (1993).

Brazelton, T. B., Koslowski, B. and Main, M. (1974). The origins of reciprocity: the early mother–infant interaction. In M. Lewis and L. Rosenblum (eds), *The Effect of the Infant on its Caregiver*. London: Wiley.

Department for Education and Skills (2001). Questions about mental health. In *Promoting Children's Mental Health Within Early Years and School Settings.* London: DfEE.

Douglas, H. (2004a). *The Solihull Approach Resource Pack: The First Five Years,* 4th edn. Cambridge: Jill Rogers Associates.

Douglas, H. (2004b). *The Solihull Approach Resource Pack: The School Years.* Cambridge: Jill Rogers Associates.

Douglas, H. (2006). *The Solihull Approach Parenting Group: Supporting Parent/Child Relationships. Facilitator's Resource Pack.* Cambridge: Jill Rogers Associates.

Douglas, H. (2007). *Containment and Reciprocity: Integrating Psychoanalytic Theory and Child Development Research for Work with Children.* London: Routledge.

Douglas, H. and Brennan, A. (2004). Containment, reciprocity and behaviour management: preliminary evaluation of a brief early intervention (the Solihull Approach) for families with infants and young children. *International Journal of Infant Observation,* 7(1), 89–107.

Douglas, H. and Ginty, M. (2001). The Solihull Approach: changes in health visitor practice. *Community Practitioner,* 74, 222–224.

Fonagy, P., Steele, H. and Steele, M. (1991). Maternal representations of attachment during pregnancy predict the organisation of infant–mother attachment at one year of age. *Child Development,* 62, 891–905.

Gianino, A. and Tronick, E. Z. (1988). The mutual regulation model: the infant's self and interactive regulation, coping and defense. In T. Field, P. McCabe and N. Schneiderman (eds), *Stress and Coping.* Hillsdale, NJ: Erlbaum.

Kolb, D. (1985). *Experiential Learning: Experience as the Source of Learning and Development.* London: Prentice Hall.

Lintern, J. (2005). A follow-up evaluation of the Solihull Approach training, Middlesbrough: unpublished study.

Lock, A. (1978). The emergence of language. In A. Lock (ed.), *Action, Gesture and Symbol.* London: Academic Press.

Lowenhoff, C. (2004). Practice development: training professionals in primary care to manage emotional and behavioural problems in children. *Work Based Learning in Primary Care,* 2, 97–101.

Milford, R., Kleve, L., Lea, J. and Greenwood, R. (2006). A pilot evaluation study of the Solihull Approach. *Community Practitioner,* 79, 358–362.

Murray, L. and Andrews, L. (2000). *The Social Baby.* Richmond, Surrey: CP Publishing.

Perry, B. D. (1995). Childhood trauma, the neurobiology of adaptation and use-dependent development of the brain. *Journal of Infant Mental Health,* 16, 271–291.

Puckering, C., Mills, M., Rogers, J., Cox, A. and Mattsson-Graff, M. (1994). Process and evaluation of a group intervention for mothers with parenting difficulties. *Child Abuse Review,* 3, 299–310.

Reid, S. (1997). The development of autistic defences in an infant. *International Journal of Infant Observation*, 1(1), 51–79.

Schore, A. N. (2001). Effects of a secure attachment relationship on right brain development, affect regulation and infant mental health. *Journal of Infant Mental Health*, 22, 7–66.

Schore, A. N. (2003). Minds in the making: attachment, the self-organizing brain, and developmentally-oriented psychoanalytic psychotherapy. In J. Corrigall and H. Wilkinson (eds), *Revolutionary Connections: Psychotherapy and Neuroscience*. London: Karnac.

Shonkoff, J. P. and Phillips, D. A. (2000). *From Neurons to Neighbourhoods: The Science of Early Childhood Development*. Washington, DC: National Academy Press.

Skinner, B. G. (1938). *The Behaviour of Organisms*. New York: Appleton-Century-Crofts.

Tronick, E. Z. (1989). Emotions and emotional communication in infants. *American Psychologist*, 44, 112–126.

Tronick, E. Z. and Cohn, J. F. (1989). Infant–mother face-to-face interactions: age and gender differences in coordination and the occurrence of miscoordination. *Child Development*, 60, 85–92.

Whitehead, R. and Douglas, H. (2005). Health visitors' experience of using the Solihull Approach. *Community Practitioner*, 78, 20–23.

Wittgenstein, L. (1921). *Tractatus Logico-Philosophicus*. London: Routledge (2001).

Further information

www.solihull.nhs.uk/solihullapproach

For an information pack or details about training, resource packs or research, please contact: Solihull Approach Administrator, Vaillant Building, Dunster Road, Chelmsley Wood, Birmingham, B37 7UU. Tel: 0121 788 3787. Email: solihullapproach@solihull-ct.nhs.uk

4 Promoting development of the early parent–infant relationship using the Neonatal Behavioural Assessment Scale

Joanna Hawthorne

The aim of health professionals should be to support parents in establishing an environment where babies can grow, develop and thrive (Shonkoff and Phillips, 2000; Nugent 2006); and supporting parents as they explore the characteristics of their newborn baby has been shown to be a factor in helping parents feel confident about their parenting role (Bakeman and Brown; 1980; Beal, 1986; Cardone and Gilkerson, 1990). Appropriate support can improve resistance to risk factors and contribute to successful developmental outcomes, adaptation and child resilience (Meisels *et al.*, 1993; Nugent, 2006; Sameroff, 1993).

There are an increasing number of studies demonstrating the positive preventive effects of relationship-based interventions for infants and their families, a number of them outlined in this volume. Most successful interventions, whether they are primarily preventive or therapeutic, are based on facilitating the parent–child relationship and helping both the child and the caregiver to learn to adapt successfully to each other (Brazelton *et al.*, 1974; Nugent *et al.*, 2007a). This requires support for the parent–child relationship, but also for the professional–parent relationship.

This chapter examines the role of the Neonatal Behavioural Assessment Scale (NBAS), developed in 1973 by Dr T. Berry Brazelton, in helping parents to read their baby's behavioural signals in order to develop a practical caregiving strategy. This chapter describes how the information gathered in the thirty-minute assessment can enable parents and professionals to observe the baby's strategies for coping with changes in state (sleep and awake states), with crying, with stimulation and with social interaction.

Infant behaviour

In order to understand the relationship between baby and parent, it is important to first understand the infant's behaviour, because this provides the key to how the baby is communicating and the areas where the baby will need support (Schore, 1994). One way is to employ an interactive assessment, of which there are few designed for use during the newborn period. Often, when professionals are supporting parents with a new baby, they tend to give advice and suggestions for trying different handling techniques based on a general understanding of babies. But rarely do professionals use a hands-on approach when working with parents and their newborn baby that enables them to focus on the individual baby.

Many parents are quite anxious about whether they are 'doing the right thing', and parents often feel that there is only one way to parent a baby and that they have to get it right. The philosophy underpinning the NBAS is that the baby is the 'guide book' (Nugent, 2004), and by learning their baby's ways of communicating parents can respond appropriately. Furthermore, by providing accurate information on infant development, as well as helping them to understand that development has moments of moving forward, as well as moments of regression, we can help parents to deal with the different developmental stages (Brazelton and Sparrow, 2006).

Until fairly recently, it was thought that newborns were unable to communicate (Wolke, 1995). The caregiver was thought to be the main influence on the baby's behaviour, and the process was not viewed as a two-way interaction. However, it is now recognised that newborn babies come into the world with remarkable abilities to communicate and interact with their caregivers *(*Klaus *et al.*, 1995). Furthermore, during the last few years, there has been an explosion of knowledge and information about babies' brain development, showing that the way infants are handled and interacted with affects the structure of their brain (Als *et al.*, 2004). We know that a child's socio-emotional development depends on a positive, nurturing attachment relationship to a primary caregiver, and it is now thought that the first three months of life are a sensitive period, when the infant is most ready to learn to understand emotions (Fonagy, 1998), and to develop such a relationship. Thus, an infant who has his needs met appropriately will become a more self-confident and secure individual.

Brazelton and Cramer (1991) suggest that babies need the following in order to achieve this:

1   An observer who sees their strengths and helps them with their difficulties
2   Warm, responsive interactions with their caretakers - taking turns
3   Vocalisations reinforced by response, initially imitation
4   Structure and routine, with flexibility
5   Interesting things to look at and do
6   Establishment of a dialogue with their caretaker who understands variabilities in development and the process
7   Play, autonomy and flexibility in their interactions, leading to attachment
8   A parent confident in understanding the behaviour of their baby

Understanding baby behaviour

A baby's behaviour is his main method of communication. In the first two months of life, the baby communicates through his behaviour and his vocalisations. The baby's initial responses to stimulation are reflexive, and babies learn quickly. The parent will provide stimulation with everyday handling, and will be observing the baby to see how he responds. However, some parents are not sure of what to look for, or of the meaning of some of the behaviours, and, as a result, there may be difficulties in reading the baby's signals and cues. Some babies show very subtle reactions such as colour changes, or looking away, and some babies may have intense reactions that puzzle the parent. Some parents can impute negative intent to their baby's behaviour, thinking that the baby is trying to irritate them on purpose. It is, however, possible to work with families to help them to respond appropriately to the infant's behaviours, and understand their meaning.

Withdrawal signals

There are many ways in which babies will show their likes and dislikes, through body or facial movements, as well as through colour changes, respiratory changes and digestive changes ...

Looking away; shutting eyes; spitting up; hiccuping; yawning; sneezing; holding hands up defensively; finger splaying; clenching fists; arching back; squirming; staring with no facial expression; frown; grimace; skin colour changes; sucking; changing position; changing state

Readiness to interact signals

Babies who are ready to interact will show a different set of signals:

Wide-eyed, bright-eyed, with raised eyebrows; arms and hands relaxed and open; interested in fixing and following

Regulatory behaviours

Babies who are able to regulate themselves will show the following behaviours and strategies:

Smooth respiration; good, stable colour; stable digestion; smooth relaxed posture; even motor tone; smooth movements, efficient strategies: hand clasping, foot bracing, hand to mouth, grasping, sucking, rooting, tucking

The Neonatal Behavioural Assessment Scale (NBAS)

The NBAS, which was first published in 1973 (Brazelton, 1973), with the third edition being published in 1995 (Brazelton and Nugent, 1995), is a tool that provides an interactive, strength-based way of understanding the baby's social and emotional development. It offers a window into the baby's abilities, capturing the behavioural characteristics of the infant in the very early days. The NBAS can be used with any full-term baby from 37 weeks gestation (full term) to 8 weeks old. It can also be used with any baby who has reached term, and was born preterm, ill, or small for gestational age, or who has congenital malformations or other difficulties.

Dr Brazelton's aim was first to understand the strengths of the infant, but also to recognise their difficulties. He noted the communicative abilities of infants and developed the NBAS so that these abilities could be captured and understood. The NBAS was not developed as an objective assessment in the psychometric or medical diagnostic tradition with an emphasis on pass/fail criteria (Nugent, 2006).

In 1997, the Brazelton Centre in Great Britain was founded to make training in the Neonatal Behavioural Assessment Scale (NBAS) available outside of the USA. It is one of seventeen Brazelton Centres worldwide. At the same time in the UK, the government's early intervention policy, Sure Start, was introduced, and funding was made available for many deprived areas in Britain to support programmes for parents and children aged from birth to 4 years.

Professionals working with newborns became interested in using the NBAS as a supportive intervention with parents, and although the NBAS was designed as a research tool in 1973, it began to be widely used as an intervention in the 1980s. It was found to be a helpful tool with which to explore with parents the amazing capabilities of their baby (Nugent, 1985). It began to be used to obtain information about behaviour, and to help parents to identify ways to provide support for the baby in their efforts to self-regulate their behavioural states from sleeping to crying. It was also used to show whether the individual baby had self-soothing strategies in place, such as sucking their hand, looking at something nearby, or finding a contained position. If the baby had difficulties with self-soothing the NBAS could be used to determine how much facilitation the baby needed to remain calm.

This scale thereby became recognised as an excellent tool for understanding babies. Within thirty minutes, the examiner can observe how the individual baby manages crying, sleeping and feeding behaviours, and his or her strategies for self-regulation. By handling the infant, the examiner elicits many of the newborn reflexes, which is a helpful way of seeing how the newborn reacts to stress, and it can also be used as a neurobehavioural screening tool.

The newborn's developmental agenda

The newborn baby's developmental agenda (Higley *et al.*, 1999) is to achieve a harmonious, regulated state (internal goals). His external goals are to deal with the environment by engaging socially and with objects (Tronick, 2003). Wolff (1966) was one of the first people to describe the baby as capable of organised behaviour.

The baby is working on four systems: autonomic, motor, state, and social interactive. These systems do not work in a linear fashion but simultaneously. This information helps parents to know the 'work' of the infant and that the infant is an active partner. They can then observe the infant's strengths and difficulties or challenges, from birth.

Autonomic system

Definition

This system concerns temperature control, breathing control, digestive function and physiological functioning. At birth, the baby must adapt to the extrauterine environment. The baby's adaptation will be influenced by his intrauterine experience, the effects of drug use of the mother, drugs in labour and delivery, and other factors. We can observe how the baby's autonomic system is functioning by noticing tremors, startles, colour changes, breathing rates, etc.

What information it gives parents

If the baby is showing some signs of an unstable autonomic system, this means he will be using a great deal of energy to organise this system, and may be less available or even unavailable for social interaction. A baby with these signs will need gentle handling and containment in order to support his efforts to gain stability in this system.

Motor system

Definition

The motor system concerns reflexes and tone, activity level and maturity of movement.

At birth, the baby will be coping with gravity and beginning to develop coordinated movements. He may move smoothly or with jerky movements, and his reflexes may vary in their intensity. A baby may mould when cuddled, or he may push away, indicating that he wants to be in a different position, or perhaps that he is finding the intensity of the touch intrusive.

A baby's motor tone has been shown to influence the development of postnatal depression (Murray and Cooper, 1997). A baby with low tone may be floppy and difficult, and may be unrewarding to hold; a baby who has high tone may seem to move out of the parent's arms or move away. A baby with good tone may feel easier and more comfortable to hold. As the baby becomes more coordinated in this system, he may become more available for social interaction.

What information it gives parents

Many parents see newborn reflexes as a skill, and are amazed at their baby's ability. In the very early days after birth, seeing the baby's toes wrap over the examiner's finger in the plantar grasp may be the first time they have seen the baby respond directly to stimulation. By observing the motor activity levels and tone, parents can assess whether the baby is feeling stable and contained in his movements, or whether he may need to be swaddled or carried in a sling, helping him to remain calmer.

State system

Definition

State refers to sleep and awake conditions:

State 1 Deep sleep	*State 4* Alert
State 2 Light sleep	*State 5* Active and alert
State 3 Drowsy	*State 6* Crying

Dr Brazelton uses the six states described first by Wolff (1966), and later Prechtl (1977), ranging from deep sleep to a full-blown crying state. The baby's state will determine his performance on a particular item. For example, a baby who is in a light sleep (state 2) will not feed well. It would be better to start a feed when he is in an alert state 4. A baby who is in a state 5 or 6 may not be available for play. By assessing the baby's state, one can determine the baby's readiness for social interaction and playing, as well as feeding or sleeping.

What information it gives parents

The way the baby moves from state to state abruptly, or skips states, provides information on the baby's characteristics. Some babies may be in a deep sleep, open their eyes and move straight into a crying state. Other babies may move slowly from a deep sleep, light sleep, drowsy, to an alert state. This baby has a more organised state regulation than the previous baby, and may be easier to be with. During the habituation items (or response decrement items), it is possible to see how the baby reacts to a disturbing light (from a torch) or noise (from a rattle or a bell) while he is asleep. If the baby is easily disturbed by these items, he needs help to stay asleep by learning self-calming strategies, or by having his bed in a quiet, dimly lit room. This will help parents help the baby to protect his sleep and encourage good sleep.

Social interactive system

Definition

This system includes the following items: alert and responsive, looking, following and vocalising.

The baby may be organising his other systems and therefore be unavailable for interaction or only available for short periods. It helps his caregiver to understand this, and that it is better not to push him to interact until he is ready. The social interactive items are very appealing to parents as they show how the baby is ready to communicate and interact with people.

What information it gives parents

It helps parents to see how responsive and receptive a baby can be from birth. If they know he can see, follow, hear and smile, they are more likely to talk to their baby and play with him.

The baby can be shown a red ball or a red rattle so that he can track them, and this tracking is seen as a clever skill by parents. The baby can also turn to sounds such as the rattle, the examiner's voice, and the parent's voice. When the baby turns to the parent's voice, it engenders a sense of awe in the parent, and re-inforces the fact that the baby is their baby and belongs to them. It also shows the parents that the baby knows them and recognises their voice, which he has been listening to *in utero* for several weeks.

Another way to show how well the baby knows the parent's voice is to place the baby between one parent and the professional, and ask the parent to call the baby's name at the same time. When a baby chooses to turn to the parent rather than the professional, this shows again the baby's preference for their own parent's voice which they know well, over the professional's voice.

A baby who is not as responsive as a parent would like can disappoint a parent. It may be that the baby is working to stabilise his other systems so he is not as available for social interaction as they had hoped. Also, their baby may not com-municate in the way they expect, but may have another way of communicating. Accepting this enables the parents to explore and understand their baby's own ways of communication.

Stimulation

Another important factor in understanding infant behaviour is to detect the amount of stimulation a baby can cope with. This can be assessed during the NBAS, and stress signals will be shown in the baby's behaviour. A baby may show very sub-tle signs of stress, such as a slight colour change, looking away, or looking down, and these might be missed. He may also show sneezes, yawns, as well as spitting up, gagging, hiccuping and certain motor behaviours. Individual babies will have their own repertoire, and parents can be helped to recognise these behaviours. Un-derstanding why the baby is not responding as they might expect may help parents to be sympathetic to the baby's needs at the time.

Research using the NBAS

The NBAS has been used in over 800 studies worldwide, mostly as a research tool. In the USA in the 1980s it was used increasingly as a supportive intervention for parents (Nugent, 1985). Observing the capabilities of their infant, in the first month of life increased maternal self-confidence (Widmayer and Field, 1981). Anderson and Sawin (1983) found that the NBAS enhanced responsiveness in mother–infant interaction. Beal (1989) found that fathers who had helped perform the NBAS on their infants at birth felt closer to them one month later and were more involved in their care. A recent study by Cooper and Murray (2004) found that an intervention with an adapted form of the NBAS increased maternal sensitivity. A study by Nugent *et al.*, (2007b) found that an intervention with an assessment using NBAS concepts, the NBO (Newborn Behavioural Observations), at 4 days of age and at 1 month of age with healthy, full-term babies reduced the likelihood of serious postnatal depression by 75 per cent. Mothers who participated in the NBO were four times more likely to be judged as more sensitive in their interactions with their infants on the CARE-Index (Crittenden, 1979-2004). Infants who were exposed to the NBO were six times more likely to be judged as responsive compared to control group infants, also assessed on the CARE-Index.

Nugent and Brazelton (1989, 2000) describe the use of the NBAS as a preventive intervention. Other studies have shown that an NBAS intervention increased developmental scores of very low birth-weight babies (Rauh *et al.*, 1988), and mothers who actively participated in the behavioural assessment of the infant in the NICU setting showed positive effects on maternal perceptions of their infants (Parker *et al.*, 1992). Stern (1995) and Stern and Bruschweiler-Stern (1998) examined the mother's adjustment to her foetus in pregnancy, and how she imagined the baby to be. They identified that for some mothers the newborn baby is not at all like the imagined baby, and that the NBAS can help mothers adjust to the real baby.

Research suggests therefore that the NBAS is an excellent tool for supporting parents and parenting in a range of contexts.

Learning the NBAS – considerations for trainees

The NBAS is a therapeutic tool, and learning how to use it effectively with parents is an extremely important aspect of the training. Trainees are guided in their use of language with parents, omitting the use of labels and words that may be interpreted negatively by the parent. For instance, it is important to understand that the baby is a social being who likes people, and that if he does not follow the face of the professional, it does not mean that the baby does not 'like' them. Rather, it helps to examine how other factors in the newborn system might be affecting the baby's ability to attend. In contrast with many other assessments, the aim of the NBAS is to bring out the baby's best performance. The baby's communicative skills and robustness are shared with the parents, and the examiner's role is to facilitate the baby's behavioural skills. The interaction between examiner and baby can simulate the parent–infant interaction and provide an understanding of the baby's contribution to the parent–infant relationship.

It is important that NBAS assessors avoid the use of the expert model of working, thereby preventing the mother from feeling that the baby is acting differently with the examiner. The goal is to share with the parents how the baby reacts to stimulation, using words such as: 'He finds it difficult when I shake the rattle loudly'; 'She finds it hard to stay calm when she has few clothes on'; 'Have you found something that helps her manage these times?' or 'Let's see what helps her.' The parents will often have noticed these things, and during the assessment they will observe how the baby reacts to certain supports, and hear the descriptive words used by the examiner. Parents can learn more easily when modelling and observation are used. Conversing with the baby and reinforcing and validating the mother's comments and observations on her infant throughout are ways to work with the parents. This approach reinforces the fact that the mother/father is the expert about the baby, and that all relationships are about figuring out what each other needs. Most of the time, the baby will behave with the examiner similarly to the way he behaves with the mother, which can help to remove the mother's possible sense of guilt or isolation.

There are times when it may not be suitable to handle the baby, but the same goals can still be achieved. In an adaptation of the NBAS called the Family Administered Neonatal Activities (FANA) (Cardone and Gilkerson, 1990), the examiner does not handle the baby but guides the parent to do so. This approach may well be appropriate in some cases, such as 'parental fear of handling the infant, resurgence of grief due to prior perinatal loss, or distress from an especially difficult labor and delivery' (Cardone and Gilkerson, 1995). (A manual of the FANA is to be published in December, 2007.)

NBAS examiners need to have a thorough understanding of infant development as well as of the issues and influences on parenting, and need to be skilled in listening to parents. Nugent lists the qualities needed in a good NBAS examiner (2006; Nugent *et al.*, 2007a):

1. **A good observer has excellent handling techniques** – is able to observe, recognize and respond to the infant's threshold for responding, is able to read cues for stress and availability, recognize states however subtle and respond with sensitive handling, and be flexible in letting the infant lead the interaction, using appropriate pacing
2. **Good interpreter** - has a deep developmental understanding – knows how newborn behavior is organized but also appreciates the developmental challenges parents are facing
3. **Good communication skills** – has the ability to listen to and engage parents simultaneously observing the infant; collaborative relationship with parent
4. **Offers guidance that is non-didactic** – but is individualised, developmentally appropriate and culturally sensitive.

Conclusion

Parents are fascinated by their baby's behaviour, and they easily recall the NBAS intervention on follow-up (Bruschweiler-Stern, 2000). Some parents have

48   *Joanna Hawthorne*

commented on how much their baby liked the NBAS, or how it affected them as parents (Hawthorne, 2005). One parent with a preterm baby commented that 'Bonding is difficult in the NICU. Baby does not feel like your own. The assessment helps to affirm you do know your baby.'

Professionals who learn the NBAS feel that it helps them to understand infant behaviour. One midwife said: 'I am much more observant of the baby's "cues" and feel more confident sharing them with parents to help facilitate a healthy attachment, for example, by saying "look how much your baby's responding to you".' Professionals feel that they help the mother and baby, and father if present, to make that connection which they see as the beginning of an attachment relationship. There is often a moment during the NBAS when this occurs, such as when the baby turns to the mother's voice, and the mother says to her baby, 'Oh you do know me!' Any parent or worker experiencing this moment knows that the relationship has just taken another step towards becoming stronger. But it also strengthens the relationship between the professional and the parent, and most say that they would recommend it to other parents or colleagues. One midwife said she would recommend its use because 'it gives you a tool that opens the "neonatal behaviour mystery box" and brings you closer to a mum through this process, and what a privilege that is!'

References

Als, H., Duffy, E., McAnulty, G., Rivkin, M., Vajapeyam, S., Mulkern, R. *et al.*, (2004). Early experience alters brain function and structure. *Pediatrics*, 113(4), 846–857.

Anderson, C. J. and Sawin, D. (1983). Enhancing responsiveness in mother–infant interaction. *Infant Behavior and Development*, 6(3), 361–368.

Bakeman, R. and Brown, J. V. (1980). Early interaction: consequences for social and mental development at three years. *Child Development*, 51, 437–447.

Beal, J. A. (1986). The Brazelton Neonatal Behavioural Assessment Scale: a tool to enhance parental attachment. *Journal of Pediatric Nursing*, 1, 170–177.

Beal, J. A. (1989). The effect on father–infant interaction of demonstrating the Neonatal Behavioural Assessment Scale. *Birth*, 16, 18–22.

Brazelton, T. B. (1973). *Neonatal Behavioral Assessment Scale*. Clinics in Developmental Medicine, No. 50. London: Heinemann Medical Books Ltd.

Brazelton, T. B. and Cramer, B. G. (1991). *The Earliest Relationship: Parents, Infants and the Drama of Early Attachment*. London: Karnac Books.

Brazelton, T. B. and Nugent, J. K. (1995). *The Neonatal Behavioural Assessment Scale*, 3rd edn. London: Mac Keith Press.

Brazelton, T. B. and Sparrow, J. D. (2006). *Touchpoints. Birth to Three. Your Child's Emotional and Behavioral Development*, rev. 2nd edn. Cambridge, MA: Da Capo Press.

Brazelton, T. B., Koslowski, B. and Main, M. (1974). The origins of reciprocity: the early mother–infant interaction. In M. Lewis and L. Rosenblum (eds), *The*

Effect of the Infant on its Caregivers (pp. 49–77). New York: Wiley Inter-science.

Bruschweiler-Stern, N. (2000). Modèle d'intervention préventive au cours de la période néonatale. *Prisme*, 33, 126–139.

Cardone, I. A. and Gilkerson, L. (1990). Family Administered Neonatal Activi-ties: a first step in the integration of parental perceptions and newborn behavior. *Infant Mental Health Journal*, 11, 127–131.

Cardone, I. A. and Gilkerson, L. (1995). Family Administered Neonatal Activi-ties (FANA). In T. B. Brazelton and J. K. Nugent (eds), *Neonatal Behavioural Assessment Scale*, 3rd edn. London: Mac Keith Press.

Cooper, P. and Murray, L. (2004). Enriching the mother–infant relationship in the postpartum months: a preventative intervention. Paper presented at Enriching Early Parent–Infant Relationships Conference, London.

Crittenden, P. M. (1979-2004). CARE-Index Coding Manual. Unpublished man-uscript, Miami, FL. Available from the author.

Fonagy, P. (1998). Prevention, the appropriate target of infant psychotherapy. *Infant Mental Health Journal*, 19(2), 124–150.

Hawthorne, J. (2005). Using the NBAS to support parent–infant relationships in a neonatal unit. *Infant*, 1(6), 213–218.

Higley, B., Cole, J. G., Howland, E., Nugent, J. K. and Ranuga, T. (1999) The Newborn Developmental Agenda. In *Neonatal Behavioral Assessment Scale (NBAS) Handbook.* Boston, MA: Brazelton Institute.

Klaus, M. H., Kennell, J. H. and Klaus, P. H. (1995). *Bonding.* Reading, MA: Addison-Wesley Longman.

Meisels, S., Dichtelmiller, M. and Fong-Ruey, L. (1993). A multidimensional analysis of early childhood intervention programs. In C. Zeanah (ed.), *Hand-book of Infant Mental Health*, New York: Guilford Press.

Murray, L. and Cooper, P. J (1997). The role of infant and maternal factors in postpartum depression, mother–infant interactions, and infant outcomes. In L. Murray and P. J. Cooper (eds), *Postpartum Depression and Child Develop-ment.* New York: Guilford Press.

Nugent, J. K. (1985). Using *the NBAS with Infants and their Families: Guidelines for Intervention.* White Plains, NY: March of Dimes Birth Defects Foundation.

Nugent, J. K. (2004). A relationship-building approach of family-centered care beginning in the newborn period – training healthcare professionals in the Clinical Neonatal Behavioral Assessment Scale (CLNBAS). Paper presented at Enriching Early Parent–Infant Relationships Conference, London.

Nugent, J. K. (2006). Looking back, looking forward: using the NBAS to under-stand newborn behavior. Presentation at the Brazelton Study Day, Clare Col-lege, Cambridge.

Nugent, J. K. and Brazelton, T. B. (1989). Preventive intervention with infants and families: the NBAS model. *Infant Mental Health Journal*, 10, 84–99.

Nugent, J. K. and Brazelton, T. B. (2000). Preventive infant mental health: uses of the Brazelton Scale. In J. Osofsky and H. E. Fitzgerald (eds), *WAIMH*

Handbook of Infant Mental Health (Vol. II, pp. 159-202). New York: John Wiley and Sons.

Nugent, J. K., Keefer, C. H., Minear, S., Johnson, L. C. and Blanchard, Y. (2007a). *Understanding Newborn Behavior and Early Relationships. The Newborn Behavioral Observations (NBO) System Handbook.* Baltimore, MD: Paul H. Brookes Publishing Co.

Nugent, J. K., Valim, C., Killough, J., Gonzalez, J., Wides, J. and Shih, M. C. (2007b). The effects of the Newborn Behavioral Observations (NBO) system on reducing postpartum depression. Poster presented at the Society for Research in Child Development, biennial meeting, Boston.

Parker, S., Zahr, L. K., Cole, J. C. D. and Braced, M. L. (1992). Outcomes after developmental intervention in the neonatal intensive care unit for mothers of preterm infants with low socioeconomic status. *Journal of Pediatrics*, 120, 780–785.

Prechtl, H. F. R. (1977). *The Neurological Examination of the Full-term, Newborn Infant*, 2nd edn. Spastics Medical Publications. London: William Heinemann.

Rauh, V., Achenbach, T., Nurcombe, B., Howell, C. and Teti, D. (1988). Minimizing adverse effects of low birthweight: four-year results of an early intervention program. *Child Development*, 59, 544–553.

Sameroff, A. J. (1993). Models of development and developmental risk. In C. H. Zeanah, Jr (ed.), *Handbook of Infant Mental Health* (pp. 3–13). New York: Guilford Press.

Schore, A. N. (1994). *Affect Regulation and the Origin of the Self.* Hillsdale, NJ: Lawrence Erlbaum Associates.

Shonkoff, J. P. and Phillips, D. A. (eds) (2000) *From Neurons to Neighbourhoods: The Science of Early Childhood Development.* Washington, DC: National Academy Press.

Stern, D. (1995). *The Motherhood Constellation.* New York: Basic Books.

Stern, D. and Bruschweiler-Stern, N. (1998). *The Birth of a Mother.* New York: Basic Books.

Tronick, E. Z. (2003). Things still to be done on the still-face effect. *Infancy*, 4(4), 475–482.

Widmayer, S. and Field, T. (1981). Effects of Brazelton demonstrations for mothers on the development of preterm infants. *Pediatrics*, 67, 711–714.

Wolff, P. H. (1966). *The Causes, Controls, and Organization of Behavior in the Neonate.* New York: International Universities Press.

Wolke, D. (1995). Parents' perceptions as guides for conducting NBAS clinical sessions. In *Neonatal Behavioural Assessment Scale*, 3rd edn. J. K. Nugent and T. B. Brazelton (eds), London: Mac Keith Press.

Zeanah, C. H., Jr (ed.) (1993). *Handbook of Infant Mental Health.* New York: Guilford Press.

Useful websites

www.brazelton.co.uk
www.brazelton-institute.com
www.touchpoints.org
www.zerotothree.org
www.socialbaby.com

Training in the NBAS in the UK

For information see www.brazelton.co.uk

For workshops, study days, conferences or other queries, please contact: Brazelton Centre in Great Britain, c/o Box 226, NICU, Addenbrookes NHS Trust, Hills Road, Cambridge CB2 2QQ. Telephone: 01223-245791. Fax: 01223-217064.

5 'First Steps in Parenting'

Developing nurturing parenting skills in mothers and fathers in pregnancy and the postnatal period

Mel Parr, in collaboration with Catherine Joyce

Introduction

Professional observations and research have shown that a substantial number of women and their partners enter new parenthood not knowing what to expect emotionally or without the skills or support to evaluate or cope with the normal and natural changes they encounter. British antenatal classes appear to be based on the myth that, during pregnancy, women are not capable of addressing issues beyond the birth experience. Postnatal groups focus mainly on practical aspects of infant care or offer loosely structured social support. The most persistent criticisms are the narrowness of focus, the provision of just one social opportunity after the birth for new parents to meet up and talk about their experiences, and the exclusion of fathers. There is an unforeseen demand for a change of focus and for continuity in antenatal classes, and there is a need for further emotional support for early parenting after the birth, which includes fathers and emphasises non-verbal emotional-expressive communication between parents and infants (Parr *et al.*, 1997; Parr, 1998; Woollett and Parr, 1997; WHO, 1995).

'First Steps in Parenting' is an evidence-based parent–infant programme for the antenatal and postnatal period which helps fathers and mothers build strong nurturing relationships with their infants. Parents also learn communication and problem-solving skills for family life in order to help develop a framework within which potentially challenging experiences can be managed more creatively, and so that they can respond more sensitively and confidently to their infants.

This chapter describes the literature relating to the transition to parenthood, and the First Steps in Parenting programme. It concludes with a description of an evaluation of the programme using a British longitudinal study (Parr, 1996).

The transition to parenthood

The transition to parenthood refers to the fairly brief period of time from the beginning of pregnancy through to the first months of having a child, and is an important window of opportunity for promoting parent and infant mental health. Maternal stress and anxiety in pregnancy can have a permanent effect on infant outcomes in terms of increased risk of prematurity and low birth weight (Glover and O'Connor, 2006), and neuro-developmental disorders in later childhood (Glover, 2007). Postnatal depression also affects attachment and child development (Murray and Cooper, 1997).

The development of a 'secure' attachment is the central issue in the first year of life, during which the infant needs to learn trust in people and the environment. A common factor in mothers of securely attached children is 'maternal attunement' (Stern, 1985, 1995). Sensitive parents interacting with their infants modulate their infant's rhythms, facilitating the development of the infant's sense of integrated selfhood. This process of attunement is impaired in mothers of insecurely attached infants, leading to a 'mismatch' in maternal response. The quality of an infant's attachment to the parent is linked to factors present and measurable in pregnancy, such as the parents' 'internal working model' (Bowlby, 1977), their capacity to reflect on the current state of the child, the quality of the mother–infant (Ainsworth *et al.,* 1971) and father–infant relationship (Dragonas, 1990; Pruett, 1993), the couple relationship, and 'complementarities' in the couple's parenting process (Belsky and Kelly, 1994; Diamond *et al.,* 1996). Also important is 'mind-mindedness' – the mother's proclivity to treat her infant as an individual with a mind, rather than merely as a creature with physical needs that must be satisfied (Meins, 1997, 2007). What distinguishes mothers of insecure children from those of secure ones is not a general failure to respond to their children; rather their responses are more likely to be inappropriate because they are less able or willing to think about why the child is demonstrating a particular behaviour. The 'mind-minded' mother is willing and able to change her focus of attention in response to cues from her infant.

Involving fathers is also important, even when they do not take part in routine caretaking. Becoming a father brings men face-to-face with their own emotions and expectations and reflects their identification with their own father. New fathers may also become depressed, contributing to stress, anxiety and depression in mothers, and impacting on the parent–infant relationship.

Effective preparation for parenting goes beyond a mere basic ability to recognise and respond to the child's physical states, such as hunger, and emotional states, such as distress. Secure attachment is more likely to develop if intense states of mind in infancy are emotionally contained by well supported mothers and fathers, starting before birth. Programmes which focus mainly on preparation for childbirth, practical aspects of infant care or maternal mental health make no difference to infant attachment. Women and their partners who are better equipped to face the normal feelings of anxiety and ambivalence that occur in pregnancy and after birth have the capacity to tolerate and express negative feelings in their family of origin and current relationships. This is more likely to lead to less stress, anxiety and depression in the parents and the development of secure attachment (Fonagy, 1998; Perry *et al.,* 1995).

A four-stage integrative model

First Steps in Parenting is designed to complement traditional antenatal classes, and provides thirty-seven hours of structured support to four to six couples and their infants in a closed group setting through eight weekly two-hour group sessions in pregnancy, a one-hour home or hospital visit soon after the birth, and ten weekly postnatal group meetings. The programme is manualised but flexible and non-prescriptive. There are four stages to the programme: antenatal, review, home visit, and postnatal group.

Antenatal

In the antenatal stage of a typical First Steps in Parenting group, which begins around three to five months into pregnancy, pregnant women and their partners meet weekly and begin to 'wonder aloud' about their infants by reflecting on their own experiences of being parented and their hopes and expectations of themselves and their partners as parents. Meetings focus on topics such as 'changing feelings and relationships', 'roles and responsibilities' and 'parent–infant relationships'. Participants are encouraged to share experiences and to learn listening, communication, and problem-solving skills to help them feel less overwhelmed and cope more creatively with problems as they arise. The skills are practised in same-sex pairs and small groups. Partners then come together to practise the skills with each other around the session theme, to help them make choices based on their own needs and values. A large group discussion draws together key messages and learning from the session, and ideas for putting the skills into practice over the week are drawn up. This is reviewed and further developed at the beginning of the following session.

Review

In late pregnancy the group meets less often, perhaps fortnightly or every three weeks, while participants are encouraged to attend traditional antenatal classes. During this time, the programme provides ongoing emotional support as births are celebrated and infants join the group (the youngest member in a group being 1 day old).

Home visit

Each family receives an individual one-hour home visit from one of the facilitators within two weeks of the birth. Based on a specialised adaptation for this programme of the 'Family Administered Neonatal Assessment' (FANA) (Cardone and Gilkerson, 1989, 1990), this provides an opportunity for parents to process the labour and delivery experience if needed. It also provides parents with an opportunity for observing and exploring how they respond to their infant and how the infant responds to them. Facilitators adopt a 'hands off' approach and encourage parents to discover their infant for themselves (Parr, 1996), by posing the question: 'Tell me what you have noticed about your baby so far?' – in order to minimise future challenges in the parent–infant relationship.

Postnatal group

Support issues raised during the home visit are further addressed in weekly postnatal group sessions until infants are around 3-4 months old. The focus remains on parent–infant relationships in the context of the normal concerns of new parents (such as crying, sleeping, feeding, health, balancing work and home, and the changing couple relationship). Parents also further review whether they have adequate support from each other, family, and friends, to meet the demands of early parenting, and develop strategies to overcome any problems using the skills learned in pregnancy. Facilitators pose questions relating to issues which arise naturally during the groups. For example, when a baby begins to cry, they might ask 'What do you notice happening for your baby right now?', 'What do you notice about how you are feeling?', 'What do you think your baby is trying to do or tell you?' or 'Why might your baby be so upset?' Facilitators acknowledge parents' feelings and make verbal observations to help parents focus on meaningful behaviours and read their infant's cues, and help parents reflect on whether a given approach 'works' for their infant. As they learn about their own and others' feelings and perspectives about parenting and observe the different ways their infants communicate their wants, needs and personalities, parents shift from an emphasis on controlling the infant so that sensitivity, empathy and respect develop naturally.

Parents are encouraged to continue to meet socially between sessions and after the programme has ended. Facilitators adhere to professional boundaries and limits of the programme and refer parents to local specialist professional support if needed (which is rare because of the emotional containment provided by the programme).

Facilitation

Each programme group is run by a pair of specially trained facilitators (Parr, 1996, 1999) using a core humanistic model of group work (Glassman and Kates, 1990). Groups are delivered at an 'educational and counselling skills level'; no analysis or interpretation of parent or infant behaviours is offered, even where unconscious processes are evident. Parents are viewed as sources of knowledge about their infant, rather than recipients of the expertise of others. Facilitators model the skills and attitudes of healthy family and parent–infant communication and relationships through their interactions with their co-worker, parents and infants. Group process is used to promote and reinforce change and provide social support.

Evaluation

The primary data for the evaluation of the programme were obtained from a British longitudinal study (Parr, 1996) carried out between 1989 and 1993, in which 106 couples expecting their first baby were recruited from an NHS antenatal clinic in North Hertfordshire. Ages ranged from 17 to 45 years; the mean for women was 29 years, and 31 years for men. Educational backgrounds varied; 30 per cent had received further or higher education. Most were employed and 57 per cent of the women returned to work after birth. A wide range of jobs and family income was represented.

All couples were offered the opportunity to take part in the new programme at recruitment and were allocated at random to a group depending on due dates, until nine groups were filled. Most couples (92 per cent) were interested in the offer of the programme: eight couples expressed no interest and fourteen couples who were interested were unable to attend because due dates or work schedules were incompatible with programme dates. Partners were interviewed together at home and completed individual questionnaires during pregnancy, two weeks after birth, and six months after birth. All interviews were audio-taped and transcribed. Qualitative data were analysed using content analysis in order to explore the experiences and processes by which women, men and couples adjust to parenthood, and to provide illustrative case studies. A wide range of standardised measures was also used at each time point, which included satisfaction with the couple and parent–infant relationship, sensitivity and reciprocity in relation to infant needs, coping styles, and emotional well-being. Couples who did not take part in the groups were interviewed and assessed in the same way. As well as assessing individual adjustment, absolute agreement or discrepancy between scores for each couple (treated as matched pairs) was ascertained as an index of satisfaction for some measures.

A total of 212 adults (106 women and 106 men) were pre-tested in pregnancy and again at two weeks and six months postnatally. The findings reported here summarise results comparing 98 adults (49 couples) who participated in the groups and 114 adults (57 couples) who did not. Most of the differences reported were statistically significant with a probability of .05 or less, suggesting that changes which occurred for parents who took part in the programme did not occur by chance alone.

Becoming parents

A substantial number of the clinically 'low-risk' sample of women and their partners recruited to the study reported moderate to high levels of stress, strain, depression and anxiety. Many gender differences were found and adjustment was significantly and consistently less positive for women than for men. Satisfaction with the couple relationship declined after childbirth and men felt strongly about their role in the family. They were frequently confused and distressed at the lack of support available for them from health professionals. Women and men also reported more need for support around emotional aspects of becoming parents. These findings are in keeping with other studies of the transition to parenthood (Clulow, 1982; Cowan *et al.*, 1985; Belsky and Kelly, 1994; Feeney *et al.*, 2001). One father said:

> One of the low spots for me was the birth ... It was a feeling of helplessness ... it was such a difficult time for me too ... Up until the moment he came out it was horrible ... I was trying to help her breathe through the pain and more often than not I got a bit of abuse. As a man you are left in limbo, you don't know how well you are doing ... I would be interested to see how other men coped. Perhaps if that sort of thing was brought into antenatal classes as well ...

how men feel ... what was going on ... I felt like crying ... breaking down,
I couldn't cope.

(Parr, 1996: 235)

Programme benefits

No differences were found in pregnancy at pre-test between individuals or couples allocated to programme groups and the control group in terms of either
socio-demographic or assessment data. A number of significant benefits of the
programme ($p < 0.05$ or less) were found when assessed two weeks after birth and
at six months.

Satisfaction with the couple and parent–infant relationship, confidence as a
parent, coping abilities, and sensitivity and reciprocity in relation to infant needs
increased over time, and were significantly greater for women and men who had
been part of the intervention. In the control group, women tended to become easily overwhelmed by their problems and men tended to 'bottle things up'. There
were significantly more women in the control group who scored high on the Edinburgh Postnatal Depression Scale. The interpersonal skills learned in the intervention enabled men to feel more comfortable with talking about their experiences,
and a focus on father–infant relationships led to an increased desire to be more
involved in childcare. Fathers were also less likely to take out their frustrations on
their infant or partner. One father said:

> When she [baby] woke in the night I knew it was because she had a wet
> nappy, or she was hungry, or teething, or something. I knew it was not
> because she was naughty or trying to wind me up. It didn't help the tiredness
> and anger, I still felt it, but I could usually talk to her [partner] about it rather
> than arguing, or talk about it in the group with the other men and get support
> with those feelings, rather than think I was a useless father or take them out
> on my [partner] or baby.
>
> (father/intervention group, Parr, 1996: 236)

Men in the control group tended to think it was 'a waste of time' for fathers to be
involved with small babies.

> It's highly unlikely there'll be another one unless there's some serious change.
> It's been a bad six months all round. It causes problems at work. In the end
> I went to the GP ... I was so stressed because of lack of sleep ... if we're
> honest we're resentful of her [baby]. I can't think of any gains. I can fully
> understand those people, who hit their baby now ... even if I don't agree with
> it ... I was just tired in the middle of the night and she wouldn't shut up and
> you just strike ... I actually slapped her leg, I felt awful ... she was crying and
> shouting and messing around. The positive things, the first smile, crawling ...
> the negative things are outweighing them.
>
> (father/control group, Parr, 1996: 238)

He's still a bit of a blob ... I can't wait to know him better when he's a little older ... when he's about two years old and can play with me.

(father/control group, Parr, 1996: 237)

There were no differences between the two groups in terms of obstetric outcomes, infant birth weight or health. However, significantly fewer women in the intervention group were anxious about their infant's crying and they perceived their infants as 'more healthy' than the control group.

Just after she was born ... and it still happens now at times ... I looked in the bathroom mirror and thought who's that woman? It was a while before I realized it was me ... Every day is a fight. I hate getting out of bed in the morning ... simple things are so difficult, trying to feed or bathe the baby ... she's so antisocial and grizzly ... she's always ill, but the doctor says there's nothing wrong with her ... I wished she hadn't been born ... it's been so bad I've often wished something would happen to her ... I even thought of killing myself. I just couldn't cope anymore.

(mother/control group, Parr, 1996: 153)

Group process

All group sessions were audio-taped and parents and facilitators were asked to complete weekly client satisfaction and process evaluation questionnaires designed to monitor programme functioning, participation of members, perceived effectiveness of the programme, and recommendations for programme improvement (Coche and Coche, 1992). Results suggest that benefits of the programme were a result of equal attention being paid to 'content and focus' and 'the way the groups were run', in particular the focus on 'parent–infant relationships' and 'facilitation of interaction between group members'(Parr, 1996: 265).

It was good to be able to review my childhood and relate that to caring for my child ... I feel a lot calmer as a person and a parent as a result.

(Parr, 1996: 222)

My view of parenthood has changed by viewing the babies as individuals. The group also supported me in my conviction that my baby knew me from birth. I've now become more patient and tolerant of our baby's needs. It began in the group in pregnancy ... thinking about the baby and what it might look like ... and afterwards seeing how our baby and all the babies in the group got their parents' attention, learning about the babies' facial expressions, that they have a meaning ... I learned a lot.

(Parr, 1996: 237)

Sixteen of the forty-nine couples who began the intervention did not complete it. This attrition rate of one or two couples per group is within the normal expected range for any parent programme. The groups were well attended and parents' satisfaction was high. On a four-point scale (4 = strongly agree), 98 per cent of parents who completed the intervention expressed favourable perceptions of the usefulness of the programme and would recommend it to others. All parents in the study attended traditional antenatal classes. These were considered to be helpful for preparing for childbirth and as a way to meet other parents. Parents who took part in the intervention programme rated the programme as 'more helpful' than antenatal classes (p<0.01).

> The hospital class was so large, cold and clinical ... a different professional came each time and just lectured us ... it was an insult to our intelligence ... I'm glad you're interested in us men. Nothing is done to support men who are trying to make a commitment to their children. Having a baby is not just about the medical care of mother and baby, it's also about the family being created.
>
> (father, Parr, 1996: 175)

> I think that whatever anybody says about having children, you are never prepared for it. I went to all the classes ... everything is geared towards the birth ... then suddenly you are there with this helpless little thing with no instruction manual and no support.
>
> (mother, Parr, 1996: 155)

Programme dissemination

Following the conclusion of the study, First Steps in Parenting was rolled out nationally for a further eleven years (1993-2004) by midwives and health visitors who had been trained by 'Parents In Partnership–Parent Infant Network' (PIPPIN). This national organisation was set up after the study ended, with further funding from the Artemis Trust, and provided the opportunity to ensure that the intervention was available to as many parents as possible across a wide range of NHS and Sure Start settings. All groups delivered in this way were also evaluated through the continued use of some of the measures used in the original study, to ensure that programme integrity continued to be maintained. Although no control groups were used, similar outcomes to those of the original study were found. Process evaluation of the facilitator training and dissemination of the intervention in routine health settings provided important information about maintaining programme integrity during large-scale dissemination. Much of this work was carried out through nationally funded projects (by, for example, the Department of Health, Home Office Family Support Unit, the Department of Further Education and Skills and the Community Fund). The programme was frequently reported as an example of good practice and an effective preventive child mental health initiative which government should support (House of Commons Health Select Committee, 1997; British Medical Association, 1999; Royal College of Midwives, 1999; Mental Health Foundation, 1999; Kraemer and Roberts, 1996;

Robbins, 1998; Sure Start, 2002; Hosking and Walsh, 2005). Although PIPPIN no longer provides training to deliver First Steps in Parenting, the originator and colleagues trained by her continue the work through their independent roles in various settings around Britain.

Conclusions

The normal transition to parenthood is stressful and first-time parents in particular require support that goes beyond that provided by antenatal classes. The First Steps in Parenting programme provides an evidence-based method of supporting both the parents' emotional transition to becoming parents and their developing relationship with their baby, both of which are extremely important for later outcomes.

Acknowledgements

The study reported was carried out through the University of East London in collaboration with Parent Network with financial support from the Artemis Charitable Trust. The authors are also appreciative of the participating families and the expertise of colleagues in running groups and training facilitators. Most of the information provided in this chapter is based on the main author's PhD research and an invited paper read at the United Kingdom Council for Psychotherapy Tenth Anniversary Lecture Series, Tavistock, London, October 2003. Requests for further information about First Steps in Parenting and the research study should be directed to the programme originator Mel Parr (mel.parr@virgin.net).

References

Ainsworth, M. D. S., Bell, S. M. and Stayton, D. J. (1971). Individual differences in Strange Situation behaviour of one year olds. In H. R. Schaffer (ed.), *The Origins of Human Social Relations*. New York: Academic Press.

Belsky, J. and Kelly, J. (1994). *The Transition to Parenthood: How a First Child Changes a Marriage*. London: Vermilion.

Bowlby, J. (1977). The making and breaking of affectional bonds. *British Journal of Psychiatry*, 130, 201–210, 421–431.

British Medical Association (1999). *Growing up in Britain*. London: British Medical Journal Books.

Cardone, I. A. and Gilkerson, L. (1989). Family Administered Neonatal Activities: an innovative component of family centered care. *Zero to Three*, 10, 23–28.

Cardone, I. A. and Gilkerson, L. (1990). Family Administered Neonatal Activities (FANA). In T. B. Brazelton and K. Nugent (eds), *Neonatal Behavioural Assessment Scale*, 3rd edn. London: Mac Keith Press.

Clulow, C. (1982). *To Have and To Hold: Marriage, the First Baby and Preparing Couples for Parenthood*. Aberdeen: Aberdeen University Press.

Coche, J. and Coche, E. (1992). *Couples Group Psychotherapy: A Clinical Practice Model.* New York: Bruner/Mazel.

Cowan, C. P., Cowan, P. A., Heming, G., Garrett, E., Coysh, W. W., Curtis-Boles, H. and Boles, A. (1985). Transitions to parenthood: his, hers and theirs. *Journal of Family Issues* 6, 451–481.

Diamond, D., Heinicke, C. and Mintz, J. (1996). Separation–individuation as a family process in the transition to parenthood, *Infant Mental Health Journal*, 17(1), 24–42.

Dragonas, T. (1990). Turning towards the father. *Paediatric and Perinatal Epidemiology*, 4, 247–254.

Feeney, J. A., Hohaus, L., Noller, P. and Alexander, R. (2001). *Becoming Parents.* Cambridge: Cambridge University Press.

Fonagy, P. (1998). Prevention, the appropriate target of parent–infant psychotherapy. *Infant Mental Health Journal*, 19(2), 124–150.

Glassman, U. and Kates, L. (1990). *Group Work: A Humanistic Approach.* London: Sage Publications.

Glover, V. (2007). The long term effects of maternal antenatal stress/anxiety on the child. Paper presented at the Daksha and Freya Emson Annual Conference, 'Perinatal Mental Health: Back to the Future', 6 July, Anglia Ruskin University, Chelmsford, Essex.

Glover, V. and O'Connor, T. G. (2006). Maternal anxiety: its effect on the foetus and child. *British Journal of Midwifery*, 14(11), 663–667.

Hosking, G. and Walsh, A. (2005). *The WAVE Report 2005: Violence and What to Do About It* (www.wavetrust.org.uk).

House of Commons Health Select Committee (4th Report) (1997). *Child and Adolescent Mental Health, Report Proceedings.* London: HMSO.

Kraemer, S. and Roberts, J. (eds) (1996). *The Politics of Attachment: Towards a Secure Society.* London: Free Association Books.

Meins, E. (1997). *Security of Attachment and the Social Development of Cognition.* Hove: Psychology Press.

Meins, E. (2007). Maternal mind mindedness. Paper presented at the British Psychological Society (Division of Clinical Psychology) Special Interest Group in Perinatal Psychology, 6 November, Chancellors Conference Centre, University of Manchester.

Mental Health Foundation (1999). *Bright Futures: Promoting Children and Young People's Mental Health.* London: Mental Health Foundation.

Murray, L. and Cooper, P. J. (eds) (1997). *Postpartum Depression and Childhood Development.* New York: Guilford Publications.

Parr, M. (1996). Support for couples. In The transition to parenthood. Unpublished PhD thesis, University of East London.

Parr, M. (1998). A new approach to parent education. *British Journal of Midwifery*, 6(3), 160–165.

Parr, M. (1999). Integrating infant observation skills into parent facilitator training. *International Journal of Infant Observation and its Applications. Special Edition: Early Interventions*, 3(1), 33–46.

Parr, M., Whittaker, V. and Paden, L. (1997). Adjustment to family life. In C. Henderson, and K. Jones (eds), *Essential Midwifery*. London: Mosby.

Perry, B. D., Pollard, R. A., Blakley, T. L., Baker, W. L. and Vigilante, D. (1995). Childhood trauma, the neurobiology of adaptation and 'use-dependent' development of the brain: how 'states' become 'traits'. *Infant Mental Health Journal*, 16(4), 271–289.

Pruett, K. D. (1993). The paternal presence. *Families in Society: The Journal of Contemporary Human Services*, 74, 46–50.

Robbins, D. (1998). *Refocusing Children's Services Initiative*. London: Department of Health.

Royal College of Midwives (1999). *Transition to Parenting: An Open Learning Resource*. London: Royal College of Midwives.

Stern, D. (1985). *The Interpersonal World of the Infant*. New York: Basic Books.

Stern, D. (1995). *The Motherhood Constellation*. New York: Basic Books.

Sure Start (2002). *Guide to Evidence-Based Practice: Trailblazer Edition*. London: Sure Start.

Woollett, A. and Parr, M. (1997). Psychological tasks for women and men in the transition to parenthood. *Journal of Reproductive and Infant Psychology*, 15, 159–183.

World Health Organization (1995). *Improving the Psychosocial Development of Children*. Geneva: Division of Mental Health, MNH/PSF/95.4.

Useful websites

www.waimh.org
www.aimh.org.uk
www.wavetrust.org.uk
www.parentingacademy.org
www.parentinguk.org

6 The Family Partnership Model

Understanding the processes of prevention and early intervention

Hilton Davis

Current high levels of psychosocial problems in children and families are of wide concern because of their association with distress, negative developmental effects, youth crime, adult mental health difficulties, and the long-term financial costs. However, despite the development and implementation of a range of early interventions aimed at preventing such problems, many such interventions have to date shown limited success. Furthermore, where success has been achieved, research suggests the overriding significance of non-specific programme factors, such as the helper–client relationship. This implies that the lack of a clear and explicit conceptual framework of the processes involved in helping families may have played a significant role in hindering developments in this area. This chapter will argue for a 'model of process' to underpin all interventions that are directed at parents and families.

The chapter will begin by exploring the reasons why such a model of process is necessary for interventions to be effective. It will go on to examine a promotional and preventive programme that has been used in the UK and other European countries during the antenatal/perinatal period to support early parenting, alongside the Family Partnership Model, which underpins such promotional strategies and which, it will be argued, provides such a conceptual framework. The chapter will conclude with an examination of their effectiveness.

Promotional and preventive strategies

In spite of the affluence of countries such as the USA and UK, the well-being of children is compromised, as indicated in a recent UNICEF report (Adamson, 2007). The prevalence of child mental health problems is high (e.g. Meltzer *et al.*, 2000; Attride-Stirling *et al.*, 2001) and increasing (Collishaw *et al.*, 2004). The level of need is not met by services (e.g. Audit Commission, 1999), and 42 per cent of children with such problems have no contact with relevant services and 75 per cent are not in contact with specialists (Ford *et al.*, 2005).

There are also strong arguments for early promotional strategies on humanitarian grounds, in terms of the poor outcomes for untreated problems (Fonagy, 1998; Offord and Bennett, 1994) and the long-term costs to the individual, family and society (Scott *et al.*, 2001). Theoretically, it makes sense to intervene at times of major change (e.g. during pregnancy) and rapid development (i.e. the first years of life) given the importance of the early years (e.g. Cicchetti and Toth, 1995; Hay *et al.*, 2001) and the early sensitivity of the brain to parental influence (e.g. Swain *et al.*, 2007).

In practice, early prevention must involve all people working in child and family services, because of the requirements to identify all children at risk and to manage potential problems in all relevant settings. All services (educational, social, health, voluntary, police, housing and judicial) need to take a broad, holistic view of their role and to consider every interaction between staff and families as a potential opportunity for the active promotion of children's well-being.

Promotional programmes have been available for some years (e.g. Olds *et al.*, 1986), but wide-scale implementation is severely limited (e.g. Sure Start, Children's Fund). Although there is evidence to support such approaches, there remain major concerns about effectiveness. Studies (e.g. Olds *et al.*, 1997, 1999) have shown that home visiting, for example, can produce sustained benefits, whilst others have found little effect (e.g. St Pierre and Layzer, 1999; Emond *et al.*, 2002). Reviews (e.g. Kendrick *et al.*, 2000; Bull *et al.*, 2004) have concluded that there are benefits for parenting practice, attitudes and knowledge, but that effects on child health, development and behaviour, and abuse and neglect, are elusive. Gomby *et al.* (1999) regarded the results as sobering, since programmes struggle to enrol, engage and retain families, and produce modest and inconsistent benefits.

The need for a model of process

The complexity and inconsistency in this area clearly indicate the need for a model of process. Research has been largely outcomes-based to date (Jacobs, 2003) with little attention to the active ingredients and mechanisms of successful interventions. Effective intervention requires a model that makes the processes of helping explicit and this is frequently lacking (Barnes and Freude-Lagevardi, 2002). Existing models tend to address processes related to parenting and children's development but neglect equally important issues about how personnel engage families in order to tackle problems. This is supported by studies showing poor professional communication (e.g. Mitcheson and Cowley, 2003), parental dissatisfaction (e.g. Attride-Stirling *et al.*, 2001), low family recruitment and retention rates, and a deep distrust of professionals by the most vulnerable (Jack *et al.*, 2005; Barlow *et al.*, 2005).

Concern with process is growing (e.g. Hoagwood, 2005) and reviews (e.g. Moore *et al.*, 2001) suggest that positive outcomes are associated with interventions that: are theory-based; have clear aims and goals; are family-centred; ensure partnership with parents; are community-based; have a developmental focus, but address multiple needs directly or by coordination with all appropriate services; use evidence-based strategies; involve universal early identification; have effective monitoring and evaluation; and have staff who have been selected appropriately, who have been well trained, and who work consistently with families, and are supported by skilled and enthusiastic managers.

These characteristics endorse the need for a model of *how* to work with families and not just *what* to do for them. Because the style of interaction is as important as the content of interventions, the Family Partnership Model was constructed to make these processes explicit. It was intended as a guide to individual practice in working with families, but it has clear implications for the design of systems of care, for the recruitment and selection of workers, for the nature of their training, for the requirements of managerial support or supervision, and for process research. Before examining the Family Partnership Model in more detail, the next section will explore its application in supporting families during the perinatal period.

European Early Promotion Project

The European Early Promotion Project (Davis and Tsiantis, 2005; Puura *et al.*, 2005a) is a service aimed at preventing psychosocial problems developing in children by promoting the well-being of babies and families. It was designed to meet the specifications of effective prevention services derived from the research literature and listed earlier in the chapter (e.g. theory-based, family-centred). The conceptual framework had the Family Partnership Model at its foundation.

Specially designed training was provided for primary care personnel in five European countries. The people trained were mostly from a nursing background (health visitors in the UK, public health nurses in Finland, community nurses in Serbia and Cyprus), except in Greece, where the health visitors were from a non-nursing background. All the frontline workers were trained in their own languages by facilitators from child mental health specialties trained together in London. Following their training, all frontline staff received regular supervision on a fortnightly individual basis from child mental health specialists, with additional group support every six to eight weeks.

Universal early identification of need was established by the trained nurses visiting all prospective mothers in their area four to six weeks before and four weeks after birth. On each occasion the home visitors conducted semi-structured, non-directive, promotional interviews, which were designed specifically to facilitate the development of a partnership with the mothers-to-be and to enable their transition to parenthood. Each interview explored a discrete set of issues relevant to either the antenatal or postnatal period, with the intention of helping mothers to explore the issue, identify perceived problems, identify their strengths, and facilitate their own problem-solving skills. The issues covered in the antenatal interview included: the mother's feelings about pregnancy; expected family support; anticipated changes in family life and relationships; self-perceptions; anticipated perceptions of their baby-to-be; anticipations of the delivery and feeding of the baby; finance and housing issues; and life events.

The postnatal promotional interview was conducted by the same worker approximately four weeks after birth. Again, mothers were encouraged to talk about and explore in some depth the changes in their lives, in an attempt to identify and explore all possible worries and to facilitate the mothers' use of their own resources, and particularly their existing support networks. Specific questions centred on the experience of the birth, their current emotional state, the response and support of their family, their concerns about their baby, their perceptions of the child, the interaction and communication between the mother and baby, the mother's emotional resources available to the child, their financial and housing situation, and again specific life events that might be relevant.

Following the second interview and on the basis of information from both meetings, the home visitor completed a checklist of needs in order to decide on the risk for each family of the development of future child mental health problems. The needs checklist consists of a list of risk factors each rated as definitely, possibly, or not present. The factors were grouped into those associated with the child (e.g. prematurity, physical illness), the mother–child relationship (e.g. lack of feeling for the baby), the parents (e.g. physical health problems, marital discord, psychological problems, substance abuse and criminality), the more general environment (e.g. poverty, unemployment, environmental threat), and major life events. The promotional interviews and needs checklist have been published in Davis *et al.* (2002b: appendices 5 and 6).

Mothers who were thought to be at any risk were invited to continue to meet the home visitor on a weekly basis for as long as needed to deal with the problems identified. Although help was attempted in relation to all identified difficulties, a strong focus was maintained on the parent–infant relationship, since this is considered to be the organising focus of all early experience. The home visitors put considerable effort into helping parents explore and understand the importance of their interaction with their baby, enhancing their understanding of their baby as a person, and helping them develop their own skills in responding appropriately to their baby's physical and psychosocial needs. In theoretical terms this was based upon the notion of the parent–child interactive cycle (Davis *et al.*, 2002a), but in practical terms it involved drawing from a number of initiatives such as Watch, Wait and Wonder (e.g. Cohen *et al.*, 2000), Brazelton's work (1992), and baby massage (Field *et al.*, 1996).

In addition, parents were helped to explore, clarify and manage any problems such as depression, personal stress and anger or parental conflict, where these were likely to disrupt parenting and put the baby at risk. Following the model, the intention was to develop a sufficiently strong partnership with the mothers for them to be able to explore difficulties, derive useful and effective understandings of them, and therefore develop and implement appropriate goals and strategies. Although it is clear that individual non-specialist workers can have considerable benefit in helping with a range of issues, as in the case of postnatal depression for example (e.g. Cooper *et al.*, 2003), coordination with all other services, such as adult mental health, was crucial for circumstances in which referral to more specialist help was required. However, access to such services was constantly problematic.

Effects of the European Early Promotion Project

The project was set up with a research component in order to evaluate aspects of the processes of intervention and the outcomes when the children were 2 years old. The results are described elsewhere (Davis *et al.*, 2005; Puura *et al.*, 2005b) and will be illustrated here with reference to maternal satisfaction, the parent–helper relationship, and outcomes for the babies and families.

A questionnaire measure of service satisfaction was completed by mothers in the intervention group and mothers who received services in a neighbouring area from primary health carers who had not been trained on the European Early Promotion Project course. The mothers in the intervention groups in all countries rated the service they had received more positively than those in the comparison groups, with the results reaching statistical significance in Cyprus (int. 33 vs. comp. 38; p=0.003), Greece (int. 13 vs. comp. 20; p=0.0002) and the UK (int. 20 vs. comp. 25; p=0.032), but not in Finland (int. 20.5 vs. comp. 21) or Serbia (int. 16 vs. comp. 19). Lower scores indicate greater satisfaction. These results replicate consistently high levels of satisfaction found in relation to workers trained in the Family Partnership Model (e.g. Davis and Rushton, 1991; Davis and Spurr, 1998).

The findings in relation to satisfaction also indicated improvements in the parent–home visitor relationship, in terms of how the mothers felt about their helper, their relationship and its effects. However, there was also direct evidence of positive effects of the professionals' training upon relationships with parents. For example, the trained health visitors in the UK were more sensitive to the needs of families; they identified more problems in the families that they visited, even though all the families were independently assessed as having similar levels of need. The fact that the problems they identified were related to emotional and relationship concerns strongly suggests improved relationships and communication between the parents and visitors, since such problems could not have been identified unless the mothers had talked about them and had felt safe enough to do so. The trained visitors were also significantly more accurate in their identification of family need, as judged against detailed interviews conducted by child mental health specialists. The accuracy scores were 77.7 per cent vs. 32.2 per cent in Greece, 53 per cent vs. 47 per cent in Serbia, and 66 per cent vs. 32 per cent in the UK.

The outcomes for families in the European Early Promotion Project were generally positive, even though the intensity of the intervention was limited by resources in most of the countries involved. Like many other studies of this kind (Gomby *et al.*, 1999) there were inconsistencies across countries, although overall there was a general trend toward improved outcomes. The effect sizes were in a positive direction throughout, with 62 per cent of the effect sizes being positive, 13 per cent zero and 25 per cent negative. The most prominent effects were in the area of mother–infant interaction, which was the focus of the programme. In Greece and the UK, mothers in the intervention group related better to their babies. Greek mothers were found to organise the baby's environment more appropriately, provide more varied stimulation and avoid punishment. Intervention mothers in the UK were more responsive to their babies, provided more playthings, were less controlling, and tended to be more involved.

Intervention children in Cyprus were more consistent in sleep routines and less easily upset than children in the comparison group. Finnish children in the intervention group were somewhat healthier and easier to take out, and their mothers experienced fewer minor depressive episodes. Intervention women in Greece experienced less depression, as in Finland, and were also less stressed, had greater self-esteem and better relationships with their husbands and children. Their children had fewer behaviour problems, were easier to manage and had made better developmental progress. There were fewer dependency problems in children in the UK intervention sample.

These findings suggest that the Family Partnership Model, on which this programme is based, enables professionals to develop an effective (trusting) relationship with families. The remainder of this chapter will examine the key components of the model.

Family Partnership Model

The model is constructed to be accessible and usable by all people working with children and families and is therefore expressed as simply as possible in terms of a small number of concepts, each of which contains a limited number of propositions. The overall model is shown in Figure 6.1. Each box is intended to represent and elaborate a key aspect of the helping process as simply as possible.

In essence the model suggests that the outcomes of intervention must be explicit, holistic and family-centred (see Figure 6.2).

These outcomes are predominantly determined by the process of helping, which can be understood as a set of interrelated tasks as shown in Figure 6.3.

Since the task of building a relationship between the helper and the parent is crucial to the facilitation of the whole process and hence the outcomes, the nature of the relationship towards which health professionals should work must be carefully defined and represented as a specific ingredient within the overall model.

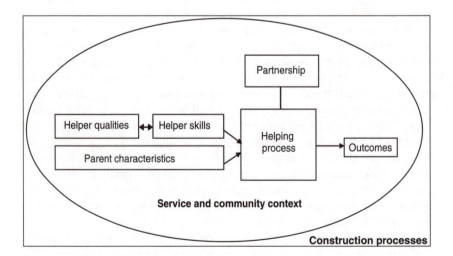

Figure 6.1 The Family Partnership Model.

- To do no harm.

- To help parents identify, clarify and manage problems.

- To enable parents (including their ability to anticipate problems).

- To enable parents to enable the development and well-being of their children.

- To facilitate families' social support and community development generally.

- To enable necessary service support from all agencies.

- To compensate for families' difficulties where necessary.

- To improve the quality of our care.

Figure 6.2 The outcomes of helping.

It is argued that a partnership is most effective for enabling the process and outcomes, as is characterised in Figure 6.4.

The model also indicates that the process of helping, including the development of the working relationship, is determined by what both the helper and parents bring to the interaction. In the case of the helper, we have attempted to specify the interpersonal skills needed to engage parents and facilitate the process (e.g. attentive and active listening, prompting them to talk and explore, responding

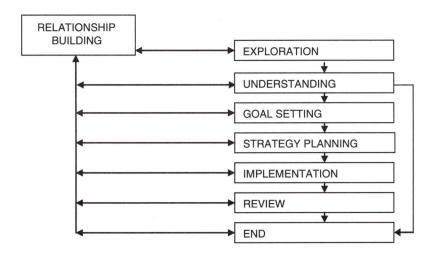

Figure 6.3 The process of helping: tasks.

- Working closely together with active participation and involvement.

- Sharing decision-making power.

- Recognition of complementary expertise and roles.

- Sharing and agreeing aims and process of helping.

- Negotiation of disagreement.

- Mutual trust and respect.

- Openness and honesty.

- Clear communication.

Figure 6.4 Characteristics of an effective partnership.

empathically and negotiating), but also to define the underlying, internal qualities of effective helpers. These include respect, genuineness, empathy, humility, quiet enthusiasm, personal integrity, attunement and technical knowledge, including an understanding of the processes of helping.

Many characteristics of parents might influence the processes involved in helping and it is difficult to be definitive, but the work of Hoagwood (2005) amongst others suggests a number of relevant variables, including, for example, parents' problems and strengths, barriers to engagement, motivation to change, attitudes and beliefs about services, and cultural and socioeconomic circumstances.

Another ingredient of the model is the service and community context, which has implications for all aspects of the model and is therefore represented as an encompassing ellipse. This includes the characteristics of the service, the population and the geographical area, but of particular importance for effective practice is the management and supervisory support available for service personnel. Within the Family Partnership framework it is assumed that the processes of such support are exactly parallel to the processes of helping and that the model as outlined here applies to both.

The final ingredient is represented as an all-encompassing box enclosing the aspects mentioned so far, because it provides an understanding of how people function psychologically and socially, and therefore has implications for all other aspects of the model. The basic ideas are listed in Figure 6.5 and present a constructionist viewpoint which assumes that both parents and helpers develop a unique understanding of their world in order to anticipate and adapt to events. A major implication of this is that the helping processes are essentially about

- People constantly take in and process information so as to make sense of their world.

- They construct a model of the world in their heads.

- This enables them to anticipate and adapt to whatever happens to them.

- The model is derived from their past experience.

- Each person has a unique set of constructions, which are not necessarily conscious or easily verbalised.

- These constructions are constantly being tested, clarified and changed.

- Social interaction is determined by our constructions of each other.

Figure 6.5 Constructing.

enabling people to develop more useful or effective 'constructions', in the terminology of Kelly (1991).

For more elaborate descriptions of the model, please refer to Davis *et al.* (2002a) and Braun *et al.* (2006).

Implications of the model

The design of systems of care must take account of these ingredients and allow for relationship development. Staff must be selected for the qualities and skills indicated in the model, and should be trained to understand the processes involved and to develop the basic qualities and interpersonal skills. They must also be supervised in ways that support them and facilitate their work in order for them to be as effective as possible with parents and to continue to develop.

To meet these requirements, training programmes (e.g. Davis *et al.*, 2002b) have been developed for people working with parents and children in whatever capacity, for facilitators to conduct the basic programme, and for managers to supervise frontline staff. The courses are based on the model and are designed to reflect or demonstrate the approach implicitly and explicitly in content, format and style. Facilitators are trained to help participants learn by using the same skills and qualities and involving them in the same processes, including the formation of relationships that have all the qualities of a partnership, as defined above.

These courses have been used throughout the UK, Europe and Australasia to train people from all agencies and disciplines working with children and families, on the assumption that, if they understand the processes better and develop their interpersonal skills, they will be more effective, whatever their technical expertise (e.g. medicine, physiotherapy, teaching). The model has also been the basis of specific interventions for families of children with a range of problems (APIP, 1998; Davis and Rushton, 1991; Davis and Spurr, 1998), of a tiered system of care (Day *et al.*, 1998), and of promotional and preventive services (e.g. Barlow *et al.*, 2003).

Training in the Family Partnership Model has been shown to enhance the work of health visitors and midwives in a number of ways. It makes the processes of helping explicit in a relatively simple way and endorses a respectful, holistic and collaborative stance which tends to be what families request (e.g. Attride-Stirling *et al.*, 2001; E. Davis *et al.*, 1997; Family Policy Alliance, 2005; Little *et al.*, 2001; Coulter, 2005). The training is seen as relevant to the professionals' work and evaluated positively (e.g. Papadopoulou *et al.*, 2005). It improves the qualities and interpersonal skills required for their work, including self-efficacy and knowledge of processes (Rushton and Davis, 1992; H. Davis *et al.*, 1997; Papadopoulou *et al.*, 2005; Lea *et al.*, 1998; McArdle and McDermott, 1994). There is also evidence that health visitors become more sensitive and accurate in identifying family problems (Papadopoulou *et al.*, 2005), more effective in relating to families (e.g. Kirkpatrick *et al.*, 2007), and more effective in terms of the outcomes for families (e.g. Davis and Rushton, 1991; Davis and Spurr, 1998).

Conclusion

The well-being of children in affluent countries like the UK has been severely compromised, and there is an urgent need for holistic, promotional and preventive strategies involving all agencies and disciplines. Such developments require a conceptual base to make the processes of helping explicit, and to guide individual practice, system design, training and research. The Family Partnership Model is a possible option with important implications for staff selection, training and managerial support. The service can be implemented in different countries and has been shown to have benefits for staff, their relationship with parents, and in terms of outcomes for families. There remains much to be done in developing, implementing and evaluating preventive services based on the model, yet one might argue that all people should show respect and empathy and work with each other in true partnership on humanitarian grounds, whatever the evidence base. How we behave is as important as what we do. Whatever our advice, showing parents respect and empathy may enable them to provide a more nurturing environment for their children, following Pawl's (1994) Platinum Principle, 'Do unto others as you would have others do unto others.' We may continue to seek multiple, independent, randomised controlled trials as evidence for effectiveness, but will make little real progress until our understanding of processes has developed sufficiently to allow interventions to be appropriately adapted to the needs of the people most likely to benefit. In this context this means of course helping the parents to become more able to understand and respond sensitively to their babies and infants.

References

Adamson, P. (2007). *Child Poverty in Perspective: An Overview of Child Well-being in Rich Countries.* Florence: UNICEF Innocenti Research Centre.

APIP (Avon Premature Infant Project) (1998). Randomised trial of parental support for families with very preterm children. *Archives of Disease in Childhood: Foetal and Neonatal Edition*, 79, 4–11.

Attride-Stirling, J., Davis, H., Markless, G., Sclare, I. and Day, C. (2001). 'Someone to talk to who'll listen': addressing the psychosocial needs of children and families. *Journal of Community and Applied Social Psychology*, 11, 179–191.

Audit Commission (1999). *Children in Mind: Child and Adolescent Mental Health Services.* London: Audit Commission Publications.

Barlow, J., Brocklehurst, N., Stewart-Brown, S., Davis, H., Burns, C., Callaghan, H. and Tucker, J. (2003). Working in partnership: the development of a home visiting service for vulnerable families. *Child Abuse Review*, 12, 172–189.

Barlow, J., Kirkpatrick, S., Stewart-Brown, S. and Davis, H. (2005). Hard-to-reach or out-of-reach? Reasons why women refuse to take part in early interventions. *Children and Society*, 19, 199–210.

Barnes, J. and Freude-Lagevardi, A. (2002). *From Pregnancy to Early Childhood: Early Interventions to Enhance the Mental Health of Children and Families.* London: Mental Health Foundation.

Braun, D., Davis, H. and Mansfield, P. (2006). *How Helping Works: Towards a Shared Model of Process.* London: Parentline Plus.

Brazelton, T. (1992). *Touchpoint: Your Child's Emotional and Behavioural Development.* Reading, MA: Perseus Books.

Bull, J., McCormick, G., Swann, C. and Mulvihill, C. (2004). Ante-natal and post-natal home-visiting programmes: a review of reviews. *Evidence Briefing*, 1st edn. London: Health Development Agency.

Cicchetti, D. and Toth, S. (1995). A developmental psychopathology perspective on child abuse and neglect. *Journal of the American Academy of Child and Adolescent Psychiatry*, 34, 541–565.

Cohen, N., Muir, E., Lojkasek, M., Muir, R., Parker, C., Barwick, M. and Brown, M. (2000). Watch, wait, and wonder: testing the effectiveness of a new approach to mother–infant psychotherapy. *Infant Mental Health Journal*, 20, 429–451.

Collishaw, S., Maughan, B., Goodman, R. and Pickles, A. (2004). Time trends in adolescent mental health. *Journal of Child Psychology and Psychiatry*, 45, 1350–1362.

Cooper, P., Murray, L., Wilson A. and Romaniuk, H. (2003). Controlled trial of the short- and long-term effect of psychological treatment of post-partum depression: I. Impact on maternal mood. *British Journal of Psychiatry*, 182, 412–419.

Coulter, A. (2005). What do patients and the public want from primary care? *British Medical Journal*, 331, 1199–1201.

Davis, E., Dibsdall, J. and Woodcock, C. (1997). *The Building Block Project: Investigating the Needs of Parents and Children Where a Parent Has a Mental Health, Drug or Alcohol Problem.* Bromley: London Borough of Bromley.

Davis, H. and Rushton, R. (1991). Counselling and supporting parents of children with developmental delay: a research evaluation. *Journal of Mental Deficiency Research*, 35, 89–112.

Davis, H. and Spurr, P. (1998). Parent counselling: an evaluation of a community child mental health service. *Journal of Child Psychology and Psychiatry*, 39, 365–376.

Davis, H. and Tsiantis, J. (2005). Promoting children's mental health: the European Early Promotion Project (EEPP). *International Journal of Mental Health Promotion*, 7, 4–16.

Davis, H., Spurr, P., Cox, A., Lynch, M., von Roenne, A. and Hahn, K. (1997). A description and evaluation of a community child mental health service. *Clinical Child Psychology and Psychiatry*, 2, 221–238.

Davis, H., Day, C. and Bidmead, C. (2002a). *Working in Partnership with Parents: The Parent Adviser Model.* London: Harcourt Assessment.

Davis, H., Day, C. and Bidmead, C. (2002b). *The Parent Adviser Training Manual.* London: Harcourt Assessment.

Davis, H., Dusoir, T., Papadopoulou, K., Dimitrakaki, C., Cox, A., Ispanovic-Radojkovic, V., Puura, K., Vizacou, S., Paradisiotou, A., Rudic, N., Chisholm, B., Leontiou, F., Mantymaa, M., Radosavljev, J., Riga, H., Day, C. and Tamminen, T. (2005). Child and family outcomes of the European Early Promotion Project. *International Journal of Mental Health Promotion*, 7, 63–81.

Day, C., Davis, H. and Hind, R. (1998). The development of a community child and family mental health service. *Child: Care, Health and Development*, 24, 487–500.

Emond, A., Pollock, J., Deave, T., Bonnell, S., Peters, T. and Harvey, I. (2002). An evaluation of the first parent health visitor scheme. *Archives of Disease in Childhood*, 86, 150–157.

Family Policy Alliance (2005). *Parent Participation: Improving Services for Children and Families.* London: Parentline Plus.

Field, T., Grizzle, N., Scafidi, F., Abrams, S., Richardson, S., Kuhn, C. and Schanberg, S. (1996). Massage therapy for infants of depressed mothers. *Infant Behaviour and Development*, 19, 107–112.

Fonagy, P. (1998). Prevention, the appropriate target of infant psychotherapy. *Infant Mental Health Journal*, 19, 124–150.

Ford, T., Hamilton, H., Goodman, R. and Meltzer, H. (2005). Service contacts among the children participating in the British Child and Adolescent Mental Health Surveys. *Child and Adolescent Mental Health*, 10, 2–9.

Gomby, D., Culross, P. and Behrman, R. (1999). Home visiting: recent program evaluations – analysis and recommendations. *The Future of Children*, 9, 4–26.

Hay, D., Pawlby, S., Sharp, D., Asten, P., Mills, A. and Kumar, R. (2001). Intellectual problems shown by 11 year old children whose mothers had postnatal depression. *Journal of Child Psychology and Psychiatry*, 42, 871–889.

Hoagwood, K. (2005). Family-based services in children's mental health: a research review and synthesis. *Journal of Child Psychology and Psychiatry*, 46, 690–713.

Jack, S., DiCenso, A. and Lohfeld, L. (2005). A theory of maternal engagement with public health nurses and family visitors. *Journal of Advanced Nursing*, 49, 182–190.

Jacobs, F. (2003). Child and family program evaluation: learning to enjoy complexity. *Applied Developmental Science*, 7, 62–75.

Kelly, G. (1991). *The Psychology of Personal Constructs. Volume 1: A Theory of Personality*. London: Routledge.

Kendrick, D., Elkan, R., Hewitt, M., Dewey, M., Blair, M., Robinson, J., Williams, D. and Brummell, K. (2000). Does home visiting improve parenting and the quality of the home environment? A systematic review and meta analysis. *Archives of Diseases in Childhood*, 82, 443–451.

Kirkpatrick, S., Barlow, J., Stewart-Brown, S. and Davis, H. (2007). Working in partnership: user perceptions of intensive home visiting. *Child Abuse Review*, 16(1), 32–46.

Lea, D., Clarke, M. and Davis, H. (1998). Evaluation of a counselling skills course for health professionals. *British Journal of Guidance and Counselling*, 26, 159–173.

Little, P., Everitt, H., Williamson, I., Warner, G., Moore, M., Gould, C., Ferrier, K. and Payne, S. (2001). Preferences of patients for patient centred approach to consultation in primary care: observational study. *British Medical Journal*, 322, 1544.

McArdle, G. and McDermott, M. (1994). From directive expert to non-directive partner: a study of facilitating change in the occupational self-perceptions of health visitors and school nurses. *British Journal of Guidance and Counselling*, 22, 107–117.

Meltzer, H., Gatward, R., Goodman R. and Ford, T. (2000). *Mental Health of Children and Adolescents in Great Britain*. London: Stationery Office.

Mitcheson, J. and Cowley, S. (2003). Empowerment or control? An analysis of the extent to which client participation is enabled during health visitor/ client interaction using a structured health needs tool. *International Journal of Nursing Studies*, 40, 413–426.

Moore, T., Ochiltree, G. and Cann, W. (2001). *Best Start: Effective Intervention Programs*. Melbourne: Centre for Community Child Health.

Offord, D. and Bennett, K. (1994). Conduct disorder: long-term outcomes and intervention effectiveness. *Journal of the American Academy of Child and Adolescent Psychiatry*, 33, 1069–1078.

Olds, D., Henderson, C., Chamberlin, R. and Tatelbaum, R. (1986). Preventing child abuse and neglect: a randomized trial of nurse home visitation. *Pediatrics*, 78, 65–78.

Olds, D., Eckenrode, J., Henderson, C., Kitzman, H., Powers, J., Cole, R., Sidora, K., Morris, P., Pettitt, L. and Luckey, D. (1997). Long-term effects of home visitation on maternal life course and child abuse and neglect. *Journal of the American Medical Association*, 278, 637–643.

Olds, D., Henderson, C., Kitzman, H., Eckenrode, J., Cole, R. and Tatelbaum, R. (1999). Prenatal and infancy home visitation by nurses: recent findings. *Future of Children*, 9, 44–65.

Papadopoulou, K., Dimitrakaki, C., Davis, H., Tsiantis, J., Dusoir, A., Paradisiotou, A., Vizacou, S., Roberts, R., Chisholm, B., Puura, K., Mantymaa, M., Tamminen, T., Rudic, N., Radosavljev, J. and Miladinovic, T. (2005). The effects of the European Early Promotion Project training on primary health care professionals. *International Journal of Mental Health Promotion*, 7, 54–62.

Pawl, J. (1994). On supervision. *Zero to Three*, 15, 3–5.

Puura, K., Davis, H., Cox, A., Tsiantis, J., Tamminen, T., Ispanovic-Radojkovic, V., Paradisiotou, A., Mantymaa, M., Roberts, R., Dragonas, T., Layiou-Lignos, E., Dusoir, T., Rudic, N., Tenjovic, L. and Vizacou, S. (2005a). The European Early Promotion Project: description of the service and evaluation study. *International Journal of Mental Health Promotion*, 7, 17–31.

Puura, K., Davis, H., Mantymaa, M., Tamminen, T., Roberts, R., Dragonas, T., Papadopoulou, K., Dimitrakaki, C., Paradisiotou, A., Vizacou, S., Leontiou, F., Rudic, N., Miladinovic, T. and Radojkovic, A. (2005b). The outcome of the European Early Promotion Project: mother–child interaction. *International Journal of Mental Health Promotion*, 7, 82–94.

Rushton, R. and Davis, H. (1992). An evaluation of the effectiveness of counselling training for health care professionals. *British Journal of Guidance and Counselling*, 20, 205–220.

St Pierre, R. and Layzer, J. (1999). Using home visits for multiple purposes: the Comprehensive Child Development Program. *The Future of Children*, 9, 134–151.

Scott, S., Knapp, M., Henderson, J. and Maughan, B. (2001). Financial cost of social exclusion: follow up study of antisocial children into adulthood. *British Medical Journal*, 323, 1–5.

Swain, J., Lorberbaum, J., Kose, S. and Strathearn, L. (2007). Brain basis of early parent–infant interactions: psychology, physiology, and in vivo functional neuroimaging studies. *Journal of Child Psychology and Psychiatry*, 48, 262–287.

Useful websites

www.cpcs.org.uk (Centre for Parent and Child Support).
www.fpta.org.au (Family Partnership Training Australia).

Training in the Family Partnership Model in the UK

For information contact: The Centre for Parent and Child Support, Munro Centre, Guy's Hospital, 66 Snowsfields, London SE1 3SS. Telephone: +44 203 228 9751. Fax: +44 203 288 9755. Email: info@cpcs.org.uk Website: www.cpcs.org.uk

7 The importance of the parental couple in parent–infant psychotherapy

Paul Barrows

The theme of this book is the central importance of keeping the baby in mind when working with parents and infants. In this chapter I seek to emphasise that in approaching this task, one of the things that we specifically need to consider is the nature of the baby that both parents have *in their minds*, that is to say, how they both see this particular infant, coloured as this will be by their own earliest experiences. In addition to this, and just as important, is the way in which the two more or less shared views of the mother and father interact with each other to produce the emotional climate in which the infant's personality will develop. It will be suggested that the implications of this are that both parents should be involved in any therapeutic interventions with infants if an optimal outcome is to be achieved.

The importance of the couple

Until recently researchers and clinicians largely focused on the mother–infant dyad, and the important role that fathers play in infant development was relatively neglected. This applies both to parent–infant specialists such as psychotherapists and infant mental health workers in their clinical work, and to researchers and developmental psychologists looking at parent–infant interactions. In a review of studies of child and adolescent research between 1984 and 1991, Phares (1992) noted that 48 per cent included only mothers whereas 1 per cent included only fathers. The author concluded that, 'although it is encouraging that 26 per cent of studies during this time period obtained and analyzed data separately for fathers and mothers, the bias towards studying mothers and therefore implicitly blaming mothers for problems in their children has continued unabated' (cited in Walters, 1997).

There are, of course, notable exceptions to such a generalisation. Fivaz and colleagues, for example, have sought to develop a model for the study of triadic interaction (i.e. the father–mother–infant relationship), noting that, 'It is probable that because of the multiple variables involved in father–mother–infant interactions the family unit has not yet been studied as a whole' (Corboz-Warnery *et al.*, 1993). However, it remains fair to say that in the infant mental health arena pride of place has been given to the study of the mother–infant relationship.

This is equally true for many clinicians, and both Cramer and Stern, for example, have tended to neglect the father's potential contribution, whether as a factor in the development of the presenting problem or in assisting in its resolution. In a work written together with his colleague Palacio-Espasa on *mother*–infant psychotherapy (Cramer and Palacio-Espasa, 1993), Cramer gave a number of responses to this charge, arguing that (1) in individual therapy one would not invite the partner along, for example, even if it were marital difficulties that prompted the request for help, since one is concerned with the patient's subjective, internal world; (2) the mother initiates the consultation and should therefore be free to decide who attends; (3) by coming alone the mother indicates that she does not wish the father to attend; and (4) the mother will in any event refer to the father, and it is her representation of the father (or its absence) that is to be worked with. The focus for Cramer is, therefore, primarily the exploration of the mother's 'ghosts' (Fraiberg, 1975) rather than the interactive system constituted by the family as a whole.

In *The Motherhood Constellation*, Stern (1995) similarly argues explicitly that the constellation made up of the triad of daughter–mother–mother's mother becomes the central organising principle of psychic life at this stage in the woman's development. In consequence fathers tend to be relegated to providing support for the mother rather than having their own particular role to play: 'It is expected that the father and others will provide a supporting context in which the mother can fulfil her maternal role' (Stern, 1995: 174). This conceptualisation of the father's role also has a long history in psychoanalytic literature. On the whole, when the father's role has been addressed (other than as the third party in the Freudian, Oedipal triangle), it has tended to be as a support to the mother. By sustaining and containing the mother, it is argued, she is enabled, in her turn, to nurture the infant. Bick's classic paper on infant observation contains a moving illustration of how crucial this role can be in the case of a mother who is very lacking in confidence in her maternal abilities, and Bick comments on how 'This supportive behaviour of the father seemed to be an important factor in the gradual improvement in the mother's closeness and tolerance towards the baby' (1964: 560).

There is also a fair amount of research which confirms that fathers remain the most important source of support to their partners (and vice versa), both men and women turning to their partners for support before any other source (Thorpe *et al.*, 1991a, 1991b).

Whilst this view of the father's role is rather limited, as I shall argue, it nevertheless supports the growing body of research suggesting that we can provide the best conditions for the infant's emotional development by involving the father in therapeutic work with the infant, in order to improve the marital relationship. We know from the work of Rutter and Quinton (1984) that children function best where the marital/parental relationship is without excessive conflict. Marital satisfaction also leads to greater father participation in family life, with its concomitant benefits: 'Families with involved fathers, by virtue of their enhanced cohesiveness, may also espouse a more coherent and constructive "world view" tending towards higher aspirations and lower criminality' (Lewis *et al.*, 1982, cited in Walters, 1997).

Moreover, infants simply do not grow up - unless in the most pathological of situations - in dyads. From the beginning they are part of a much broader social matrix. In some ways it is curiously difficult to assess whether this idea – namely that infants begin life by relating to many different people, rather than relating only to one, the mother, and gradually spreading out from this – is particularly controversial. To my mind, it seems self-evident and, indeed, over twenty-five years ago, the French analyst Colette Chiland was able to write:

> The concept of a purely dyadic relationship between infant and mother is now as unacceptable as the concept of a stage of normal autism.
>
> (1982: 377)

And yet in the same book which brought this citation to my attention another contributor wrote:

> Developmentally, interactions with an external mother precede those with any other object, thus the mother is the first object to emerge in the inner world. The father is the second.
>
> (Fakhry Davids, 2002)

It is with this point that I would like to take issue. I would suggest that, in fact, from birth the infant already has to deal with numerous relationships. Further, that within this complex network, it is above all the nature of the *parental couple* that the infant encounters that will be paramount for the infant's future mental health. This holds true even for those infants who are raised in single-parent families. Target and Fonagy write that:

> The physical availability of the father may be neither sufficient nor necessary for triangulation to evolve. What does seem critical is *a situation within which the child can envisage a relationship between two other, emotionally significant figures*.
>
> (2002: 57, italics added)

In other words, even if the father is not actually present, the infant still has to deal with the feelings that arise from being aware that his mother is not his exclusive possession and that she will have in her mind thoughts of an emotionally significant other. More specifically, the infant will be particularly affected by the nature of the parental couple that their single parent has in mind, which will be a product of that parent's more recent experience but also of their own childhood experience with their own parents (see Emanuel, 2002).

This point of view with respect to the primacy of the parental couple as a factor in emotional development has been developed particularly by some contemporary British psychoanalysts working in the tradition of object relations theory (Britton,

1989). They hold that a central feature of psychic development, and a measure of mental health, is the way in which the child manages to negotiate their relationship to the parental couple. It is the child's ability to allow the parents to come together in a creative and procreative relationship, through tolerating the painful feelings that this arouses, that lays the foundation for their own future identity as parents. It is then through identifying with such a parental couple that they will become good-enough parents in turn, as well as developing the capacity to be creative in other spheres. As Britton has put it: 'In normal development the perception by the child of the parents' coming together independently of him unites his psychic world' (Britton, 2002: 116). Thus, the infant 'internalises' not only the parents and the relationships between the parents and self, but also the relationship between the parents. When positive and mutually supporting, the presence of such a united couple is deeply reassuring for the infant and lays the foundation for his or her future emotional well-being.

Support for the idea that addressing the couple's relationship may add to the efficacy of our therapeutic interventions also comes from a number of research findings in several different areas. For example, the Cowans (2001) have been researching the factors affecting the couple's transition to parenthood and subsequently the toddler's adjustment to starting in kindergarten, for a number of years. Their work suggests that the quality of the *couple*'s functioning is a critical factor in improving outcomes for young children, and their preventive intervention programme consequently involves the use of a group-based programme for couples in which there is a focus on the couple's relationship *as a couple*, in addition to parenting. Early findings suggested that this change in emphasis resulted in improvements in the couple's relationship in addition to their parenting (Cowan and Cowan, 2002).

The following case study provides an example of the importance of including fathers in therapeutic work with infants.

Case study

John, aged 2 ½, was referred for aggressive behaviour, including attacking his mother and younger sister, swearing and tantrums. The referring health visitor described a difficult family background: the mother, Mrs A., had a history of depression dating back prior to any pregnancies; she had been depressed following John's birth and then acutely depressed when pregnant with his sister, although refusing the psychiatric admission that was offered. The father was also apparently depressed. The health visitor had offered lots of help and positive encouragement but felt she was not making progress.

When I first met them as a family (although they did not bring the sister) John behaved in an exemplary fashion, being quiet, polite and constructive in his play. His mother, however, recounted a catalogue of his awful behaviour completely at odds with his presentation in the room – she attributed this to the fact that his sister wasn't there. Father, meanwhile, sought to promote a more positive view: he reminded the mother of what a good report John had had from his day care worker – he was her 'star child'. Mother agreed, but quickly went on to say that she had then learnt that this worker said this about all the children.

I arranged to see the couple for some sessions on their own and a very sad picture emerged. On the mother's side there was a history of domestic violence and she could recall her father attacking her mother, although apparently the children were never victims themselves. Her mother was still with her father – and still at times attacked by him – though she would deny this. Her brother was also violent and irresponsible. These grandparents lived nearby and looked after the children, though Mr A. was not happy about the fact that they would swear in front of them. Mrs A. acknowledged that she herself had a very short fuse and would become fiercely angry though not actually violent, and she described how overwhelming her bouts of depression had been. She was scathing about some of the 'help' she had had with this, particularly her most recent episode of attendance at an out-patient psychiatric facility where she saw someone different on each occasion. Clearly there were enough 'ghosts' (Fraiberg, 1975) from the mother's side for it not to be surprising that she found it difficult to deal with what might be the quite ordinary boisterousness and bossiness of a 2-year-old. And indeed the referral did make it appear that this was predominantly a difficulty between mother and son, with the father trying, although not very effectively, to improve the situation.

Mr A. was himself clearly very intimidated by his wife's angry outbursts and felt that she had really given him hell in the past, although it was somewhat better now. However, if that was how the father felt then what must it be like for John? Over a few sessions Mr A.'s story also unfolded. His father had been seriously ill during his childhood and seemed to have been very dominated by his wife. He had died when Mr A. was aged 12. Thereafter Mr A. had felt very put upon by his mother, who had made him feel guilty whenever he went out with his friends, but like his father he had gone along with her demands, which also involved being very helpful around the house. However, she had subsequently found a new partner who had pretty much thrown him out of the house. He therefore now had no contact with his mother. In addition to this, relations with his sister were also very strained; this sister had lived nearby but since moving had had little to do with them. She was seen as favouring a cousin and taking very little interest in Mr A.'s own children.

It was a source of great sadness to Mr A. that he was therefore unable to provide his own children with any kind of extended family, and he felt very strongly that he had let them down. It became very clear that he had a warm image in mind of what family life should be like, and that he was failing to provide this.

Now, I think it would have been quite easy to approach this case as largely centred around a conflictual relationship between mother and son. In this context, a major factor would be the background of domestic violence in the mother's family of origin. Is this male child perhaps seen through the lens of an internal representation of a violent father (or indeed brother) such that an ordinary expression of anger is felt to be catastrophic and responded to accordingly? An additional contributory factor would be the mother's periods of depression which would have meant that she was not available at an emotional level to contain her son's more aggressive feelings and help him to manage them.

Of course all of this is true, but I believe it is only half of the story. I would suggest that the final outcome, in terms of John's actual experience, is in fact determined by the *interaction* that takes place between mother and father. For example, Mr A. appears unable to protect John from his wife's angry outbursts – just as he seems unable to protect himself from them. The reasons behind this would seem to lie with the 'ghosts' within *his* nursery (Fraiberg, 1975). There is some evidence that Mr A. struggles to deal with his own aggression in a way that leaves him prone to becoming a victim: *he* was put upon by his mother as a child (in a way that was not true for his siblings) and he seems to have subsequently also been involved in a rather masochistic relationship with another male colleague. This situation is then again recreated in his relationship with his wife, in which he feels pushed around and intimidated. His own aggression, which is not apparent in the sessions, can then be readily located in his wife who – for her own reasons – is a very suitable target for such a projection.

In the ensuing interaction, as became much clearer in a later session, both parties then find themselves taking up more and more polarised positions. In one session, I commented on Mr A.'s tendency to always play the role of peacemaker, trying to make sure everyone is OK (he had typically begun the session with several enquiries about how I was getting on and if I was all right). We talked about how he also does this at home in an attempt to smooth things over between John and his wife, partly out of anxiety about the aggressive feelings being expressed but also because of his concern for his son and his wish to provide a family life akin to the internal image he has of what family life should be like. When this happens, though, Mrs A. seems to experience it as her husband failing to deal with John's angry feelings – and, of course, to some extent she is right. This then raises her anxiety about these feelings getting out of control and prompts her to become more harsh and punitive, which in turn pushes him to work even harder at trying to calm things down, whilst raising his anxiety about his wife's feelings getting out of control, thereby trapping them in an escalating vicious spiral.

To some extent, what this couple share, albeit for quite different reasons, is a lack: the lack of a representation of a father who can be firm and yet tolerant of, and able to acknowledge, more aggressive feelings. *Mrs* A.'s father was himself unable to manage such feelings and acted them out; *Mr* A.'s father had been in a fragile and damaged state and there was reason to suppose he had had his own difficulties in this area and had been somewhat dominated by his wife. Whilst the role played by this 'lack' highlights the importance of one aspect of the father's function, what I would particularly wish to emphasise is the way in which the *interaction* between the two parents is most critical, because it is the product of that interaction that creates the emotional atmosphere in which the infant is born and lives.

This example shows why – clinically – it is important to try to work with both parents together whenever this is possible. This means not only encouraging the father to attend but also trying to keep a balance between the needs and contributions of the two parents within the session. An over-emphasis on the role of either parent is likely to be less helpful.

So, whilst it is important to ensure that fathers are included, it would, of course, be equally mistaken to focus our attention too exclusively on the father–infant or father–child dyad. Rather, fathers (and indeed mothers) are important primarily *as part of a parental couple* and it is that couple and their relationship that should be at the heart of our work.

Co-parenting and the family

While infant mental health workers are beginning to address this issue, there is still a long way to go. This proposed approach requires not only more attention to the father's role but also to the family as such. A number of writers have recently been seeking to redress the balance and to give due weight to the importance of the father's contribution to the family system, such as Kai von Klitzing (von Klitzing *et al.*, 1999a, 1999b) and James McHale (McHale and Cowan, 1996; McHale and Fivaz-Depeursinge, 1999).

McHale, whose particular area of interest is what he refers to as *co-parenting*, notes that: '[the] enduring qualities of the marital partnership play an important role in shaping subsequent triadic family process' (McHale and Fivaz-Depeursinge, 1999: 121). However, his main contention is that we continue to neglect the complexity of the family process and the fact that this constitutes a distinct entity in its own right, which is not reducible to the sum of its parts. He describes how there is a strong bias in developmental research toward conceptualizing the family as a collection, and occasionally as a network of interlocking dyadic relationships. Furthermore, studies of the family continue to place the mother–infant relationship at the family's core, although this is seldom acknowledged.

In fact, he goes on to argue, 'the interpersonal dynamics of such [family] groups often significantly diverge from the dynamics of dyadic relationships … the family triad of mother, father, and infant develops its own way of being, unique unto itself'. This point of view is echoed by Corboz-Warnery and colleagues (1993) who note that although the contributions of each partner in the triad are important, describing them is not sufficient to convey the full context of the infant's development. It is also necessary to *move beyond these additive approaches to capture the ways in which the family operates as a small group'* (Parke, 1990: 182).

In his most recent paper on this subject McHale likewise reiterates the need to operate 'with a mindset that it is important to view other care-giving figures in families not as background or supportive context but as integral to an understanding of the family group dynamic' (2007: 386).

This line of argument is undoubtedly compelling in linking into the whole field of family and systemic therapeutic approaches. It is, after all, this complex web of family relationships that the infant is born into and has to begin to learn about from day one. Moreover, this is not only a matter of triads. For the second-born there is also another sibling already present, not to mention, for many children, the grandparental generation. Given what we know from, for example, Stern's work on *The Motherhood Constellation* (1995), maternal grandmothers may also have a particularly important role to play. Here too, though, the partner's attitude towards the mother-in-law will be a powerful factor in determining how the grandmother's influence is expressed.

Clinically, of course, this is quite challenging since the logical conclusion of this line of argument is that we should not be working just with the couple – as I began by arguing – but with the whole family across the generations!

Conclusion

This chapter points to the importance of including the father in therapeutic work with the infant. However, it also stresses that the key issue is to see the father as part of the parental couple, based on the premise that it is the couple who, essentially, provide the emotional matrix in which the infant develops. When the couple can be enabled to see how fundamental an influence they have on their infant's development, they are also more likely to become willing partners in the exploration of those family relationships.

This is not, however, to minimise the difficulty of such an endeavour. Most parents will not have sought help with this in mind and many may find it difficult to see how a discussion of their relationship has anything to do with the fact that their child will not settle at night. Moreover, if there are indeed difficulties in the relationship, it may also be experienced as very threatening to bring them out into the open. There is no ready answer about how to engage parents in this task but what is essential is that the clinician approaches the work with a mindset that takes full account of the complexity of these dynamics and family systems.

References

Bick, E. (1964). Notes on infant observation in psychoanalytic training. *International Journal of Psychoanalysis*, 45, 558–566.

Britton, R. (1989). The missing link. In J. Steiner (ed.), *The Oedipus Complex Today*. London: Karnac.

Britton, R. (2002). Forever father's daughter. In J. Trowell and A. Etchegoyen (eds), *The Importance of Fathers*. Hove: Brunner-Routledge.

Chiland, C. (1982). A new look at fathers. *Psychoanalytic Study of the Child*, 37, 367–379.

Corboz-Warnery, A., Fivaz-Depeursinge, E., Bettens, C. G. and Favez, N. (1993). Systemic analysis of father–mother–baby interactions: the Lausanne triadic play. *Infant Mental Health Journal*, 14, 298–316.

Cowan, P. and Cowan, C. P. (2001). A couple perspective on the transmission of attachment patterns. In C. Clulow (ed.), *Adult Attachment and Couple Psychotherapy*. London: Brunner-Routledge.

Cowan, P. and Cowan, C. (2002). Partners, parents, and intergenerational change: what do we know and how can we help? Paper given at the Tavistock Marital Studies Institute Summer Conference, London.

Cramer, B. G. and Palacio-Espasa, F. (1993). *La Pratique des psychothérapies mères-bébés*. Paris: PUF.

Emanuel, L. (2002). Parents united: addressing parental issues in work with infants and young children. *International Journal of Infant Observation*, 5(2), 103–117.

Fakhry Davids, M. (2002). Fathers in the internal world: from boy to man to father. In J. Trowell and A. Etchegoyen (eds), *The Importance of Fathers*. Hove: Brunner-Routledge.

Fivaz-Depeursinge, E. and Corboz-Warnery, A. (1999). *The Primary Triangle*. New York: Basic Books.

Fraiberg, S. (1975). Ghosts in the nursery: a psychoanalytic approach to the problems of impaired infant–mother relationships. In *Clinical Studies in Infant Mental Health*. London: Tavistock (1980).

McHale, J. P. (2007). When infants grow up in multiperson relationship systems. *Infant Mental Health Journal*, 28(4), 370-392.

McHale, J. P. and Cowan, P. A. (eds) (1996). *Understanding How Family-level Dynamics Affect Children's Development: Studies of Two-parent Families*. San Francisco: Jossey-Bass/Pfeiffer.

McHale, J. P. and Fivaz-Depeursinge, E. (1999). Understanding triadic and family group interactions during infancy and toddlerhood. *Clinical Child and Family Psychology Review*, 2(2), 107-127.

Murray, L. and Cooper, P. J. (1997). *Postpartum Depression and Child Development*. New York: Guilford Press.

Parke, R. D. (1990). In search of fathers: a narrative of an empirical journey. In I. E. Sigel and G. H. Brody (eds), *Methods of Family Research: Biographies of Research Projects, Vol. 1, Normal Families* (pp. 154–187). Hillsdale, NJ: Lawrence Erlbaum Associates.

Phares, V. (1992). Where's poppa? The relative lack of attention to the role of fathers in child and adolescent psychopathology. *American Psychologist*, 47, 656–664.

Rutter, M. and Quinton, D. (1984). Parental psychiatric disorder: effects on children. *Psychological Medicine*, 14, 853–880.

Stern, D. (1995). *The Motherhood Constellation*. New York: Basic Books.

Target, M. and Fonagy, P. (2002). Fathers in modern psychoanalysis and in society. In J. Trowell and A. Etchegoyen (eds), *The Importance of Fathers*. Hove: Brunner-Routledge.

Thorpe, K., Dragonas, T. and Golding, J. (1991a). The effects of psychosocial factors on the mother's emotional well-being during early parenthood: a cross-cultural study of Britain and Greece. *Journal of Reproductive and Infant Psychology*, 10, 205–217.

Thorpe, K., Dragonas, T. and Golding, J. (1991b). The effects of psychosocial factors on the mother's emotional well-being during early pregnancy: a cross-cultural study of Britain and Greece. *Journal of Reproductive and Infant Psychology*, 10, 191–204.

Von Klitzing, K., Simoni, H. and Burgin, D. (1999a). Child development and early triadic relationships. *International Journal of Psychoanalysis*, 80(1), 71–89.

Von Klitzing, K., Simoni, H., Amsler, F. and Burgin, D. (1999b). The role of the father in early family interactions. *Infant Mental Health Journal*, 20(3), 222–237.

Walters, J. (1997). Talking with fathers: the inter-relation of significant loss, clinical presentation in children and engagement of fathers in therapy. *Clinical Child Psychology and Psychiatry*, 2(3), 415–430.

Part II

Targeted approaches

8 Empowering parents through 'Learning Together'

The PEEP model

Alison Street

> I learned children have lots of abilities and if we give them opportunities to explore
> … go out and talk about things … they are not just a plant that we water. We have to
> give them opportunity. I learned how to play, touch, and feel and enjoy being with my
> child. I learned the importance of music and song. I learned confidence that I could
> cope with the early months and child behaviour.
>
> (Roberts, 2001: 126)

These are the thoughts of a parent in 2001 who had attended a PEEP group with
her baby. When her baby was born she had felt isolated from her own family.
Now she works as a PEEP practitioner. This mother's story illustrates the sense of
empowerment felt by many parents and carers who have experienced PEEP since
the start of work with families in 1995.

This chapter focuses on elements in the 'Learning Together' programme developed by PEEP, and in particular those that have been found to help adults
feel confident in their role as their children's first educator. The chapter starts by
providing an outline of the theoretical background and then describes how the
Learning Together curriculum is used to enhance relationships between parents
and young children. Particular attention will be given to the rationale for using
music in the programme. The chapter will describe how the project works with
families and young children, what was found from two evaluation studies, and the
implications of these findings for the future.

PEEP beginnings

Peers Early Education Partnership (PEEP) began with the idealism, determination
and generosity of key figures in the education community in Oxford in 1989. It
was born of the conviction that an initiative involving parents was needed to address the imbalance of opportunity for learning in a generation of children across
a distinctive, disadvantaged community in south Oxford. The momentum to foster
a culture of learning in the area, which would have a practical long-term effect,
was driven by the head and governors of Peers School, a senior school for students
aged from 14 to 18 years. However, rather than seek a remedial solution, their
vision was to devise a preventive programme that would start with babies and

their families. Since October 1995, when the first families in PEEP pilot groups ventured cautiously through the door in the local community centre, the project has expanded to become a nation-wide intervention, its curriculum and principles adopted by a variety of organisations in all regions of the UK.

The aim of PEEP was, and is, to bring about a significant improvement in the educational attainment of whole communities of children by working with parents and carers. Its rationale emerges from and contributes to the growing body of evidence that focuses on the supportive role of the home learning environment (HLE). One of the most comprehensive and influential studies in this field was the Effective Provision of Pre-School Education project (EPPE). EPPE showed that a range of activities that parents undertake at home can have a positive effect on children's development (Sylva *et al.*, 2003). The home learning environment was found to be only moderately associated with mothers' own educational levels, thus emphasising what parents *do* at home rather than who they *are*. This was borne out by Evangelou and Sylva (2003) who found that children who had experienced PEEP improved in vocabulary, language comprehension, understanding of books and print, number concepts and self-esteem. Parental support has been found to influence not only children's adjustment to school, but also their aspirations and long-term self-concept as learners (Desforges and Abouchaar, 2003).

Evidence about 'what works' in terms of support for early learning can be found in a review of international evidence (Moran *et al.*, 2004). However, there is still a need to determine what works, for whom, and in what circumstances. For example, while the term 'parent' usually refers to mothers there have been some impressive findings in recent UK studies about the positive effects of fathers in supporting their children's learning. Surveys have shown that increased paternal involvement in parenting is associated with higher social expectations about the amount of time that men spend with their young children (Dex and Ward, 2007), and stems from their genuine wish to take part in family life (Henwood and Procter, 2003). Flouri and Buchanan (2004) found that early father involvement can last into adolescence, and that both father's and mother's involvement at age 7 independently predicted a child's educational attainment by age 20.

Theoretical foundations of 'Learning Together'

Three strands of thinking have been influential in the development of the curriculum, materials and activities that make up the Learning Together programme. The first emerges from research in developmental psychology that focuses on the significance of social interactions with babies and young children for healthy cognitive development. This research highlights the competencies that babies and toddlers have in reaching out and relating to other people (Stern, 1977, 1985, 2000), and the role adults play by responding, imitating, joking, singing, playing games and turn-taking (Trevarthen, 1987, 1990, 1993). The potential opportunities for talking and listening afforded by everyday life, and the meanings and negotiations that are exchanged, are also highlighted (Bruner, 1990). Songs and rhymes are important components of the PEEP programme, and they have been found to enhance relationships, to build mutual understanding and to encourage interactions between adults and babies (Street, 2006).

The second strand of thinking is found in the expanding body of research on the infant brain. This has shown how susceptible babies' brains are to environmental influences, and how they respond and develop through affectionate relationships with others (Gerhardt, 2004; Hobson, 2002).

The third area of thinking is about the parent as a baby's first educator. PEEP supports parents and carers essentially as communicators rather than as teachers. Emphasis is placed on those aspects of parenting that support affectionate bonding and learning through relating. A central aspect of Learning Together is an emphasis on ways of enhancing young children's and adults' self-esteem and thereby confidence in facilitating successful early learning (Roberts, 1995, 2006). In the curriculum, aspects of learning are presented within the ORIM framework, originally devised by Hannon (1995). This recognises the important role of parents and carers, across a wide spectrum of abilities, in providing *Opportunities* for learning, *Recognition* of their children's achievements, *Interaction* around playful activities, and *Modelling* of attitudes to learning and ways of using literacy at home. This framework is based on a Vygotskyan view of child development. Learning is conceived as a social activity where young children's capacity to grow and learn can be encouraged and maintained by an attentive adult who 'tunes in' to a child's interests and supports them by watching and assisting their activities. By supporting the child within their 'zone of proximal development' (Vygotsky, 1978), adults can help a child to become increasingly independent in their learning and confident in their decisions.

The PEEP programme: aims, principles and curriculum

The aims of the PEEP programme are sixfold:

1　To promote parents' and carers' awareness of children's very early learning and development, through making the most of everyday activities and interactions.
2　To support parents/carers in their relationships with their children, so that the children's self-esteem will be enhanced.
3　To affirm the crucial role of parents/carers as their children's first educators.
4　To support parents/carers in the development of their children's literacy and numeracy.
5　To support parents/carers so that they can encourage the development in children of positive learning dispositions.
6　To promote and support parents' and carers' lifelong learning.

At the heart of the programme are key principles about relationships with carers and about learning together with young children. These principles have their roots in the theory on which the programme is based, and have evolved through discussion and review with practitioners. They reflect the importance of awareness of diverse cultural child-rearing practices and are seminal to the PEEP model.

PEEP principles

The principles on which the programme is based (see below) are embedded within the curriculum and all aspects of the materials and resources. The curriculum is based on five themes: self-concept and disposition to learn, listening and talking, reading, writing, and numeracy. These are organised within the ORIM framework in a cyclical structure, which enables repetition of topics and allows flexibility for families' changing circumstances and patterns of attendance.

Principles about relationships with parents and carers

PEEP:

- values parents'/carers' knowledge and experience of their children, using this as a starting point and building on it by offering ideas and information;
- works with parents as equal partners (PEEP is done *with* parents, not *to* them);
- has a non-judgemental approach towards families;
- values diversity, welcoming people from all backgrounds and cultures;
- creates opportunities for parents to share experiences and ideas in a safe and supportive environment.

Principles about learning with children

PEEP recognises that:

- parents/carers are a child's first and most important educators;
- self-esteem is central for learning;
- learning works best when the world is understood from the child's point of view;
- children learn through play and interaction;
- singing, stories and books are extremely important in the education of children, beginning at birth;
- relationships are at the heart of learning;

and encourages:

- parents and carers to learn together with their children;
- high expectations of what children and adults can achieve together.

Applying the curriculum with babies in mind

The Learning Together curriculum for families with babies focuses mainly on oral language (talking and listening) and on self-concept. For example, topics for discussion with parents centre on: watching and noticing the small differences in the baby's sounds and gestures; the adults' responses; the usefulness of songs and rhymes to help understanding and relating; and the balance between allowing choices and developing caring routines that are mutually helpful. For families who feel confident about attending groups with others the following core activities are offered in the weekly sessions:

- Talking time
- Songs, rhymes and playful activities
- Sharing books and stories

Resources used in groups include a variety of treasure baskets; collections for heuristic play (Goldschmied and Jackson, 2004), the PEEP *Singing Together* songbooks with CDs, props to enliven the stories, and playful activities. Talking time centres on parents' existing practices and attitudes, and builds on these to support learning at home. Parents develop their own networks of support and gain in confidence as their experiences are valued and their views sought.

For those families who have difficulty in attending groups or who choose not to engage with a curriculum-based programme, PEEP practitioners adapt the activities and focus for talking one-to-one. The following illustrates the potential in a story to help one mother to reflect on her situation. The practitioner, whose thoughts opened this chapter, wrote:

> We shared 'Little Beaver and the Echo'. The story went really well especially for the mother. The children enjoyed story pictures and the sounds which I was making as an echo, but the mum said, 'I needed a friend like little beaver and PEEP heard my Echo'. We had good discussion about the mum's own inner feelings; how she had never had a chance to share them openly and safely.

The need for active listening to help understanding is a strong theme throughout Learning Together. The focus on listening is explored through sharing playful songs and rhymes.

The use of music in PEEP

Music supports interactions between mother and baby, helps one get to know the other (Street, 2001), and plays an important part in facilitating group activities. The musical materials in the programme focus on using songs and rhymes in everyday situations, rather than on playing instruments or listening to recorded or live instrumentalists. How can music be helpful in supporting interaction?

The musicality of early interactions

Research has shown that around the time of their birth, babies are ready and able to communicate with and mimic other people (see, for example, Trevarthen *et al.*,

1999). Their ears have been able to pick up vibrations and sounds from outside the mother's body from three to four months before birth (Lecanuet, 1996). Once born, they are often able to recognise familiar voices and even TV tunes they had heard while still inside the womb (Hepper, 1988). During early infancy, communication between caregiver and baby moves on through a continuous dance of sounds, gestures and exaggerated facial expressions. As the baby matures, this is enhanced by jokes, games and 'proto-conversations' (Bateson, 1979). Communication is regarded here as being fluid and reciprocal, involving feelings and responsiveness to each other's emotional states (Fogel, 1993). Timing is crucial – the turn-taking and synchronous stream happen intuitively but may be disrupted by maternal circumstances such as depression, feelings of loneliness or social alienation. Trevarthen (1999-2000) defined these communication patterns as 'communicative musicality', referring to the *'pulse'* of behaviours happening through time, the *'quality'* or character of vocal or body gesture, and the *'narrative'* of the experiences and common understandings that make up everyday life with a baby.

Singing to babies

When adults sing to babies, the presence of the baby has been seen to influence how the adult uses their voice. Compared with singing to another adult, the tone is warmer, the pitch usually higher and the tempo slower (Trainor *et al.*, 1997). These elements appear to be widespread across different cultures (Trehub and Trainor, 1998) and to emerge within a repertoire of lullabies, playsongs and singing games with associated movements and playful gestures. Some studies suggest that this traditional repertoire has been forgotten and needs to be re-taught to parents (Baker and Mackinlay, 2006). But recent research has demonstrated that mothers sing repeatedly to their babies, although they do not necessarily consider their singing in a musical context (Street, 2004). Instead, for them singing to babies is about incorporating many imitative behaviours, in mimicking babies' sounds, babbles and gestures or the jingles on radio, television and digitised toys. Moreover, where mothers use more sustained voice play or the measured structure of a song or rhythmic chant, the baby will often look attentive and engaged, listening with more alert concentration than to the spoken word (Street, 2006). The tuneful 'doodles' emerging during chatter with babies can therefore be helpful for parents in regulating a baby's mood, and in being a resource for play.

PEEP practitioners draw attention to voice play, and suggest that singing or playful chants can help both adult and baby in day-to-day caring routines to show each other how they feel. How the rhymes and songs are used depends on the carers and practitioners, who watch and listen, and on the purposes of their choice of songs.

Evaluation of PEEP

Two major studies were conducted to evaluate the effectiveness of PEEP, using a range of outcomes for children and their families: the Birth to School Study

(BTSS) and the Enabling Parents Study. The BTSS followed a cohort of children and their families over a six-year period (see the BTSS full report (SSU/2005/FR/017) for full details). One important finding (Evangelou *et al.*, 2005) was that improved early parenting skills resulted in improved child outcomes in later years. Thus, improved parenting pre-empted improvements in children's literacy and self-esteem, and was the result of the PEEP focus on enhanced communication, sensitivity, responsiveness and modelling.

Furthermore, the design of the BTSS made it possible to analyse the *whole community* effects of the programme (i.e. over the whole PEEP catchment area). PEEP activities were delivered by trained practitioners in nurseries and community playgroups and in outreach work. The cognitive and self-esteem effects found in the children living in the PEEP catchment area suggest that even where parents chose not to take part in the programme itself, they nevertheless benefited from receiving aspects of the programme through their interaction with practitioners in family centres and preschool settings.

The second study, entitled Enabling Parents (Sylva *et al.*, 2004), employed quantitative and qualitative methods to evaluate the effect of PEEP on parenting skills and on parental perceptions about the support they received. It compared the attitudes and experiences of a group of parents who had attended at least five sessions with those of a matched group of similar socioeconomic status, but who had no knowledge of PEEP. Only mothers participated in the study. Compared with the matched group, the PEEP mothers:

- reported taking more basic skills courses;
- significantly improved their socioeconomic status;
- reported significantly greater awareness of their child's literacy development and ways to foster it through modelling skills, play and music;
- developed more occupation-related skills;
- reported more understanding of their child's general development.

In addition, both groups found that attendance at groups with other parents provided support and encouragement and a chance for their children to socialise. An associated finding was the anxiety and stress some parents expressed about attending a group for the first time. This illustrates the importance of making delivery as accessible as possible, and of increasing diversity, for example, through the use of open-access, and drop-in sessions.

The support and encouragement parents have experienced through the programme is reflected in the diaries and portfolios they have kept about their babies' development. These often include photographs, their child's mark-making, mementoes from visits, and their own thoughts and observations. The diaries qualify for Open College Network (OCN) accreditation at levels 1 and 2, and practitioners provide support in the production of these records. Many parents have expressed pride in being awarded certificates in recognition of their role, and have used it as proof of attainment on their CVs and job applications, especially where employment is educational.

Looking to the future

The positive outcomes from these studies reinforce the need for preventive programmes that seek to empower parents while their children are very young. If intervention occurs at a later stage, disaffection, cynicism and a sense of powerlessness may occur as a result of social disadvantage. The challenges for projects like PEEP are to ensure the relevance of curriculum and practice for families who may, for a variety of reasons, choose to opt out of both group and individual home-based provision. Such families are often labelled 'hard to reach' by services that aim to help. Targeted provision to families who are 'at risk' may result in stigma. With this in mind, in April 2006 the Oxford PEEP opened 'Room to Play'. This initiative aims to be accessible to families locally, rather than being based in a location to which families have to travel. It was set up in collaboration with Sutton Trust with support from the Garfield Weston Foundation, and is a 'drop in' facility in a busy local shopping centre, where parents go to pass time. In the 'shop' people can get a cup of tea, talk with each other, or with a PEEP worker who is available all day, change, feed and wash their baby, and obtain information about other services in the area. Here, they will find many books, in addition to indoor and outdoor play activities based on the 'Learning Together' curriculum.

PEEP's philosophy is to provide a universal service, where all families are welcome. In this spirit, 'Room to Play' opens its doors to anyone who chooses to visit. This open-access approach presents new challenges for practitioners who make themselves available to respond to a variety of families' needs. It raises questions, which have been highlighted by preliminary research (Evangelou, *et al.*, 2006), such as which aspects of the curriculum, normally structured for groups or individuals, are appropriate to offer in this kind of unpredictable, open-ended situation, where a mother and baby may stay for five minutes or five hours. Another question concerns the relationship between client and practitioner, where the boundaries that define roles and associated expectations are often fluid and continuously being drawn and redrawn. One finding emerging from discussions with practitioners is that the ORIM framework is helpful in underpinning all interactions and activities, and that parents, children and practitioners are benefiting mutually from each other.

These three-way patterns of interaction between practitioner, child and parent/carer constitute the relational factors that ebb and flow in a constant interplay in this kind of situation. Their characteristics contribute to the feelings of challenge, frustration, excitement and satisfaction of day-to-day work in parent support. What 'works' for families in PEEP seems to depend ultimately on the flexibility of provision which enables practitioners to respond sensitively, to be non-didactic, to accept parents as they are, and to strike a balance between PEEP's goals and those of the parents. The Birth to School Study reported that PEEP had worked with a cohort of children over a six-year period to improve self-esteem, literacy skills, and parental attitudes to learning. There is a need for further research on the relational factors pertaining to staff and parental roles and attitudes, which are harder to define, and which fluctuate according to context. Moreover, there is a need to understand more about them to inform practice and to plan ahead for this challenging kind of work.

Conclusion

PEEP empowers parents by helping them to realise the learning potential of everyday interactions with their children. The programme emphasises parental strengths and competencies, through the use of an approach that aims to be both optimistic and pragmatic. This is in contrast to the large number of interventions that seek to prevent known risk factors by concentrating on deficits in parenting skills. If risks to parenting arise from 'the absence of normal, expectable opportunities' (Garbarino *et al.*, 2002), then, through its curriculum and ORIM framework, PEEP is pioneering an approach that redresses the balance. Viewed from this perspective, PEEP contributes to a view of practice, research, and policy based on 'accumulated opportunities' instead of 'accumulated risk'. Future research might focus on the interpretations and significance parents attach to these opportunities and should aim to help us understand more about what 'empowerment' means from the parents' point of view.

Acknowledgements

This chapter is dedicated to Mumtaz Shabir and her family. I am grateful to Nuzhat Abbas for her thoughtful insights and to colleagues at PEEP for their helpful comments on the script.

References

Baker, F. and Mackinlay, E. (2006). Sing, Soothe, Sleep: a lullaby education programme for first time mothers. *British Journal of Music Education*, 23(2), 147–160.

Bateson, M. C. (1979). The epigenesis of conversational interaction: a personal account of research development. In M. Bullowa (ed.), *Before Speech: The Beginning of Human Communication* (pp. 63–77). London: Cambridge University Press.

Bruner, J. (1990). *Acts of Meaning*. Cambridge, MA: Harvard University Press.

Department for Education and Skills (2001). *Schools: Building on Success* (Green Paper). London: DfES.

Desforges, C. and Abouchaar, A. (2003). *The Impact of Parental Involvement, Parental Support and Family Education on Pupil Achievement: A Review of Literature*. London: DfES Publications.

Dex, S. and Ward, K. (2007). *Parental Care and Employment in Early Childhood*. Working Paper No. 57. London: Institute of Education.

Evangelou, M. and Sylva, K. (2003). *The Effects of the Peers Early Education Partnership (PEEP) on Children's Developmental Progress*. Research Report 489. London: DfES Publications.

Evangelou, M., Brooks, G., Smith, S. and Jennings, D. (2005). *The Birth to School Study: A Longitudinal Evaluation of the Peers Early Education Partnership (PEEP) 1998-2005*. London: DfES Publications.

Evangelou, M., Smith, S. and Sylva, K. (2006). *Evaluation of the Sutton Trust Shopping Centre Project: A Preliminary Report*. Oxford: Oxford University Department of Education.

Flouri, E. and Buchanan, A. (2004). Early father's and mother's involvement and child's later educational outcomes. *British Journal of Educational Psychology*, 74, 141–153.

Fogel, A. (1993). *Developing Through Relationships. Origins of Communication, Self and Culture*. Hemel Hempstead: Harvester Wheatsheaf.

Garbarino, G., Vorrasi, J. A. and Kostelny, K. (2002). Parenting and public policy. In M. H. Bornstein (ed.), *Handbook of Parenting*, Vol. 5 (pp. 487–507). Hillsdale, NJ: Laurence Erlbaum Associates.

Gerhardt, S. (2004). *Why Love Matters: How Affection Shapes a Baby's Brain*. Hove: Brunner-Routledge.

Goldschmied, E. and Jackson, S. (2004). *People Under Three: Young Children in Daycare*, 2nd edn (pp. 96–110). London: Routledge.

Hannon, P. (1995). *Literacy, Home and School: Research and Practice in Teaching Literacy with Parents*. London: Falmer Press.

Henwood, K. L. and Procter, J. (2003). The 'good father': reading men's accounts of paternal involvement during the transition to first time fatherhood. *British Journal of Social Psychology*, 42, 337–355.

Hepper, P. G. (1988). Fetal 'soap' addiction. *Lancet*, 1, 1147–1148.

Hobson, P. (2002). *The Cradle of Thought: Exploring the Origins of Thinking*. London: Macmillan.

Lecanuet, J. P. (1996). Prenatal auditory experience. In I. Deliège and J. Sloboda (eds), *Musical Beginnings: Origins and Development of Musical Competence* (pp. 3–34). Oxford: Oxford University Press.

Moran, P., Ghate, D. and van der Merwe, A. (2004). *What Works in Parenting Support? A Review of the International Evidence*. Research Brief No. RB574. London: DfES Publications.

Roberts, R. (1995). *Self Esteem and Successful Early Learning*. London: Hodder and Stoughton Educational.

Roberts, R. (2001). *PEEP Voices: A Five Year Diary*. Oxford: PEEP Publications.

Roberts, R. (2006). *Self Esteem and Early Learning: Key People from Birth to Three*. London: Paul Chapman Publishing Sage Publications.

Stern, D. (1977). *The First Relationship: Infant and Mother*. London: Fontana/Open Books.

Stern, D. N. (1985). *The Interpersonal World of the Infant: A View from Psychoanalysis and Developmental Psychology*. New York: Basic Books.

Stern, D. N. (2000). Introduction. In *The Interpersonal World of the Infant: A View from Psychoanalysis and Developmental Psychology*, 2nd edn. New York: Basic Books.

Street, A. (2001). *The Use of Music in the PEEP Programme*. Oxford: PEEP Publications.

Street, A. (2004). Singing with infants: balancing control with collaboration. Proceedings of British Psychological Society, Developmental Section Annual Conference, Leeds Metropolitan University, 2-5 September. pp. 268–269.

Street, A. (2006). The role of singing within mother–infant interactions. Unpublished PhD thesis, Roehampton University, London.

Sylva, K., Melhuish, E., Sammons, P., Siraj-Blatchford, I., Taggart, B. and Elliot, K. (2003). *The Effective Provision of Pre-School Education (EPPE) Project: Findings from the Pre-school Period*. London: Institute of Education.

Sylva, K., Evangelou, M., Taylor, R., Rothwell, A. and Brooks, G. (2004). *Enabling Parents: The Role of PEEP in Supporting Parents as Adult Learners*. Sheffield: OUDES and School of Education, University of Sheffield. (http://www.edstud.ox.ac.uk/fell.html).

Trainor, L. J., Clark, E. D., Huntley, A. and Adams, B. (1997). Comparisons of infant-directed and non-infant directed singing: a search for the acoustic basis of infant preferences. *Infant Behaviour and Development*, 20, 383–396.

Trehub, S. E. and Trainor, L. J. (1998). Lullabies and playsongs. *Advances in Infancy Research*, 12, 43–77.

Trevarthen, C. (1987). Sharing makes sense: intersubjectivity and the making of an infant's meaning. In R. Steele and T. Threadgold (eds), *Language Topics: Essays in Honour of Michael Halliday*, Vol. 1 (pp. 177–199). Amsterdam: John Benjamins.

Trevarthen, C. (1990). Signs before speech. In T. A. Sebeok and J. Umiker-Sebeok (eds), *The Semiotic Web*, (pp. 689-755). Berlin: Mouton de Gruyter.

Trevarthen, C. (1993). The function of emotions in early infant communication and development. In J. Nadel and L. Camaioni (eds), *New Perspectives in Early Communicative Development* (pp. 48–81). London: Routledge.

Trevarthen, C. (1999-2000). Musicality and the intrinsic motive pulse: evidence from human psychobiology and infant communication. *Musicae Scientifae, special issue*, 155–215.

Trevarthen, C., Kokkinaki, T. and Fiamenghi, G. A. Jr (1999). What infants' imitations communicate: with mothers, with fathers and with peers. In J. Nadel and G. Butterworth (eds), *Imitation in Infancy* (pp. 127-185). Cambridge: Cambridge University Press.

Vygotsky, L. S. (1978). *Mind in Society: The Development of Higher Mental Processes*. Cambridge, MA: Harvard University Press. (Originally published in 1930, 1933 and 1935).

Useful websites

www.peep.org.uk
www.education.ex.ac.uk/music-one2one
www.talktoyourbaby.org.uk

9 Promoting a secure attachment through early screening and interventions

A partnership approach

P. O. Svanberg

Fifty years ago Bowlby (1958) theorised that secure attachment in infancy could predict mental health and well-being even into adulthood (see, for example, Sroufe *et al.*, 2005), and Ainsworth and her colleagues (1978) created the procedure (i.e. the development and validation of the Strange Situation) by which attachment behaviour in infancy could be assessed in a reliable and valid manner. Over the years this procedure has become the gold standard in the assessment of an infant's attachment behaviour. Having established that attachment behaviour was a significant predictor of a child's future emotional regulation and resilience (Svanberg, 1998), and the means by which to assess it, the antecedents or the determinants of secure attachment became the focus of attention, and sensitive responsiveness on the part of the parent was demonstrated to be significantly associated with secure attachment in the infant (De Wolff and Van IJzendoorn, 1997). This growing body of research demonstrated that a sensitively responsive parent is more likely to have a securely attached child who is more likely to grow into a secure and empathic adult.

Video feedback as a therapeutic intervention to promote such sensitively responsive parenting was first developed in the Netherlands (Wels, 2002), where it was initially used as an adjunct to family interventions (van der Does, 2002), as well as a tool to intervene in the parent–infant relationship (Weiner *et al.*, 1994). This approach has become increasingly common in the field of parent–infant therapy or infant mental health, as is reflected in a number of chapters in this volume in which video feedback is discussed. Although the videoing may focus on a range of situations (e.g. a play situation, a feeding situation, etc.), the procedures used are very similar in that a brief video clip of the parent and the infant interacting is recorded. The purpose of the procedure is to use the videotape to illustrate positive, reciprocal interaction, which is done using reflective discussion between the parent/family and the therapist/intervener. The approach to feedback may vary according to the emphasis placed on the actual interactional behaviour between the mother and the infant, and the opportunity for reflection the video provides for the mother to consider her own attachment organisation. These different approaches are aptly illustrated in a recent book by Juffer *et al.* (2007).

This chapter describes the development and use of a videotape feedback protocol delivered by health visitors in partnership with parent–infant psychologists working in a primary care context to improve maternal sensitive responsiveness and secure infant attachment behaviours. The chapter begins by briefly summarising the research evidence, and goes on to provide a detailed description of the intervention protocol, concluding with a description of a recent evaluation of the intervention.

The research context

Although video has very frequently been utilised as a research tool it has only recently been used in clinical work with parents and infants. Crittenden and Snell (1983), in one of the very first intervention studies, improved the sensitivity of maltreating mothers by getting them to watch and analyse their interactions with their infants, specifically focusing on what mothers did that 'pleased' the infant. The interaction guidance approach developed by Susan McDonough (1993) was one of the first relationship-focused interventions using video feedback and has been found to produce positive improvements in mother–infant relationships even in highly stressed at-risk samples (Robert-Tissot *et al.*, 1996; McDonough, 2004). In an early case study, Juffer *et al.* (1997) demonstrated an improvement in parental sensitivity and infant attachment following video feedback, and later used the intervention in a group of families with adopted children to improve the children's attachment status (Juffer *et al.*, 2004). Since this early pioneering work, the video has become more widely used as a part of intervention work with parents and infants (Schechter *et al.*, 2006; Tucker, 2006; Veldeman *et al.*, 2006; Woodhead *et al.*, 2006).

A number of clinicians, some working from a psychoanalytic perspective, have also used positive reinforcement, modelling, and information giving, in addition to psychoanalytic interpretations, while watching and reflecting on videotaped interaction with the parent (Beebe, 2003; Zelenko and Benham, 2000; Madigan and Benoit, 2002; Jones, 2006). Initial reports from the 'Minding the baby' programme, which uses video feedback as part of a wider approach aimed at increasing parents' reflective functioning, have also shown encouraging results in terms of improvements in mothers' sensitive responsiveness (Slade *et al.*, 2005). Others have used video feedback as part of a comprehensive infant mental health service (Weatherston and Tableman, 2002), and it was also central to the development of the Minnesota-based STEEP programme (Farrell-Erickson, 2002; Egeland and Ericksson, 2004), in which it was used to improve the interaction between the mother and baby by enabling the mother to perceive the infant's cues from a different perspective. This aspect of offering or providing a different perspective to the dyadic interaction, so that the parent has an opportunity to see the interaction 'from the outside', is central to the approach (Juffer *et al.*, 2007).

The Sunderland Infant Programme

Building on this work, a new primary prevention-based service model, which became known as 'the Sunderland Infant Programme', was developed. The programme aimed to provide a cost-effective service to help parents support their infants to develop a secure attachment by their first birthday. The overarching purpose of the programme was thereby to increase the proportion of children who were securely attached through the development of collaborative community work between health visitors and clinical parent–infant psychologists, working in partnership with families to enable the parents (in particular the mothers) to more accurately perceive their infants' communicational cues, and to respond in an appropriate and timely way (i.e. to increase mothers' sensitive responsiveness).

Engaging parents in preventive work is notoriously difficult. In comparison to many other countries, however, the British health service is fortunate to have a community-based group of nurses (i.e. health visitors), whose function is related to child development and monitoring, and who have considerable 'street credibility' with families, and particularly parents of young children. This credibility increases the likelihood of an improved therapeutic alliance (Browne, 1995; Elkan *et al.*, 2001; Robinson, 1999) between the nurse and the family, particularly in terms of trying to develop sensitive attunement to the mother. Some health visitors were quite ingenious in their pursuit of 'hard-to-reach' families, but, as a rule of thumb, where mothers made it clear that they did not want to participate, either overtly by saying so or covertly by 'never being available', no further action was taken.

Screening mother–infant interactions using the CARE-Index

The process of engaging parents focused on the 'unique' opportunity for the parents to better 'know their baby' and to better understand 'babyese'. Thus at the primary visit (ten to fourteen days post-delivery) the programme was introduced as an opportunity for a mother to learn more about the unique way her baby communicates. In addition she was provided with an information leaflet about the programme. As this primary visit is often the first time the mother meets 'her' health visitor and it is also a visit which contains a great deal of information giving, it was not used to engage mothers in the programme, but rather to draw their attention to it. At around six weeks post-delivery, in a clinic, through a home visit or via telephone contact, the health visitor then invited the family to participate. Any anxieties about the programme on the part of the mother (or the father or grandmother) were discussed, and if she was in agreement, a formal consent form was signed. A home visit was then arranged at eight to twelve weeks post-delivery to undertake the video recording.

At this first 'video' visit the health visitor videotaped a brief (3–4 minutes) interaction between the mother and the baby, 'playing and talking together as they would normally do'. If the father wanted to participate a separate video clip was made of him and his child playing together.

Having completed the initial video, together with any relevant family history, the health visitor met weekly with her colleagues and the parent–infant psychologist for a consultation to discuss the video clip. In the consultation meeting the video clip was copied to a DVD to be returned to the parent, and the interaction was assessed using the CARE-Index (Crittenden, 1997–2004). Where appropriate, an intervention plan was formulated. The psychologist provided a very brief, written report for the health visitor with a tentative formulation of the issues, intervention advice, and recommendations.

The CARE-Index provides scores for seven aspects of behaviour for both caregiver and infant (see below), which are collated into a set of coding scales for both mother and baby (see below), and can be reliably used for caregivers and children up to the age of 3 years (Crittenden, 2005).

CARE-Index aspects of behaviour
- Facial expressions
- Vocal expressions
- Position and body contact
- Expression of affection
- Turn-taking contingencies (within bouts of play)
- Control (between bouts of play)
- Choice of activity

CARE-Index coding variables

Caregiver	Infant
Sensitive	Cooperative
Controlling	Difficult
Unresponsive	Compulsive
	Passive

For the purpose of identifying parent–infant dyads at increased risk for insecure attachment, the score for maternal sensitivity was used. This score can vary between 14 (when the interaction is described as 'mutual delight, joy in one another, a dance') and 0 (described as 'a total failure to perceive or attempt to soothe infant's distressed state, no play'). A score of 8–14 on the maternal sensitivity scale indicates that the interaction is 'good enough', so that the likelihood of the child developing a secure attachment to the mother is high. A score of 4–7 indicates that the interaction is 'of concern', and a score of 0–3 indicates that the interaction between the mother and the infant is seriously compromised. In other words, the CARE-Index analysis was used for screening, to guide the intervention, and also as a baseline assessment for the formal evaluation.

Three levels of intervention were provided based on the CARE-Index score – a minimal one-session video feedback; a series of health visitor-provided video feedback sessions; or video feedback provided by the health visitor plus tailor-made psychological therapy. Thus at the least complex level (CARE-Index score between 8 and 14) only a minimum intervention was necessary as the interaction was at least 'good enough'. The health visitor arranged only one feedback visit to discuss the video and to use it to emphasise and underline the various instances of the mother's sensitive responsiveness and the positive reactions this generated in the baby. The health visitor also provided developmental guidance and would give the mother a copy of an in-house 'Positive Parenting' leaflet. Where the interaction gave cause for concern (CARE-Index score between 4 and 7) the mother was offered a series of visits by the health visitor, working to an intervention protocol providing reflective video feedback. Finally, where interactions gave rise to serious concern (CARE-Index score between 0 and 3) with regard to the quality of the interaction, the health visitor facilitated a clinical psychologist's access to the family so that he or she could offer appropriate psychological therapy, in addition to the video feedback.

Reflective video feedback protocol

When a health visitor intervention was agreed to be appropriate, the health visitor arranged up to four additional visits to implement the video-focused reflective discussion with the mother or both parents. She also used the consultation opportunities with the psychologist between these visits for support and guidance in the delivery of the intervention.

Video-focused reflective discussion was aimed at accentuating the positive aspects of the interaction, was strengths-based, and built on the snippets of sensitive interaction that were almost invariably present. The health visitor would also open up reflective discussions with, for example, a focus on the mother's own upbringing, thereby endeavouring to make links between her own experiences of being parented and her current parenting practices. There were four foci or 'areas of concern' for the health visitor's intervention, which were developed into a protocol (Svanberg, 2001). These were:

• Developing mindfulness
• Acknowledging ambivalence
• Making links to mother's own childhood and her emotional roots
• Dealing with separation

The central aim of the whole programme was to help mothers become more sensitively attuned to their babies, and the protocol therefore also stressed how important it was for the health visitor to try to be sensitively attuned to the mother. This meant that the four foci had to be used very flexibly, so that if the mother was eager to talk about her own upbringing following the first 'video' visit a focus on mindfulness was not imposed. Similarly it sometimes happened that in one visit all four areas were touched upon. The father was included as much as possible in the discussions.

Focus 1: Developing mindfulness

The purpose of the first visit was to help parents understand the baby's mind as expressed by the baby's way of communicating. Thus, as part of the initial feedback of the video clip and the focus on the interaction between the mother and the baby, the health visitor discussed infant signals and their meaning (see also Chapter 4). Ideally there was also some discussion about the parent using 'containment' strategies when the baby was fretful, such as covering the baby with a blanket, and cuddling and holding, rather than using 'silencing' strategies such as dummies or immediately offering a distressed baby something to eat.

This process was undertaken by focusing on the video and jointly identifying what the baby was trying to communicate. A range of questions were used as prompts to explore this, for example: 'Does she like that?', 'What do you think she is trying to say here?', 'What do you think this (gaze avoidance/grimace/smile/hiccup, etc.) means?'

Engagement cues: bright-eyed, focused expression, calm attentiveness, relaxed posture including arms, shoulders and hands
Disengagement cues: gaze aversion, yawning, arching, grimacing, anxious tongue poking, and arms and legs held stiffly
Self-regulation cues: hand-to-mouth, foot clasping, leg bracing

---

In order to help the mother to recognise 'behavioural contingencies', the health visitor also asked her to recall what she did preceding the baby's behaviour, i.e. did she do anything which triggered the behaviour, such as 'Did you smile?', 'Did you vocalise?', 'Did you reflect/mirror the baby's behaviour?' Where necessary the tape would be rewound and the mother and health visitor would look again at the segment until they felt they could make sense of the interaction. This was aimed at helping mothers to ask 'What is it that I do that particularly pleases my baby?' The discussion also provided the health visitor with an opportunity to discuss a number of areas, e.g. temperament, in which some infants are more highly stimulus-sensitive and others are less so (see also Chapter 4), which often leads to a focus on the need to attune to baby's communication by slowing down and giving enough time for baby to organise herself and mobilise a response. This was aimed at providing the mother with an opportunity to understand that attuned mirroring and imitation (i.e. 'taking her cue from the baby') were not about spoiling the baby but instead about providing him or her with crucial experiences in order to build a sense of self-esteem and mastery. This could then lead into a discussion about baby's competence. The health visitors tried to convey that, small as they are, babies are very competent, that they can set their own pace at feeding time, are able to fall asleep unassisted, and can self-soothe if they get over-stimulated and stressed. This provided an opportunity to discuss what the mother can do if baby can't self-regulate when he or she becomes distressed (i.e. the central importance of being able to soothe and comfort quickly and consistently). This was once again undertaken with an explanation aimed at helping the mother to understand that this response would not spoil baby or make him or her dependent.

As potential 'homework' the mother was asked to keep a diary and explore with the baby what he or she liked and disliked in their day-to-day interactions, also including the father, where possible. The health visitor then asked the mother whether they could film a second video to be discussed at the second intervention visit.

Focus 2: Acknowledging ambivalence

In addition to developing the mother's sensitive responsiveness through video feedback the purpose of this intervention was to explore the mother's possible ambivalence about her baby. The focus of the second visit was on discussing anything that may have made her thoughtful from the previous visit. 'Was there anything she puzzled about, anything that didn't make sense, anything she wanted to talk about more?'

The second video was then discussed and fed back, again focusing entirely on positive reciprocity and mutual engagement. This was followed by the 'homework' from the last visit, for example: 'What had she learned about her baby's likes and dislikes?'

These discussions often led naturally into an exploration/discussion about how baby makes the mother feel, i.e. 'What in baby's behaviour does the mother find difficult? How does she feel when baby turns away and avoids her gaze? How does she react emotionally when baby is fractious or difficult?' This allowed the mother an opportunity to talk about her own negative feelings towards the baby and to 'normalise' these, i.e. to help her to understand that everybody feels such ambivalence from time to time.

Where possible it was also helpful if the health visitor was able to engage the father, in order to discuss his feelings of ambivalence, and in particular his 'sense of displacement'. As the mother becomes fully engaged with the baby through the process of 'primary maternal pre-occupation' (Winnicott, 1975), father at times may feel excluded and abandoned. In vulnerable men this may result in anger and violence. By openly acknowledging these feelings, and by father also becoming more aware of mother's absolute need to bond, the intention was to reduce the risk of conflict in the new threesome.

Focus 3: Making links to mother's own childhood and her emotional roots

The purpose of the third visit was to help the mother to make links between her current relationship with her baby and the relationships she experienced when she was growing up, in order to help her to begin putting the 'ghosts in her nursery' to rest.

The health visitor and the parents viewed and discussed the third video, and the health visitor was again particularly sensitive to any positive changes. This involved the health visitor praising any attempts on the part of the mother (and father if present) to recognise engagement cues. The homework was then discussed to explore what she had learned about baby's communications and her own reactions to them. This provided an opportunity to explore the mother's relationship with her own parents, including:

- How was she played with?
- How was she comforted when distressed/upset?
- How was she disciplined?

By reflecting on how the mother was brought up, the health visitor aimed to help her to explore how she wanted to bring up her own baby. At times, of course, this exploration resulted in disclosures of serious abuse, neglect or trauma in the mother's childhood, and having a clinical psychologist available for both consultation and 'shared care' proved invaluable in these circumstances.

Focus 4: Dealing with separation

The purpose of the fourth visit was to focus on separation, in particular the parents' own experiences of separation; the mother's feelings when the baby begins to separate from her; and her feelings about separating from the health visitor.

In addition to abusive experiences, which are by definition traumatic, the most common childhood experience which may have caused lasting problems for the mother or father as they grew up would be separation. Consequently the health visitor enquired as to how the mother felt about separations from baby. 'How did baby react at these times?' This focus provided an opportunity to talk about baby's emerging attachment to mother at 6 to 7 months and how separations from then on would be difficult for baby until she was old enough to talk and understand at around age 3. The health visitor explored with the mother whether she had any unresolved issues about separation because this could have an effect on her parenting and cause a dilemma for baby's developing autonomy (e.g. a 'struggle' between baby (wanting to do it herself) and mother (being over-anxious) could create problems in the relationship). 'Did she find it difficult to "let go"? Was she anxious about baby sleeping by herself? Did she have fears about baby "crawling away"?'

Impact of training on health visitors

The training of the health visitors proceeded in two phases. The initial phase consisted of an intensive week-long training in the use of the CARE-Index, while the second phase involved developing the skills, expertise and confidence to use video feedback through weekly consultations and supervisions with the parent–infant psychologist. Jennings (2004) compared the ability of health visitors, trained and untrained in the use of the CARE-Index, to estimate the maternal sensitivity score. She found that in the group who had received the CARE-Index training, there was a significant positive correlation (n=27, r=.74, p=.0005) between the estimated score and the assessed score on maternal sensitivity. In the untrained group, there was a significant *negative* correlation (n=11, r=-.62, p=.041) between the estimated and assessed scores. The trained health visitors' estimates of maternal sensitivity were thus highly correlated with the actual CARE-Index scores, while the untrained health visitors estimated maternal sensitivity consistently and significantly incorrectly (Jennings, 2004). These findings suggest that the future basic training of this professional group should incorporate the skills to observe and analyse parent–infant interaction. In addition, Dodds and Svanberg (in preparation) undertook a qualitative study of eight health visitors two years after the termination of the project to explore their perceptions about the impact of the programme on their practice. Amongst the most significant themes which emerged was the perceived improvement in relationships between parents and health visitors, thereby facilitating increased feelings of empowerment on the part of both. Another theme was the sense of containment for the health visitors (see Chapter 3), which was provided through the regular psychology-led supervision to help them manage the emotional impact of their work.

Evaluation

A detailed analysis of outcomes for the three levels of intervention outlined above will be reported elsewhere (Svanberg, under revision), and this chapter therefore provides an overview of only the most significant findings. Three main findings will be reported: the infants' attachment behaviour at 12–13 months; the differences in maternal sensitivity and infant cooperativeness between the baseline assessment and the follow-up assessment at 12 months; and finally differences in service utilisation between the two groups at the follow-up.

A controlled evaluation with a total of 194 participants, in an intervention group (n=134) and a control group (n=60), was undertaken with two measurement points, i.e. at eight to twelve weeks pre-intervention baseline and at twelve to thirteen months follow-up. The results of the Strange Situation assessment at the follow-up showed an approximate doubling of the proportion of securely attached children in comparison with the control group receiving 'routine care'. The Strange Situation was analysed using Crittenden's 'Modified and Extended Protocol' (Crittenden, 2005). This analytical method is informed by her work using the Pre-School Attachment Assessment (Crittenden, 1994), which has been extensively validated (see, for example, Crittenden *et al.*, 2007). It differs from the Main protocol (Main and Solomon, 1986) by identifying a number of non-normative and complex, organized attachment behaviours such as Compulsive Compliance, Compulsive Care Giving (Type A+) or Aggressive/Helpless (Type C+) in addition to Disorganization. The Modified and Extended Protocol can also be used to identify a small number of children as Compulsive (i.e. at risk) who would be considered securely attached in the Ainsworth–Main system (Crittenden, personal communication).

Table 9.1 Strange Situation procedure codes at twelve months follow-up

	Intervention group		Control group	
Type B	59	55 per cent	16	30 per cent
Type A 1-2	19	18 per cent	9	17 per cent
Type C 1-2	14	14 per cent	6	11 per cent
Type A+, C+, A/C	15	14 per cent	23	43 per cent

Note: Types A+, C+, A/C are non-normative, clinical attachment patterns derived from Crittenden's Dynamic-Maturational Model of Adaptation (Crittenden, 2000).

Table 9.1 shows that the interventions provided lowered the risk of the infant developing along a less than optimal pathway (Bowlby, 1977), in comparison with the substantial proportion (43 per cent), in the control group where this risk remained, i.e. where the infant showed non-normative and complex insecure, attachment behaviour.

As noted in the introduction, the CARE-Index was used as a baseline assessment and it was also used at the twelve-month follow-up. At the follow-up, mothers' sensitivity and infants' cooperativeness in the intervention group had increased significantly in comparison with the control group (i.e. mothers in the intervention group had become significantly more sensitively responsive and their infants consequently more cooperative).

An effect size of $d=0.73$ for maternal sensitivity is very acceptable in comparison to the average reported (van IJzendoorn *et al.*, 2005). The differences between the groups on mothers' sensitivity were in part explained by *deterioration* in sensitivity in the control group mothers. These findings replicate those of Killen *et al.* (2006) in which a reduction in maternal sensitivity between the ages of 4 and 7 months was found in a large, normative Norwegian sample (see also Chapter 13).

Finally the participants' utilisation of health and social services in the two months preceding the follow-up was ascertained using a Service Utility Inventory (Browne *et al.*, 1990). In spite of the considerable additional resources for the intervention group (e.g. increased nurse home-visiting, psychology and psychological therapy time, etc.), the costs of the control group were still on average £35 higher per family in the two months before the follow-up assessment (Netten and Curtis, 2002). This would mean an annual saving per family of £210 (£35 × 6). In an average English health district of 2,500 births/year and with an uptake of 60 per cent (reflecting the engagement patterns of this study) this would mean an accrued annual saving of £315,000 at 2005 cost levels.

Table 9.2 CARE-Index variables

	Intervention group mean (SD)	Control group mean (SD)	d (effect size)*
Sensitivity	8.06 (2.28)	6.37 (2.39)	0.73 (medium)
Cooperativeness	7.82 (2.41)	6.39 (2.50)	0.59 (medium)

* See Thalheimer and Cook, 2002.

Conclusions

Health visitors are uniquely placed to develop a helping alliance with the mother and to use video feedback in the context of an intervention protocol such as the one described. Working in close partnership with psychology staff enabled health visitors to become agents of positive change in the lives of the families with whom they worked. The evidence suggests that for a substantial minority of mothers who struggled with the relationship with their babies in the early months, this very brief series of interventions had a significant impact on maternal sensitivity and subsequently on their children's attachment security, thereby increasing the likelihood that the children's developmental pathways would be positive.

Acknowledgements

Implementing and evaluating the programme was very much a collaborative task involving many people. Particular thanks go to the participating parents. A thousand thanks to Trudie Jennings and Joyce Powell, and to all the participating health visitors and colleagues at Sure Start, Thorney Close, Sunderland during 1999–2004. Particular thanks to Chris Colbourn at the University of Teeside for his help with the statistical analysis. Finally many thanks to Dilys Daws for her support and to Patricia Crittenden for her inspiration.

References

Ainsworth, M. D. S., Blehar, M. C., Waters, E. and Wall, S. (1978). *Patterns of Attachment: A Psychological Study of the Strange Situation.* Hillsdale, NJ: Lawrence Erlbaum Associates.

Bakermans-Kranenburg, M., Juffer, F. and van IJzendoorn, M. (2002). Sensitivity and attachment: Home-based, short-term intervention with insecure mothers. Paper presented at the World Association for Infant Mental Health, 8th Congress, Amsterdam.

Beebe, B. (2003). Brief mother–infant treatment: psychoanalytically informed video feedback. *Infant Mental Health Journal*, 24(1), 24–52.

Bowlby, J. (1958). The nature of a child's tie to his mother. *International Journal of Psychoanalysis*, 39, 350–373.

Bowlby, J. (1977). The making and breaking of affectional bonds. *British Journal of Psychiatry*, 130, 201–210 and 421–431.

Browne, G. B., Arpin, K. *et al.* (1990). Individual correlates of health service utilization and the cost of poor adjustment to chronic illness. *Medical Care*, 28(1), 43–58.

Browne, K. (1995). Preventing child maltreatment through community nursing. *Journal of Advanced Nursing*, 21(1), 57–63.

Crittenden, P. M. (1994). *Preschool Assessment of Attachment Manual.* Miami: Family Relations Institute.

Crittenden, P. M. (1997-2004). *Care-Index; Manual*. Miami: Family Relations Institute.

Crittenden, P. M. (2000). A dynamic-maturational exploration of the meaning of security and adaptation: empirical, cultural and theoretical considerations. In P. M. Crittenden and A. H. Claussen (eds), *The Organisation of Attachment Relationships: Maturation, Culture and Context*. Cambridge: Cambridge University Press.

Crittenden, P. M. (2005). Der CARE-Index als Hilfsmittel für Früherkennung, Intervention und Forschung. *Frühförderung interdisziplinär* (Early Interdisciplinary Intervention). Special issue: Bindungsorientierte Ansätze in der Praxis der Frühförderung, 24, S.99–106. (In English at www.patcrittenden.com.)

Crittenden, P. M. and DiLalla, D. L. (1988). Compulsive compliance: the development of an inhibitory coping strategy in infancy. *Journal of Abnormal Child Psychology*, 16(5), 585–599.

Crittenden, P. M. and Snell, E. B. (1983). Intervention to improve mother–infant interaction and infant development. *Infant Mental Health Journal*, 4(1), 23–31.

Crittenden, P. M., Claussen, A. M. *et al.* (2007). Choosing a valid assessment of attachment for clinical use: a comparative study. *Australian and New Zealand Journal of Family Therapy*, 28, 78–87.

De Wolff, M. S. and Van IJzendoorn, M. H. (1997). Sensitivity and attachment: a meta-analysis on parental antecedents of infant attachment. *Child Development*, 68(4), 571–591.

Dodds, N. and Svanberg, P. O. (in preparation). The use of video for screening and feedback: a qualitative study on the impact on health visiting practice.

Egeland, B. and Ericksson, M. F. (2004). Lessons from STEEP: linking theory, research and practice for the well-being of infants and parents. In A. J. Sameroff, S. C. McDonough and K. L. Rosenblum (eds), *Treating Parent–Infant Relationship Problems*. New York: Guilford Press.

Elkan, R., Robinson, J., Williams, D. and Blair, M. (2001). Universal vs. selective services: the case of British health visiting. *Journal of Advanced Nursing*, 33(1), 113–119.

Farrell-Erickson, M. (2002). Seeing is believing: using videotaping and guided self-observation to promote parental sensitivity. Paper presented at the World Association for Infant Mental Health, 8th Congress, Amsterdam.

Jennings, T. (2004). Can maternal sensitivity be enhanced by health visitor intervention, guided by clinical psychology consultation, using video feed back? Unpublished doctorate thesis in Clinical Psychology, University of Teeside, Middlesbrough.

Jones, A. (2006). How video can bring to view pathological defensive processes and facilitate the creation of triangular space in perinatal parent–infant psychotherapy. *Infant Observation*, 9(2), 109–123.

Juffer, F., Hoksbergen, R. A. C., Riksenwalraven, J. M. and Kohnstamm, G. A. (1997). Early intervention in adoptive families: supporting maternal sensitive responsiveness, infant–mother attachment, and infant competence. *Journal of Child Psychology and Psychiatry and Allied Disciplines*, 38(8), 1039–1050.

Juffer, F., Stams, G. J. J. M. and van IJzendoorn, M. H. (2004). Adopted children's problem behavior is significantly related to their ego resiliency, ego control, and sociometric status. *Journal of Child Psychology and Psychiatry*, 45(4), 697–706.

Juffer, F., Bakermans-Kranenburg, M. J. and van IJzendoorn, M. H. (2007). *Promoting Positive Parenting: An Attachment-based Intervention*. Monographs in Parenting. Hillsdale, NJ: Lawrence Erlbaum.

Killen, K., Klette, T. and Arnevik, E. (2006). Tidlig mor-barn samspill i norske familier (Early mother–infant interaction in Norwegian families). *Tidskrift for norsk, psykologforening (The Norwegian Psychological Association)*, 43, 694–701.

McDonough, S. C. (1993). Interaction guidance; understanding and treating early infant–caregiver relationship disorders. In C. Zeanah (ed.), *Handbook of Infant Mental Health*. New York: Guilford Press.

McDonough, S. C. (2004). Interaction guidance: promoting and nurturing the caregiving relationship. In A. J. Sameroff, S. C. McDonough and K. L. Rosenblum (eds), *Treating Parent–Infant Relationship Problems*. New York: Guilford Press.

Madigan, S. and Benoit, D. (2002). Reducing atypical caregiver behaviour using modified interaction guidance. Paper presented at the World Association for Infant Mental Health, 8th Congress, Amsterdam.

Main, M. and Solomon, J. (1986). Discovery of an insecure disorganized/disoriented attached pattern: procedures, findings and implications for classification of behaviour. In M. Yogman and T. B. Brazelton (eds), *Affective Development in Infancy* (pp. 95–124). Norwood, NJ: Ablex.

Netten, A. and Curtis, L. (2002). *Unit Costs of Health and Social Care*. Canterbury: University of Kent.

Robert-Tissot, C., Cramer, B., Stern, D. N., Serpa, S. R., Bachmann, J. P., Palacioespasa, F. *et al.* (1996). Outcome evaluation in brief mother–infant psychotherapies: report on 75 cases. *Infant Mental Health Journal*, 17(2), 97–114.

Robinson, J. (1999). Domiciliary health visiting: a systematic review. *Community Practitioner*, 72(2), 15–18.

Schechter, D. S., Myers, M. M., Brunelli, S. A. and Coates, S. W. (2006);. Traumatized mothers can change their minds about their toddlers: understanding how a novel use of video feedback supports positive change of maternal attributions. *Infant Mental Health Journal*, 27(5), 429–447.

Slade, A., Sadler, L. and Mayers, L. (2005). Minding the baby: enhancing parental reflective functioning in a nursing/mental health home visiting program. In L. Berlin, Y. Ziv, L. Amya-Jackson and M. T. Greenberg (eds), *Enhancing Early Attachments: Theory, Research, Intervention and Policy*. London: Guilford Press.

Sroufe, L. A., Egeland, B., Carlson, E. and Collins, A. W. (2005). *The Develop-ment of the Person: The Minnesota Study of Risk and Adaptation from Birth to Adulthood*. New York: Guilford Press.

Stern, D. (2004). The motherhood constellation: therapeutic approaches to early relational problems. In A. J. Sameroff, S. C. McDonough and K. L. Rosen-blum (eds), *Treating Parent–Infant Relationship Problems*. New York: Guilford Press.

Svanberg, P. O. (1998). Attachment, resilience and prevention. *Journal of Mental Health*, 7(6), 543–578.

Svanberg, P. O. (2001). *Intervention Protocol for Health Visitors*. Sunderland: Sure Start.

Svanberg, P. O. (2006). Promoting a secure attachment; the Sunderland Infant Programme. Poster presented at the World Association for Infant Mental Health, 10th Congress, Paris.

Svanberg, P. O. (under revision). *Promoting a secure attachment; a primary pre-vention practice approach*.

Thalheimer, W. and Cook, S. (2002). How to calculate effect sizes from published research; a simplified methodology. http://work-learning.com/white_papers/effect_sizes/Effect_Sizes_pdf5.pdf.

Tucker, J. (2006). Using video to enhance the learning in a first attempt at 'Watch, Wait and Wonder'. Infant Observation, 9(2), 125–138.

van der Does, J. (2002). The Video Interaction Training Method: a revolution in thinking about child psychology and psychiatry? Paper presented at the World Association for Infant Mental Health, 8th Congress, Amsterdam.

van IJzendoorn, M., Bakermans-Kranenburg, M. and Juffer, F. (2005). Why less is more: from the dodo bird verdict to evidence based interventions on sen-sitivity and early attachments. In L. Berlin, Y. Ziv, L. Amya-Jackson and M. T. Greenberg (eds), *Enhancing Early Attachments: Theory, Research, Intervention and Policy*. London: Guilford Press.

Veldeman, M. K., Bakermans-Kranenburg, M. J., Juffer, F. and van IJzendoorn, M. (2006). Preventing preschool externalising behaviour problems through video feedback intervention in infancy. *Infant Mental Health Journal*, 27(5), 466–493.

Weatherston, D. and Tableman, B. (2002). *Infant Mental Health Services; Sup-porting Competencies/Reducing Risks*, Southgate: Michigan Association for Infant Mental Health.

Weiner, A., Kuppermintz, H. and Guttmann, D. (1994). Video home training (the Orion project): a short-term preventive and treatment intervention for fami-lies with young children. *Family Process*, 33(4), 441–453.

Wels, P. M. A. (2002). *Helping with a Camera. The Use of Video for Family In-tervention*. Nijmegen: Nijmegen University Press.

Winnicott, D. W. (1975). *Through Paediatrics to Psycho-analysis*. London: Hog-arth Press and the Institute of Psycho-analysis.

Woodhead, J., Bland, K. and Baradon, T. (2006). Focusing the lens: the use of digital video in the practice and evaluation of parent–infant psychotherapy. *Infant Observation*, 9(2), 139–150.

Zelenko, M. and Benham, A. (2000). Videotaping as a therapeutic tool in psychodynamic infant–parent therapy. *Infant Mental Health Journal*, 21(3), 192–203.

10 Perinatal home visiting

Implementing the Nurse–Family Partnership in England

Ann Rowe

Introduction

Home visiting programmes that begin during pregnancy and continue during the postnatal period can be highly effective in supporting parents and parenting (Bull *et al.*, 2004). Perhaps one of the most successful and extensively researched programmes is the Nurse–Family Partnership (NFP). Developed by David Olds and colleagues, this intensive home visiting programme is delivered by trained and well supervised nurses who visit first-time mothers from pregnancy until the child is 2 years of age. In a recent article, Olds *et al.* (2007) outlined the painstaking validation any successful intervention programme needs to go through before it becomes routinely implemented. During 2006–2008 the first steps to validate the NFP in England (where it is known as the Family Nurse Partnership) were undertaken across ten trial sites, following a governmental decision to explore the possibilities of implementing the US-developed Nurse–Family Partnership in England (Cabinet Office, 2006).

This chapter outlines the research evidence for the NFP and the difference it can make for first-time pregnant mothers and their children. It then examines the first trial of the programme in England, describes how it has been implemented across the first ten sites, and concludes by examining its content, highlighting differences compared with existing English universal home visiting services.

Background

As a young developmental psychologist working in a preschool environment in Baltimore with a desire to work with and help disadvantaged children, Olds rapidly realised that even for preschool children it was late in the day to intervene to produce beneficial change. As a result he developed what became known as the Elmira project, after the small upstate New York town in which the intervention trial of a new model of home visiting was conducted (Olds *et al.*, 1986b). Based on Bronfenbrenner's human ecology theory (Bronfenbrenner, 1986), attachment theory (Bowlby, 1969) and self-efficacy theory (Bandura, 1977), the project had a number of aims: to improve prenatal health with positive impact on foetal development; to make the infants' lives safer by reducing childhood injuries; to support mothers to make positive life decisions with regard to future pregnancies and maternal employment; and finally to have a positive impact on children's emotional and cognitive development.

Programme model

The programme is designed for low-income, socially disadvantaged mothers who have had no previous live births. The home visiting nurses have three major goals: to improve the outcomes of pregnancy by helping women improve their prenatal health; to improve children's health and development by helping parents provide more sensitive and competent care; and to improve parental life-course by helping parents plan future pregnancies, complete their education, and find work (Olds *et al.*, 2007).

Evidentiary foundations

The programme has been tested in a series of three randomised controlled trials with different populations, living in different contexts (Olds *et al.*, 2007). In each of the three trials, women were randomised to receive either home visitation services or comparison services. The first trial, conducted in Elmira, New York, enrolled a primarily white sample (n=400). The second, conducted in Memphis, Tennessee, enrolled a sample that was nearly entirely African-American (n=1,138 for the prenatal phase and n=743 for the infancy phase of the trial). The third study, conducted in Denver, Colorado (n=735), registered a large sample of Hispanics and systematically examined the impact of the programme when delivered by paraprofessionals (individuals who shared many of the social characteristics of the families they served) and by nurses. The following findings were present in at least two of the three trials, and in most cases where the programme effects were not present in the third the absence of effect can be attributed to differences in measurement design, or to shifts in social and policy contexts in the history of the United States (Olds *et al.*, 2007).

Women visited by nurses during pregnancy, compared to women randomly assigned to comparison services, improved their diets, reduced their use of cigarettes, and had fewer hypertensive disorders of pregnancy. In the first two trials, in which the investigators were able to reliably assess all of the children's healthcare encounters in the first two years of life, nurse-visited children, compared to their control group counterparts, had fewer encounters for injuries. The programme consistently reduced the rates of subsequent pregnancies and increased the intervals between births, and nurse-visited mothers entered the workforce in the second year of the child's life to a greater extent, and used welfare less than did women assigned to the control condition (although this finding was not replicated in the Denver trial).

Children visited by nurses during pregnancy and during the first two years of the child's life exhibited fewer mental health problems at school entry and fewer antisocial behaviours in the first half of adolescence. Nurse-visited children, and especially those born to mothers with fewer psychological resources to support their children's learning, had improved language and cognitive development, improved achievement in maths, and improved behavioural adjustment at school entry.

The long-term follow-up results showed that nurse-visited mothers had 61 per cent fewer arrests, 72 per cent fewer convictions, and 98 per cent fewer days of incarceration during the fifteen-year period following the birth of their first child – an effect that the investigators think is due to nurse-visited mothers making appropriate choices about their lives that led to the protection of themselves and their children (Olds *et al.*, 1997, 1998). By their fifteenth birthday, children visited by nurses, as compared to controls, had 48 per cent fewer substantiated cases of child abuse and neglect, 59 per cent fewer arrests, and 90 per cent fewer adjudications as a 'person in need of supervision' for incorrigible behaviour.

In the third trial of this programme, the investigators found that nurses produced beneficial effects for children that were approximately twice as large as those produced by paraprofessional visitors. These findings are consistent with the disappointing findings of separate randomised trials of home visiting programmes delivered by paraprofessional visitors (Olds *et al.*, 2007).

In 2004, the Washington State Institute for Public Policy estimated that government and society save $17,000 for every family served in the Nurse–Family Partnership (Aos *et al.*, 2004). The Rand Corporation has produced similar estimates (Karoly *et al.*, 2005).

Testing the Family Nurse Partnership in England

In response to concerns about social exclusion in England, the government decided, following a review of the international evidence, that the NFP should be tested in England. Following the decision in September 2006 (Cabinet Office, 2006) to trial the NFP, a small team was put together as a joint DCSF/DH (Department of Children, Schools and Families/Department of Health) initiative to work closely with the US team to devise a programme of activities to attempt to successfully replicate the programme. An ambitious target of implementing the programme in ten primary care trust/local authority sites was proposed. This was seen as an opportunity to learn about the extent to which the programme could be applied successfully within the UK provision of universal services, and its acceptability to young families in a range of sites in England.

Ten sites were selected, which included two London boroughs, a large metropolitan city, a number of smaller cities, two suburban towns and two rural locations. The selected sites were provided with details regarding the programme's fidelity measures and the organisational requirements, and were offered job descriptions and advice regarding recruitment of supervisors and nurses. This approach to running an NHS-based programme, where a 'central team' to some extent dictate the requirements of organisations and monitor the delivery of a standardised, manualised programme, is new to many organisations delivering services to parents and children.

In many areas of the NHS a protocol-driven approach to care is now wide-spread and utilised as a way to improve care standards. Nevertheless, although protocols advise clinicians of best practice, they are still required to use professional judgement when circumstances are complex (e.g. where patients have more than one medical condition), in order to ensure appropriate individualised care. In the same way, the NFP expects that nurses will employ the methods and materials of the programme in a way that is sensitive to the circumstances of individual clients and feels personal to each one. Thus, whilst a protocol-driven or manualised programme can lead employers to believe that the skill levels needed to deliver it are relatively low, in fact the opposite is the case. Consequently the trial sites were asked to recruit very able nurses with experience in community work. Most came to the programme from a background of midwifery or health visiting, but, following consultation, the practitioners themselves chose to use the name 'family nurses' whilst working within this programme. Consequently the English programme has been named the Family Nurse Partnership (FNP).

Selection of target population group

It was known that, in the US, the women who benefited most from the programme were those who were young and had low levels of psychological resources (as measured by intellectual functioning, maternal mental health and self-efficacy). It was also a requirement arising from the research that mothers recruited to the programme were pregnant for the first time. However, within the context of universal services in England there was a need to ensure that the programme was offered to families at greatest risk. Hall and Hall (2007) reviewed a range of literature, needs assessment tools and engagement methods to consider the range of factors which could be used to identify and approach families who would be offered the FNP programme. Much is known about the characteristics of families where children are likely to under-achieve and become involved in antisocial behaviours. However, most indicators only become identifiable after the child is born, and families within which children are more likely to suffer adverse outcomes are easier to identify as the child grows and a range of impacts become evident. Hall and Hall (2007) recommended maternal age as the primary indicator of family social exclusion and therefore the main characteristic that should determine an offer of the programme. Women becoming parents under the age of 20 years continue to be more likely to suffer social disadvantage (Berrington *et al.*, 2007), and their children are more likely to experience lower educational achievement, economic inactivity, and lower income than those of older mothers (Berthoud *et al.*, 2007). However, there is also evidence to suggest that women having children in their early twenties have similar outcomes to teenage mothers (Berrington *et al.*, 2007), and it was therefore decided that whilst all sites would offer the service universally to first-time pregnant women under the age of 20, some sites would also recruit pregnant women aged between 20 and 24 with additional criteria of need (lack of education, employment, training or social support) (Hall and Hall, 2007).

Training programme

The participating nurses were prepared for their new role using an intensive and high-level course of training and development. The training covered a range of areas and involved a number of national experts. It involved two residential weeks and a number of single-day events. The author acted as lead trainer in the central team. She visited Denver to observe the US training in relation to pregnancy, then adapted the contents for the English trial. The training included a range of important issues including the following: recruitment and engagement of families; perinatal mental health and parenting; understanding key concepts about parent–infant interactions (e.g. co-regulation, containment, affect synchrony, mentalisation); interventions to build self-efficacy; behaviour change strategies; client-centred approaches; building therapeutic relationships; involving fathers; domestic abuse and working with parental relationships; safeguarding children and young people; understanding and recognising infant cues; and use of a range of tools including NCAST teaching scales, motivational interviewing, and the 'Partners in Parenting Education' (PIPE) protocol.

Delivery

The programme has a number of facets, and there are a set of manuals detailing the expected content and materials for use in visits. Each visit has a structure and planned content, covering six domains. Although the expected content of each visit is detailed, the home visitor is expected to use her professional judgement to ensure that the programme content is delivered flexibly, so that it is individualised for each client. Much of the material used supports the client in consideration of her current circumstances, motivations and behaviours, and the setting of goals for herself.

The consistent structure of the visits gives the client a regularity that is often missing in her life and as such is a model for the future. The visit structure includes a section on the client's immediate concerns and issues, and is aimed at containing these in order that the visit can also focus on planned work together. Materials used are interactive with an element of 'taught content' alongside many materials which invite the young women, their partners, and on occasion other family members, to reflect on a range of their experiences and attitudes in order to consider the impact these may have on both their own and their child's future. The PIPE programme (see above), an integral part of FNP, is more interactive and the nurses are advised to use it to encourage 'playful' activities to explore a range of parenting topics, and dolls, toys, rhymes and drawings are all used to work on these themes.

The programme also has a physical clinical element with nurses supporting the pregnant woman to assess her own health status and her child's health, and take action to improve these. The approach is underpinned by the assumption that the client is the expert in her own life and that her hopes and dreams are the 'powerhouse' from which the energy to achieve the programme goals is derived. This respectful and strength-based approach, in which the nurse enables the young woman to articulate her aspirations and align herself to them, is central to the methodology of the programme.

The planned content of the programme focuses on six domains: personal and child health; parenting and maternal role; personal goals; friends and family; local and home environment; and use of local services. The emphasis on each domain, in each phase of the programme (pregnancy, infancy and toddlerhood), varies, and the nurses' activities are monitored to ensure that they pay attention to the domains in the same proportions as in the original research.

A number of minor changes were made to the FNP materials including the Anglicising of spellings and the services referred to. Additional UK NHS information documents (e.g. 'Birth to Five') were added to the materials. No substantial changes were made to the content of the programme.

Early learning

A great deal has been learned during the first nine months of the trial. Once implemented, it was evident that the Family Nurse Partnership was different in many ways to pre-existing universal health services in England. Differences in intensity of contact with families were evident, but other more subtle differences of approach and methodology have also been noted, and, if successful within this programme, this will present the NHS with an opportunity to rethink and reinvigorate universal service provision to families of young children. Some of the key features of the FNP and its clinical delivery are described below.

Clear programme aims and theoretical framework

The FNP aims to improve pregnancy outcomes, child health and development, future school readiness and achievement, and parental economic self-sufficiency. Having clear but challenging goals of this nature focuses the delivery of the service towards these desired outcomes. The FNP is also underpinned by a clear theoretical framework, i.e. human ecology theory, attachment theory and self-efficacy theory, which runs throughout the programme content. For example, during pregnancy families are introduced to the concept of attachment. They are encouraged to see the growing child as more than a 'bump' and, through simple activities such as discussing names, and more challenging ones such as singing to the unborn child and considering their own experiences as a child, the young parent(s) are encouraged to consider the imminent arrival of an infant who will need security and love from his or her caregivers. This work is strengthened in infancy and explored further in toddlerhood.

Likewise the theories of self-efficacy and human ecology strongly influence the construction and delivery of the programme. Improved self-efficacy is sought as an outcome of the programme and clients are supported to examine and understand the outcomes they can expect from a range of behaviours, both as caregivers and for their own health and relationships. More importantly still, through the use of skilled interventions, clients are enabled to articulate their dreams, work toward goals in small steps and have their strengths and achievements reinforced. Through this process clients are able to believe that they can achieve healthy behaviours, both for themselves and for their child, and actively change their lifestyle.

The client's systemic, social and material context will of course impact on her chances of successfully parenting her child. Many activities are used to support the client and her family in addressing such influences and the changes required, from household smoking, education and training to the use of local resources such as children's centres. A major facet of the programme is the focus on the development of appropriate and long-term social support for the family. This is especially important within the context of this programme, as social support has been shown to aid the development of resilience in young people (Rutter *et al.*, 1998).

Therapeutic alliance between nurse and clients

The intensity of the relationship that is established in this programme and its explicitly therapeutic nature constitute a change in terms of the delivery of preventive universal health services for parents in the UK. The families receiving the FNP programme often have a very complex and difficult history, making successful parenting and achievement of life goals a real challenge. The explicitly therapeutic nature of the work, with an emphasis on examining and reflecting on the life experiences of clients, alongside a consideration of their health and well-being, and input designed to improve their knowledge base, enables them to explore their past and articulate their dreams. The preventive nature of the programme and the fact that it begins during a woman's first pregnancy mean that the invitation to consider her hopes and plans in relation to her future family life can be given without the burden of being seen to be addressing a pre-existing 'failure' on the client's part. The relationship with the nurse is seen as a temporary 'scaffold' which will enable the client to grow and develop so that she has the confidence, knowledge and experience to move on and achieve her goals once the programme ends. The intensity of the relationship means that boundaries need to be carefully considered, and the role of supervision is central in addressing safeguarding issues, alongside a consideration of the nurses' efficacy and support needs.

Involvement of fathers and other family members

Father involvement in the FNP is encouraged wherever possible and the family nurses report much higher levels of interest from young men in the programme than they would have expected from their previous experiences of home visiting. Indeed, in many families, the nurses are working with both mother and father to achieve successful outcomes for the child. The expectations of both mother and father in relation to the child are raised as a topic for discussion by the nurses during pregnancy visits and both partners are invited to share their hopes and dreams for parenthood along with their life experiences. The subject of domestic violence is explicitly raised by the programme, together with some discussion of positive role models, and families are encouraged to consider the best environment within which the child should be raised.

The pregnant young woman's mother and other family members may also be present during home visits, especially when clients are young adolescents. The nurses aim to involve other family members in the programme as appropriate and be respectful of the role played by the client's mother in the family.

Expectation of behaviour change and personal growth

This programme is underpinned by the expectation that the clients enrolled on it will change their behaviour. Approaches such as motivational interviewing (Rollnick and Mason, 1999) and techniques developed in solution-focused therapy (Berg, 1994) are used to enable clients to consider a range of issues through the life of the programme, and reflect on their own behaviours in relation to them. These range from a consideration of their own experience of being parented, to their diet, and expectations for the future. Clients are encouraged to set themselves goals and to plot steps to achieve them. Each step achieved, however small, is reinforced with praise.

The ability of the nurses to move effortlessly between the different 'modes' of dialogue, defined by Rollnick *et al.* (2008) as 'directing', 'guiding' and 'following', and in particular to be skilled in the difficult area of guiding (Rollnick *et al.*, 2005), is key to the success of this programme. The guiding dialogue needs to be offered within a genuinely respectful context where the Rogerian principles of empathy, acceptance and genuineness are also applied. The length and intensity of the programme enables nurses to build the relationship with families slowly and to be sensitive to their individual circumstances and life histories.

Role and level of supervision

The intensity of the programme, the level of challenge facing the families involved, and the therapeutic nature of the work make good quality supervision for the family nurses an imperative. The programme requires that all nurses receive an hour of individual supervision every week along with group supervision with their team colleagues every two weeks, as a fidelity measure. This ensures that nurses receive adequate opportunities to gain personal support, to reflect on their practice, and to share and develop plans for working with challenging issues, including safeguarding.

The role of the supervisor has been pivotal to the successful delivery of this programme. The intensity of supervision and its multifaceted agenda have been a new experience for all sites and for many of the nurses, and the opportunity to share experiences has been challenging. The emotional nature of the programme has meant that containment has been an important part of the supervisory process, and the support provided to nurses by supervisors aims to parallel the process employed by the nurses with families.

In addition, an experienced clinical psychologist offers expert clinical supervision across the sites on a six-weekly basis. This augmentation to the programme has generated very positive feedback to the extent that all sites in future will be required to arrange for a local clinical or counselling psychologist or child psychotherapist to offer monthly, expert clinical supervision, to complement the weekly reflective supervision provided by the nurse supervisor.

Programme ethos – focus on strengths and goals not problems and deficits

The programme is strength-based, focusing on resources, capacity, expertise and opportunities in individuals and families rather than problems and deficits (Saleebey, 1992). Nurses in the FNP work to understand the unique talents and strengths of each family and will explicitly detail these for the clients. They focus on things that are going well and encourage clients to learn and draw strength from these. Eliciting goals and preferred futures from clients and families, and supporting them to understand the positive possibilities that are available to them, are key aspects of the practitioner role within the FNP.

In the initial phase of the programme in England, families seem to be responding very positively to this approach, and a number have commented that very few other professionals have previously seen potential in them. Working from strengths in this way enables the nurse within the FNP to see potential in families that other services often see only very negatively. This brings with it a tension when dealing with the most difficult issues, especially safeguarding children. However, identifying strengths within families, and agreeing those areas where things are going well, brings with it opportunities to establish goals for child safety, and nurses within the FNP have successfully referred families to social care agencies for safeguarding reasons whilst remaining actively involved in the family and working with them to enable a change in circumstances.

Discussion

The use of a programme developed in the USA within the universal services of England has been a challenging issue for a number of clinicians and commentators external to the programme. The ethos of this first trial has always been to test how well the programme fits within service provision and to establish whether it is acceptable to families, clinicians and public sector organisations.

This programme has made great demands on the nurses and supervisors who have become involved. Most staff recruited had previously been health visitors and/or midwives and although they had a number of skills that could be directly transferred into the family nurse role, they also needed a considerable amount of additional learning in order to fulfil the requirements of the role. The nurses also needed to 'unlearn' certain practices and adopt a new ethos, especially the strength-based approach and working within a structured programme.

The FNP is also a challenging programme for health-care organisations to accommodate. Organisations need to comply with a range of fidelity measures and the scrutiny of external monitoring arrangements. In addition, the ethos, philosophy and clinical work of the FNP can challenge current organisational cultures. The strength-based approach and emphasis on psychological work and containment of anxiety and other strong emotions for families by nurses, and for nurses by supervisors, can bring into stark relief the range of systems and practices to defend against anxiety in place in many organisations (Huffinton and Armstrong, 2005). Working within the milieu of strong emotions, nurses need supportive organisational structures that acknowledge their commitment and the level of personal challenge they encounter. Many organisations are not ready to provide this and indeed have a range of practices that are designed to distance health-care providers from the emotional impact of the work, such as breaking the work down into discrete tasks, discontinuity of practitioner, rigid rules for clinically associated tasks such as record keeping, etc. The tension caused by this discrepancy has surfaced in this testing phase in relation to issues such as normal organisational rules (e.g. mileage, petty cash, record keeping, etc.) and a focus on premature outcomes. However, bringing this issue to the surface and working with site managers has enabled a more open approach between the central team and senior site managers.

The pilot of the Family Nurse Partnership programme has been a stimulus for much debate and reflection in the field of preventive health care for children and families in England. Early results, albeit tentative at this time, suggest that the programme can effectively make the transition from a US setting to the English health and social care arena. With funding secured for further rigorous research in years to come, it will be tested in a way that few other programmes have been. In the meantime, those working within the programme, both clinically and administratively, have developed great respect for a programme that has been carefully constructed and tested over many years by its architects, and which, it is hoped, will play a central part in improving outcomes for generations of children to come.

Acknowledgements

With grateful thanks to Professor David Olds at the University of Colorado, Denver for his careful development of the NFP and his support in writing the review of the evidence for this chapter. Thanks also to Pilar Baca, who has shared her expertise and time so generously and whose clinical insights into the programme are always so rich. Special thanks to Kate Billingham who has led the central team delivery of the FNP trial so inspiringly and has contributed so much to the development of the programme in England. Thanks also to academic colleagues who have offered support and training, and especially Professor Stephen Rollnick who has shared his expertise and insights with great generosity. Final thanks go to colleagues at DCSF and all the family nurses, supervisors and managers in the pilot sites who have committed hearts, minds and hours to the programme, and have shared their learning so willingly.

References

Aos, S., Lieb, R., Mayfield, J., Miller, M. and Pennucci, A. (2004). *Benefits and Costs of Prevention and Early Intervention Programs for Youth* (No. 04-07-3901). Washington, DC: Washington State Institute for Public Policy.

Bandura, A. (1977). Self-efficacy: toward a unified theory of behavioral change. *Psychological Review*, 84, 191–215.

Berg, K. I. (1994). *Family Based Services: A Solution-Focused Approach.* Scranton, PA: W. W. Norton.

Berrington, A., Stevenson, J., Ingham, R., with Borgoni, R., Cobos Hernandez, M. I. *et al.* (2007). Teenage Pregnancy Research Programme Research Briefing No 7: Consequences of Teenage Parenthood: Pathways which minimise the long term negative impacts of teenage childbearing. London. Department for Education and Skills. Available at: http://www.gone.gov.uk/nestore/docs/cyp/young_people/tp_conf/appendix10.pdf.

Berthoud, R., Ermisch, J., Fransesconi, M., Liao, T., Pevalin, D. and Robson, K. (2007). Long term consequences of teenage births for parents and their children. Teenage pregnancy research programme briefing, Teenage Pregnancy Unit, London.

Bowlby, J. (1969). *Attachment and Loss. I: Attachment.* New York: Basic Books.

Bronfenbrenner, U. (1986). Ecology of the family as a context for human development: research perspectives. *Developmental Psychology*, 22(6), 723–741.

Bull, J., McCormick, G., Swann, C. and Mulvihill, C. (2004). *Ante- and Postnatal Home-visiting Programmes: A Review of Reviews.* London: HDA.

Cabinet Office (2006). *Reaching Out: An Action Plan on Social Exclusion.* London: HM Government.

Department of Health (2007). *Facing the Future: A Review of the Role of Health Visitors.* http://www.amicus-cphva.org/pdf/Facing%20the%20Future%20-%20HV%20report.pdf.

Hall, D. and Hall, S. (2007). Family Nurse Partnerships; developing an instrument for identification, assessment and recruitment of clients. Department for Children, Schools and Families Research Report No. 22. http://www.dfes.gov.uk/research/programmeofresearch/projectinformation.cfm?projectid=15301&resultspage=1.

Huffinton, C. and Armstrong, D. (2005). *Working Below the Surface: The Emotional Life of Contemporary Organisations.* London: Tavistock.

Karoly, L. A., Greenwood, P. W., Everingham, S. S., Hoube, J., Kilburn, M. R., Rydell, C. P. *et al.* (1998). *Investing in Our Children: What We Know and Don't Know about the Costs and Benefits of Early Childhood Interventions.* Santa Monica, CA: Rand Corp.

Karoly, L. A., Kilburn, M. R. and Cannon, J. S. (2005). *Early Childhood Education, Proven Results, Future Promise.* Santa Monica, CA: RAND Corporation.

Kitzman, H., Olds, D. L., Henderson, C. R., Hanks, C., Cole, R., Tatelbaum, R. *et al.* (1997). Effect of prenatal and infancy home visitation by nurses on pregnancy outcomes, childhood injuries, and repeated childbearing. A randomized controlled trial. *Journal of the American Medical Association*, 278(8), 644–652.

Kitzman, H., Olds, D. L., Sidora, K., Henderson, C. R., Hanks, C., Cole, R. *et al.* (2000). Enduring effects of nurse home visitation on maternal life course: a 3-year follow-up of a randomized trial. *Journal of the American Medical Association*, 283(15), 1983–1989.

Miller, W. R. and Rollnick, S. (2002). *Motivational Interviewing: Preparing People for Change*, 2nd edn. New York: Guilford Press.

Olds, D., Henderson, C. R., Chamberlin, R. and Tatelbaum, R. (1986a). Preventing child abuse and neglect: a randomized control trial of nurse home visitation. *Paediatrics*, 78, 65–78.

Olds, D. L., Henderson, C. R., Tatelbaum, R. and Chamberlin, R. (1986b). Improving the delivery of prenatal care and outcomes of pregnancy: a randomized trial of nurse home visitation. *Pediatrics*, 77(1), 16–28.

Olds, D. L., Henderson, C. R. and Kitzman, H. (1994). Does prenatal and infancy nurse home visitation have enduring effects on qualities of parental caregiving and child health at 25 to 50 months of life? *Pediatrics*, 93(1), 89–98.

Olds, D., Kitzman, H., Cole, R. and Robinson, J. A. (1997). Theoretical foundations of a program of home visitation for pregnant women and parents of young children. *Journal of Community Psychology*, 25(1), 9–25.

Olds, D., Henderson, C. R., Cole, R., Eckenrode, J., Kitzman, H., Luckey, D. *et al.* (1998). Long-term effects of nurse home visitation on children's criminal and antisocial behavior: 15-year follow-up of a randomized controlled trial. *Journal of the American Medical Association*, 280(14), 1238–1244.

Olds, D. L., Henderson, C. R., Kitzman, H. J., Eckenrode, J. J., Cole, R. E. and Tatelbaum, R. C. (1999). Prenatal and infancy home visitation by nurses: recent findings. *Future of Children*, 9(1), 44–65.

Olds, D. L., Robinson, J., O'Brien, R., Luckey, D. W., Pettitt, L. M., Henderson, C. R. *et al.* (2002). Home visiting by paraprofessionals and by nurses: a randomized, controlled trial. *Pediatrics*, 110(3), 486–496.

Olds, D. L., Kitzman, H., Cole, R., Robinson, J., Sidora, K., Luckey, D. W. *et al.* (2004a). Effects of nurse home-visiting on maternal life course and child development: age 6 follow-up results of a randomized trial. *Pediatrics*, 114(6), 1550–1559.

Olds, D. L., Robinson, J., Pettitt, L., Luckey, D. W., Holmberg, J., Ng, R. K. *et al.* (2004b). Effects of home visits by paraprofessionals and by nurses: age 4 follow-up results of a randomized trial. *Pediatrics*, 114(6), 1560–1568.

Olds, D. L., Sadler, L. and Kitzman, H. (2007). Programs for parents of infants and toddlers: recent evidence from randomized trials. *Journal of Child Psychology and Psychiatry*, 48(3-4), 355–391.

Rollnick, S., and Mason, P. (1999). *Health Behaviour Change: A Guide for Practitioners*. Philadelphia, PA: Elsevier Health Sciences.

Rollnick, S., Butler, C., McCambridge, J., Kinnersley, P., Elwyn, G. and Resnicow, K. (2005). Consultations about changing behaviour. *British Medical Journal*, 331, 961–963.

Rollnick, S., Miller, W. and Butler, C. (2008). *Motivational Interviewing in Health Care: Helping Patients Change Behavior*. London: Guilford Press.

Rutter, M., Giller, H. and Hagel, A. (1998). *Antisocial Behavior by Young People*. Cambridge: Cambridge University Press.

Saleebey, D. (ed.) (1992). *The Strengths Approach in Social Work Practice*. New York: Longman.

Stevenson, J., Ingham, R., Borgoni, R., Hernandez, M. and Smith, P. (2007). Consequences of teenage parenthood: pathways which minimise the negative impacts of teenage childbearing. Teenage pregnancy research programme briefing, Teenage Pregnancy Unit, London.

11 Working with parents from black and minority ethnic backgrounds in Children's Centres

Lucy Marks, Sandy Hadley, Antonia Reay, Tamara Gelman and Anne Mckay

There is a large body of evidence suggesting that maternal depression and social adversity have a negative impact on the quality of the mother–infant relationship (Murray and Cooper, 1977). It has also been suggested that children from poor communities are especially vulnerable because high levels of deprivation are associated with increased psychological distress (Stafford and Marmot, 2003), and parents are more likely to be experiencing both economic strain *and* depression (Harpham, 1994). This chapter describes work with parents from black and minority ethnic groups in one of the most deprived parts of the UK, the London borough of Tower Hamlets. Almost 50 per cent of the local population belong to an ethnic group other than White British, and at least ninety different languages are spoken within the borough. A third of the population are Bangladeshi and 7 per cent come from African/Caribbean backgrounds. The Bangladeshi population in east London is the largest in the world outside of Bangladesh. Despite major structural changes and economic development over the last few decades, this borough remains one of the most deprived areas in the country; there are high rates of unemployment, and major problems with overcrowding and poor quality housing.

Whilst access to psychological therapies in the perinatal period is patchy across the country (see antenatal and postnatal mental health NICE guidelines, 2007), it has been widely documented that there is significant inequality of access to psychological therapies for people from black and minority ethnic (BME) groups (NIMHE, 2003), and the independent inquiry into the death of David Bennett (2003) described an institutionally racist mental health service. The theory and practice of delivering psychological therapies has often been based on a white western model and may therefore need to be adapted so that it is accessible and acceptable to BME groups, particularly in the perinatal period.

The authors work as a team focusing on services to Sure Start Children's Centres, which are part of the NHS-based Primary Care Psychology and Counselling Service in Tower Hamlets, providing clinical work, psychological consultation and support in health centres and community settings. The Children's Centre team provides early intervention and prevention in relation to psychological problems for parents with under-fives. The Psychology and Counselling Service has always had a commitment to provide high quality services to an ethnically diverse population, and has for many years employed Somali- and Sylheti-speaking counsellors, assistant psychologists, clinical psychologists and graduate mental health workers.

The parents using the psychology services in the Children's Centres roughly reflect the ethnic diversity of the borough. At the time of writing, our ethnicity monitoring information for new clients indicated that over the previous five months 41 per cent were White, 40 per cent were Asian, including 30 per cent Bangladeshi with 10 per cent having another Asian background, 16 per cent were Black or Black British (including those of African and Caribbean backgrounds), and 3 per cent were from other backgrounds.

Facilitating access

Mental health services are frequently associated with shame and stigma, particularly for people from BME groups (Hatfield *et al.*, 1996). One reason for the lower uptake of psychological therapies amongst non-western communities could be related to the different ways of thinking about emotional distress in these cultures, and the fact that it may be more unusual to seek help outside the family. The Sylheti language, for example (spoken by the Bangladeshi community), does not have words for concepts such as 'depression' or 'stress'.

Datta (2005) and Laungani (1997) argued that much of South Asian society is community-orientated and therefore the needs of individuals are often subordinate to the family and the greater community, so discussion of a mental health condition might be seen to breach the integrity of the family or the local community. In addition, the impact of a mental health problem on a particular family member can have negative consequences in relation to the status of the family and, possibly, the marriage prospects of siblings, particularly within certain sections of the Bangladeshi community. It is therefore necessary to work proactively to increase understanding about emotional distress and psychological problems, and ensure that BME communities are aware of the available services.

Psychologists and other mental health workers need to be willing to move outside the consulting room, particularly if they are to be able to offer timely help to mothers and infants, ensuring accessibility for harder-to-reach parents. It is thus very helpful that the nature of Children's Centre services and their ethos provide opportunities to see families in a variety of local settings, from general practitioner (GP) practices to community organisations and Children's Centres, all of which are associated with universal and non-stigmatising community services. Successful Children's Centres know how to engage with parents from local communities, and with family support workers from those local communities carrying out effective outreach, so that local people feel motivated to attend activities run by the Children's Centre.

Offering 'psychological education' groups

One way of facilitating access and of raising the profile of the service has been to use established Children's Centre groups to run open sessions in community centres to increase mothers' awareness of psychological distress during the perinatal period. Psycho-educational talks, with titles such as 'Stress Management for Mums', 'Understanding Stress and Depression', and 'Assertiveness for Mums', presented in an interactive manner, have been well attended and received.

These groups are often largely made up of Bengali mothers, usually a mixture of first, second and third generation immigrants, and either the group facilitator or a Sylheti-speaking assistant psychologist to help with language and cultural knowledge. It was extremely useful, for example, to work with a Bangladeshi senior family support worker to adjust the original material used for an assertiveness training course in order to address women's concerns that increased assertiveness might be construed as disrespectful to elders and undermine their roles as good mothers, wives and daughters-in-law.

Initially a group may be quiet during one of these psycho-educational sessions, because, as one young mother put it, 'we never talk about these things', but the sessions quickly warm up as the more confident mothers begin to share their experiences of stress and depression. Mothers often express relief that they are talking more openly about the strains and isolation of parenting very young children. Parents are asked what helps them feel better, and handouts are provided summarising the discussion and highlighting self-care messages, including the idea that talking about how you feel can help. Information is also given about the range of services that are available. Regular visits to Children's Centre groups run by other staff also help to establish the psychologist as an approachable professional.

The team also provides a six-session psycho-educational course for parents with babies of 6 months and younger, focusing on the transition to parenthood, the key aims of which are to promote positive attachment between parent and infant, and to support the development of social networks. The course is promoted by health visitors, midwives and Children's Centre staff and provides a supportive environment in which participants can discuss issues and concerns. It includes the use of videos, small and large group discussions/activities, and practice of relaxation techniques. Each session focuses on a different topic, for example: 'The Family Blueprint: what parents hope to get out of being a parent and different parenting styles'; 'What parents and babies need'; 'Your feelings and babies' feelings'; 'How babies communicate their feelings/needs'; 'Looking after yourself'; 'Learning about stress management and postnatal depression'; 'Changing relationships (couples, family, friends, work) and looking after those relationships'; and 'Developing a support network and finding local services for parents'.

The concept of providing a 'course' rather than a 'therapy group' has been used because there is some evidence that this increases access due to the fact that it is perceived as less stigmatising and intimidating for participants (White, 2000).

Approximately half the participants who have attended this course have been from BME groups and all have been English-speaking. The team wanted to ensure that the group was promoted in a way that made sense to BME parents, and so a Sylheti-speaking assistant psychologist attended an existing Children's Centre group to talk to Bangladeshi mothers about the course, and asked them what name would be most attractive to them. The title 'Raising Happy Babies' was suggested and is now incorporated in leaflets and information to parents. The feedback from the groups has been positive and participants have suggested that such groups should also be run in the antenatal period. In terms of outcomes, the preliminary results are promising, with a positive change in mental health, as measured by the General Health Questionnaire (GHQ) scores (Goldberg and Williams, 1988), for the majority of participants.

There is evidence that preparing group therapy participants improves retention and outcomes (Vinogravdov and Yalom, 1989), which suggests that the preparation of parents for the 'courses' may also be helpful. The Bangladeshi assistant psychologist therefore telephoned potential participants and visited them at home to explain the content and answer any concerns or questions that they might have. This was time-consuming but it increased attendance significantly.

Issues about language

Parvin *et al.* (2003), in their study examining experiences and understandings of social and emotional distress in the postnatal period among Bangladeshi women living in Tower Hamlets, found that the language women used to describe their emotional experiences was different from the language used by the indigenous population. For example, women talked about feeling 'restless or without peace' in their minds, feeling sad or having an 'aching heart'. They concluded that these descriptions fitted a psychosocial model of understanding psychological distress, as the women explained their distress as caused by their own particular social circumstances. This contrasts with the common view that people from this BME group are more likely to express emotional problems as somatic symptoms. However, Parvin *et al.* noted that women in their study chose not to talk to their GP about emotional issues because they thought the GP's role was to focus on physical health. As a consequence, their presentation in GP consultation sessions may differ compared to white British women when they seek help in the postnatal period.

In a service such as the one described, careful thought needs to be given to the words that can be used to express different mental health states, given for example that there is no word for 'depression' or 'stress' in the Sylheti language as we suggested earlier. It is the role of the psychologist and the interpreter to be aware of this and to think through how to talk about psychological problems before the start of the session.

Effective use of interpreters is crucial to facilitate access to and use of any health or support services. Good practice guidelines have been developed for the whole of the Primary Care Psychology and Counselling Service (Parvin *et al.*, 2003). These stress the importance of working with the same interpreter for each individual client, briefing the interpreter before seeing the client, debriefing afterwards, and making sure there is an agreement as to how to structure the session together, including the frequency of interpreting back what has been said. It is beyond the scope of this chapter to detail the complexity of working with an interpreter; for a full account see Tribe and Raval (2003).

Kirmayer *et al.* (2003) argue that there is a need for additional training of interpreters to increase their expertise in mental health, particularly when working with potentially distressing or traumatising situations. Indeed, some of the most effective work across the language divide in Tower Hamlets has been undertaken with Sylheti-speaking assistant psychologists or graduate mental health workers who have basic training in mental health skills and are able to make a therapeutic connection with the client.

Close working relationships with bilingual family support workers are also important in enabling access both directly and indirectly to the service. One of the roles for the psychology team in the Children's Centre is to provide teaching and 'reflective practice' groups for these staff. The aim is to enable them to contain the emotional content of interactions with their clients and families more effectively. This may take the form of monthly groups as well as informal discussion and teaching sessions. Family support workers are often central to forging and maintaining contact with a family. Complex difficulties and family secrets are sometimes disclosed to them, and they have to manage anxiety about the well-being of vulnerable parents and children. Part of their role is 'signposting', which includes offering information in a non-threatening way to families to enable them to better access community resources. However, where the signposting is to mental health services, particularly where the family is anxious about or rejecting of this option, the family support worker can be influential in allaying fears and supporting the family or parent to make a leap of faith and accept a referral.

Family support workers are usually the staff group who have received the least amount of formal training in mental health. Often recruited from local communities, they have a particular struggle to maintain boundaries. In Tower Hamlets they have been provided with training in a number of areas, such as: 'Communication skills'; 'Having difficult conversations: talking about domestic violence'; and 'Managing your mother-in-law'.

Adapting Clinical Practice

Loshak (2003: 53) points out that professionals working with migrants or refugees may be 'confronted with family patterns and traditions so distant from their own experience, and without a shared language, [that they] can become overwhelmed and paralysed in their thinking and capacity to be of use'. Service providers can feel overwhelmed by hopelessness when faced with the complexities of both psychological distress and external difficulties such as overcrowding, poor housing, extended family dynamics and racism. Loshak (2003: 57) points out that particularly when working with migrants and refugees one has to tolerate a 'constant confusion between factors arising from cultural norms and those arising from the individual's internal world of object relations'.

Faced with the complexities of many immigrants' experience, professionals may find themselves clinging to bits of cultural knowledge gleaned through experience with a particular community. It is then tempting to apply this knowledge as a 'recipe' in an overly concrete way, in order to contain their anxiety about facing difference. This may lead to the use of stereotyped assumptions as opposed to a real understanding of an individual's experience. There is no absolute truth where cultures are concerned; they are not homogeneous and may change over generations, especially after migration (Helman, 2007).

Emigration involves losses – often of family networks and community – and earlier losses may well be stirred up. Where these losses are not worked through, they can become entrenched in chronic depression (Garland *et al.*, 2002). As in any infant mental health work it is important to hold onto the value of listening to a mother's experience and helping her to reflect on it, thereby reducing the mother's preoccupation with her distress and the possible impact on the infant (Fraiberg *et al.*, 1980).

Case example

An asylum seeker from the Middle East was referred by her GP in the last stages of her pregnancy. She was significantly depressed and had seriously considered suicide. She had lost contact with her lawyer; and the father of her baby had been repatriated and had disappeared. She was living with a friend of his who wanted her out of his house, and she was unable to work because of the imminent arrival of the baby. She presented for an assessment soon after the birth of her baby boy, and sat listlessly in the chair, not supporting her child's head as he attempted, with some vigour, to breastfeed. Talking about her previous life uncovered a desperate history of loss. If she was sent home, she had no family to return to and, with no childcare for her son, she did not think she would find work to survive.

A risk assessment indicated she still had suicidal ideas. At times she thought of killing the baby together with herself, as there would be no one to love him, a painful echo of her own experience. An alternative in her mind was giving her child into care, so she could at least work, and not be passive about her fate. The potential threat to the child evoked huge anxiety in the psychologist, the GP and health visitor, and their ability to tolerate knowing about this mother's desperation seemed to in part contain it for her.

However, she still needed support in mobilising herself to engage with her very difficult situation. Together with the GP, the psychological therapist organised a psychiatric assessment. This was partly to manage their own anxiety, but seemed to have a positive impact on the mother's mood, in that she felt taken seriously. She became more active in seeking help. She was helped to access legal advice; social services were involved to assess the risk of harm to the child; and her health visitor made weekly contact.

During this period, this mother was able to attend therapy sessions, in which she could think about her options. It pained her deeply to talk about her past, but she said it made sense that this was part of why she felt so desperate. However, after some time she said that she needed not to be reminded of painful things and wanted to talk about the present. The therapy focused more on helping her to enjoy her lively baby. She needed repeated reassurance that the health staff would not contact immigration authorities and that she could decide to present for repatriation when she thought she could manage it. Initially, fear kept her in her room most of the day, and the therapist had to work gently to encourage her to use local resources.

She subsequently found new accommodation through a voluntary sector organisation and she stopped coming to sessions as her new home was too far away, but the therapist maintained regular phone contact for several months, and kept in communication with the local health visitor. A year after the original referral, the health visitor reported that both mother and baby seemed more cheerful and active, although their legal status remained unclear.

This case illustrates the importance of multi-disciplinary services when working with this client group, who often have social or financial needs that override any psychological ones and must be resolved if the mother, baby or family are to prosper in the long term.

Engaging with different belief systems

Beliefs around supernatural powers or black magic can be found in many different cultures and are often used as alternative explanations for psychological ill health. In the Bangladeshi community, some people believe in Jin (ghosts or spirits) and black magic curses as a way of explaining a number of problems, including those of a psychological nature, which supposedly occur in individuals who have been cursed. In a qualitative study exploring the experience of four first generation Bangladeshi mothers who had received a diagnosis of postnatal depression, Parvin (2001) notes that the Bangladeshi mothers she interviewed drew on a range of discourses to make sense of their difficulties. One key discourse involved religious beliefs about spiritual possession, where difficulties were understood as a result of being possessed by the 'Bai', which took control over the mother's body which was vulnerable after childbirth. Alternatively, difficulties were explained as a 'fara', which is a dangerous task set by Allah to test the faith of his believers during a difficult time.

When working with any client or family, clinicians need to explore and understand the client's or family's belief system. Whether these are schemas (Young *et al.*, 2003), internal representational models (Bowlby, 1969) or family scripts (Byng-Hall, 1990), exploring belief systems is central to most psychological therapies. This process is no different when working with BME clients, but the content may be different, and alternative ways of thinking about problems or psychological difficulties without this process invalidating the original beliefs should be explored. This helps to build rapport and trust between the therapist and client.

Striving to work in a culturally sensitive way with this kind of material has been greatly facilitated in Tower Hamlets by a consultation group in the wider psychology service led by team members who are experienced psychological therapists from Bangladeshi and Somali backgrounds. This group meets bi-monthly and provides an opportunity to discuss cases and develop an approach which can be culturally sensitive.

A similar 'cultural consultation model' has been used in primary care in Canada to supplement existing services in order to improve diagnostic assessment and treatment for a culturally diverse urban population, with good outcomes in terms of satisfaction (Kirmayer *et al.*, 2003). Kirmayer *et al.* report that the multiple-perspective skills and background represented in a culturally and professionally diverse team can facilitate critical analysis of conventional practices and case formulation, and lead to creative intervention. They argue further that this diversity can also sustain a cohesive collegial group able to support efforts to change systemic problems including institutional racism.

Case example

Mrs X was a 27-year-old Bangladeshi woman with five children who was referred for help with her depression following the birth of her sixth child. She believed that her depression was a result of a curse being placed upon her by an estranged family member. Following discussions in the bi-monthly consultation group, the therapist used an approach developed by a colleague when working with beliefs about spirit (Jin) possession. This involved exploring with the client her beliefs and attempts to address these, such as saying special prayers and taking advice from her Imam. Once she had tried all of these approaches and none had helped to lift her mood, the therapist explored with her whether she would like to view her difficulties from the western perspective and see whether any of these techniques were helpful. Thus, it became possible to work on her depression by introducing an alternative way of looking at these symptoms without invalidating or challenging her belief system.

Engaging with non-western ways of organising family life

Extended families are found in many different cultures. Often the families of clients in Tower Hamlets exhibit a considerable degree of what in western terms would be considered as 'enmeshment' (Green and Werner, 1996). As individual autonomy is much less valued in South Asian culture than it is for example in North American culture, this can mean a lack of separateness for each individual member, and that the married couple sometimes find emotional and practical support from the extended family to a greater extent than from each other. Parvin *et al.* (2003) noted that the Bangladeshi women in their focus groups did not expect support or practical help from their husbands after the birth of their baby.

The Tower Hamlets team has also had the experience of meeting mothers who complain about difficult relationships with their mothers-in-law, often feeling bullied and concerned that their mothers-in-law have more control over their children than they do.

Case example

Mrs B was a 26-year-old Pakistani woman who was referred for help with depression following the birth of her first baby. She lived with her parents-in-law, husband, and his three brothers (one of whom was also married). The baby was the first grandchild. In the therapy sessions she gave an account of feeling very unconfident about how to care for her baby, and her belief that she was failing as a mother. She also described how her mother-in-law was very controlling and monitored when and where she went out. Mrs B felt her attempts to care for her baby were constantly undermined. She had stopped going out of the house in order to avoid conflict.

The therapist helped Mrs B to think about the potential meaning of the baby for her mother-in-law, as the first grandchild and in relation to different generational approaches to childcare. She encouraged Mrs B to enlist her husband's help in setting clear limits with her mother-in-law about who provided what care for the baby, and in discussing how they wanted to provide this. The therapist reflected with Mrs B on the intense emotional experience of having a baby, and about the feelings it can stir up. She arranged for Mrs B to attend baby massage classes at her local Children's Centre with a view to helping her build up her confidence in caring for her baby on her own and in order to meet other first-time mothers. She helped Mrs B to problem-solve how she would introduce the idea of attending the classes to her mother-in-law.

Conclusion

A range of adaptations to usual clinical practice have been developed in Tower Hamlets in order to proactively address the challenge of making a psychological therapy service both accessible and helpful for parents and infants from diverse communities. The Children's Centre model offers a unique opportunity for developing psychological work with BME communities because of the model's capacity to address social exclusion. There is, however, still an urgent need to research and audit comparative outcomes and attrition rates for different communities, and to develop referral routes for other black and minority ethnic groups such as the Chinese/Vietnamese and Somali communities.

Acknowledgements

We wish to thank Mahbuba Khatun, assistant psychologist, for her help with the preparation of this chapter, and Gulrook Begum, Fatema Zaman and Amina Hassan, who facilitate the case consultation group and have provided much valuable help and advice.

In order to protect confidentiality, details in the case examples have been radically altered, the examples often being an amalgamation of different parents we have seen.

References

Bowlby, J. (1969). *Attachment and Loss. I: Attachment*. New York: Basic Books.

Byng-Hall, J. (1990). Attachment theory and family therapy; a clinical view. *Infant Mental Health Journal*, 11, 228–236.

Clarkson, P. (2000). *Values in Counselling and Psychotherapy. Ethics: Working with Ethical and Moral Dilemmas in Psychiatry*. London: Whurr Publishers.

Datta, P. (2005). Predictors of postnatal distress in Asian mothers in Britain. Unpublished D.Clin. Psychology doctoral thesis, Canterbury Christ Church University College.

Fraiberg, S., Adelson, E. and Shapiro, V. (1980). Ghosts in the nursery: a psychoanalytic approach to the problems of impaired infant–mother relationships. In S. Fraiberg (ed.), *Clinical Studies in Infant Mental Health* (pp. 146–169). New York: Basic Books.

Garland, C., Hume, F. and Majid, S. (2002). Remaking connections: refugees and the development of 'emotional capital' in therapy groups. *Psychoanalytic Psychotherapy*, 16, 197–214.

Goldberg, D. and Williams, P. (1988). *A User's Guide to the General Health Questionnaire*. Windsor: NFER-Nelson.

Green, R. J. and Werner, P. D. (1996). Intrusiveness and closeness-caregiving: rethinking the concept of family 'enmeshment'. *Family Process*, 35, 115–136.

Harpham, T. (1994). Urbanisation and mental health in developing countries. *Social Science and Medicine, 39*, 139–145.

Hatfield, B., Mohamad, H., Rahim, Z. and Tanweer, H. (1996). Mental health and the communities: a local survey. *British Journal of Social Work*, 26, 315–336.

Helman, C. G. (2007). *Culture, Health and Illness*, 5th edn. London: Hodder Arnold.

Independent inquiry into the death of David Bennett (December 2003). http://www.blink.org.uk/docs/David_Bennett_report.pdf.

Kirmayer, L. J., Groleau, D., Guzder, J., Blake, C. and Jarvis, E. (2003). Cultural consultation: a model of mental health service for multicultural societies. *Canadian Journal of Psychiatry*, 48(3), 145–153.

Laungani, P. (1997). Mental illness in India and Britain: theory and practice. *Medicine and Law*, 16, 509–540.

Loshak, R. (2003). Working with Bangladeshi young women. *Psychoanalytic Psychotherapy*, 17(1), 52–67.

Murray, I. and Cooper, P. J. (1977). Postpartum depression and child development. *Psychological Medicine*, 27, 253–260.

NIMHE (2003). *Inside Outside: Improving Mental Health Services for Black and Minority Ethnic Communities in England.* http://www.dh.gov.uk/prod_consum_dh/groups/dh_digitalassets/@dh/@en/documents/digitalasset/dh_4019452.pdf.

Parvin, A. (2001). Investigating the meanings of maternal distress following childbirth: comparing the understandings and accounts of general practitioners and Bangladeshi women with a diagnosis of postnatal depression. Unpublished doctoral thesis, University of East London.

Parvin, A. (2003). Guidelines for working with interpreters. Psychology and Counselling Department, Tower Hamlets Primary Care Trust, London.

Parvin, A., Jones, C. and Hull, S. (2003). Experiences and understandings of social and emotional distress in the postnatal period among Bangladeshi women living in Tower Hamlets. *Family Practice*, 21(3), 254–260.

Stafford, M. and Marmot, M. (2003). Neighbourhood deprivation and health: does it affect us all equally? *International Journal of Epidemiology*, 32(3), 357–366.

Tribe, R. and Raval, H. (2003). *Working with Interpreters in Mental Health.* Hove: Brunner-Routledge.

Vinogravdov, S. and Yalom, I. D. (1989). *Concise Guide to Group Psychotherapy.* London: American Psychiatric Press.

White, J. (2000). *Treating Anxiety and Stress: A Group Psychoeducational Approach Using Brief CBT.* Chichester: Wiley.

Young, J. E., Klosko, J. S. and Weishaar, M. E. (2003). *Schema Therapy: A Practitioner's Guide.* New York: Guilford Press.

Part III

Indicated approaches

12 Working with the hidden obstacles in parent–infant relating

Two parent–infant psychotherapy projects

Tessa Baradon, Sue Gerhardt and Joanna Tucker

Parents are at times mystified about why things go wrong in the perinatal period: why they don't enjoy their babies, why they are depressed, or why the baby isn't sleeping or feeding well. There is a lack of awareness in our culture that all of us operate on two levels – our intentional, conscious behaviours and our unintentional, unconscious behaviours. Having a baby powerfully triggers many previously excluded or repressed behaviour patterns that are held in memory but outside awareness, some of which are based on our early emotional experiences. In moments of heightened negative emotion these early relationship 'templates' or internal representational models (Bowlby, 1977) may come to the fore, taking over from the more reasoned, mature behaviours of the adult. For example, most parents 'instinctively' want to comfort their crying baby. This response will be based on their own implicit memories of how their own parents responded to them when they were babies. Others may feel so anxious hearing their baby's cries, that they feel driven to silence the noise. These parents may be bewildered about their responses, which may feel and even appear inappropriately harsh. Routine health visitor advice to the parent about the baby's vulnerability may have failed to help them become more responsive and we may then assume that unconscious factors beyond the parent's control have come into play. Psychoanalytically informed parent–infant psychotherapy aims to help parents to understand these factors and, through making what is unconscious *meaningful*, help the parent to develop an understanding of their past relationships, and how these may have played out in the present relationship with their baby. This process enables the parents to change.

This chapter will discuss the concept and practice of psychoanalytic parent–infant psychotherapy as a form of therapy which has been shown to be helpful when parents and infants present with a wide spectrum of disturbances of attachment in the infant. Our approach emphasises a clinical focus on the relationship between parent (or primary caretaker) and baby. By always working with parents and baby our aim is to develop or restore the bond between them. This chapter describes the work of two projects: the Parent Infant Project (PIP) at the Anna Freud Centre in London, and the Oxford Parent Infant Project (OXPIP) in Oxford. The chapter begins with a description of the approach used by these two projects, and then examines two case studies which show how each approach works. The chapter concludes with an examination of recent evaluations of both PIP and OXPIP.

The theoretical model

Psychoanalytic parent–infant psychotherapy derives its theoretical framework and techniques of intervention from psychoanalysis, attachment theory and developmental research. At its core, parent–infant psychotherapy is a relationship-based intervention, where change is brought about *in* the parent–infant relationship *through* the new, emergent relationships between the parent(s), the infant, and the therapist. How the therapist *relates* with the parent(s) and baby – his or her attitudes, manner, conscious, thought-out interventions and unconscious, spontaneous gestures – is all part of the intervention process.

The therapeutic work attempts to create symbolic meaning in the transactions between parent and infant and therapist. Meaning is offered both to conscious thoughts and behaviours and also to those motivations or actions the roots of which may be outside the conscious awareness of the participants. In this approach the theoretical assumption is that behaviours are triggered by emotions, often unconsciously.

Mother, father and therapist are sitting in a circle with baby in the centre. Mother is crying and father touches her arm, offering comfort. James, 5 months, slides in a rolling movement and stops close to the therapist. It could be suggested that he was just practising his developmentally-driven motor movement, and it was coincidence that it overlapped with mother's crying. We would be more likely to think that it was not a random physical movement but an emotional communication the meaning of which would be along the lines of 'it feels very scary when mummy is sad', and that the therapist was at that point the safest person in the room. We would suggest to the parents that James used his motor development to meet his own need for safety when he was feeling threatened by mother's distress – thus, his behaviour is explained by his emotions and intentions at that particular moment and has meaning.

The primary aim of this therapeutic approach is to help the caregiver to provide a growth-promoting environment for the baby by helping the parents to understand their baby as well as their own difficulties resulting from their past, often 'forgotten' experiences. By a growth-promoting environment we mean one in which the parent provides physical and emotional safety, is contingently responsive to the infant's communications of need, sees the baby as a separate but dependent individual, and can think about the baby's experience and age-appropriate emotional needs (see Schore, 2001, 2004; Gerhardt, 2004) (i.e. is truly able to 'hold the baby in mind').

Despite most parents' conscious intentions and wishes to do well by their baby, psychological factors may prevent them from responding sensitively to the infant, creating 'hidden obstacles' to parenting.

In particular, traumatic relationships from the past can be unconsciously re-evoked and come into play with the newborn baby. For example, a father who as a young child was expected to cope with adversity and was not 'allowed' to be vulnerable or show distress may, despite his best intentions, repeat his parents' expectations by overriding his baby's cues of stress or distress in order to 'toughen him up'. Or, a parent who has had a baby who has died may find themselves constantly waking up a sleeping baby 'just to check that she is still breathing'. In response, the new baby may then develop strategies to reassure the parent that she is going to live, giving up some of her developmentally appropriate dependency.

These examples highlight the fact that the mental processes which interfere with growth-promoting caregiving may often be unconscious. The parents may be quite unaware of the impact of their own mental states and behaviours on their baby's emotional state.

In early development, psychological regulation is linked to physiological regulation. A baby's inner equilibrium will inevitably be disturbed by physiological discomforts – hunger, cold, fatigue – and by psychological stimuli – fear, confusion, overwhelming excitation. Young infants have only a few options available to regulate their level of stimulation – such as gaze aversion or sucking their fingers (see also Chapter 4). Fundamentally, young infants are entirely dependent on their caretakers for regulation, to understand and respond to their bodily and mental states.

Recent research has found that the parent's capacity to regulate emotion in herself and in her infant is linked to the capacity for mentalisation (Fonagy, 1998; Fonagy *et al.*, 2001). Mentalisation is the psychological capacity to give meaning to actions and behaviours in oneself and in others in terms of underlying feelings and thoughts. Without this process of giving meaning, human behaviour can be experienced as random and unpredictable. The capacity to think reflectively allows us to understand ourselves as well as others. It develops from early experience of having been thought about, and a parent's attempts to understand what is in our minds, and what our intentions are[1] (i.e. not so much in terms of keeping the baby in mind but more in terms of *keeping the baby's mind in mind*).

Good emotional regulation depends on an ability to pay attention to feelings, to tolerate them and to respond appropriately to them. Most people have had sufficiently good experience to find that this comes naturally, but a significant minority of parents, often those who have not been well regulated by their own parents, may struggle throughout their lives to manage their states and those of their children in turn. For the baby this has significant implications: a baby who is in a state of physical and/or psychological dysregulation experiences this as a threat to integrity and survival. If the baby does not have an adult available to help him regain a state of equilibrium, he will need to focus his energies on attempting to regulate himself. The consequences of this range from less than optimal neurological development, both cognitive (Meins, 1999) and emotional (Gerhardt, 2004), through increasingly insecure attachment strategies (Lyons-Ruth and Jacobvitz, 1999; Main and Hesse, 1992), to increased likelihood of developing psychopathology in childhood and adulthood (see, for example, Sroufe *et al.*, 2005). A baby in a state of dysregulation is also unable to address the ordinary developmental tasks of feeding, sleeping, exploration, and play.

However, this model does not assume that parents need always get it right in terms of understanding and responding to their baby's communications. Detailed examination of the emotional exchanges between parent and infant shows that most infants are not in a constant, continuous state of balanced regulation. Most interactions are instead characterised by frequent, small mismatches between the partners – 'ruptures' – which a sensitive parent notices and repairs again without being aware of it. The parent misunderstands, recognises this, adjusts and matches his or her response, which re-establishes the baby's emotional regulation. This concept of 'interactive repair' (Tronick and Weinberg, 1997) is fundamental to 'good enough' parenting. Thus 'growth-promoting' parenting manages to repair the myriad small ruptures which occur in day-to-day interaction, whilst parenting that is 'growth-inhibiting' often fails to repair, thereby leaving the baby in prolonged states of distress and dysregulation, with a significant risk of creating insecure attachment strategies.

The clinical approach

The concepts of emotional 'regulation', 'mentalisation' and 'interactive repair' shape not only our understanding of the developing relationship between parent and baby and the difficulties in it, but also the way we make our therapeutic intervention. The therapist will constantly be working with the emotional states of parent(s) and infant, observing and trying to understand the triggers to dysregulation, and working with them to re-establish emotional regulation. The therapist will become part of the relational system in order to address the difficulties between parent(s) and baby. The therapist's own capacity to think about the parent and baby as individuals, to reflect on their emotions and behaviours – her own 'mentalising stance' – is pivotal in helping the parent and baby have an actual experience of being thought about and understood. This, in turn, 'supports the parent(s) in reflecting on the meaning of their baby's experience and actions' (Baradon *et al.*, 2005).

Russell sought help for his baby Dwaine who was driving him to distraction because of his excessive crying. The therapist observed in the sessions that when Dwaine cried he did not settle and his father became very anxious. The therapist learnt that Russell grew up with a drug-addicted teenage mother, and often had to look after himself. It seemed to the therapist that baby Dwaine's crying was putting Russell back in touch with his own helplessness and vulnerability as a crying, fearful, child, and that he did not know how to regulate his feelings then, or now.

In an early session, as baby Dwaine's cries became louder and stronger, the therapist observed the baby turn away from his father, arching his back and closing his eyes in an attempt to avoid his father's intrusive gaze – seeming to need to look away in order to regulate his heart rate, blood pressure and respiration. Dwaine then posseted some milk. The therapist reflected that father and baby were in a vicious spiral of mutual distress, what Beatrice Beebe describes as a state of 'mutually escalating arousal' (Beebe, 2000: 436). In such a state, it is hard to think and to find meaning – to 'mentalise'.

In one session, Russell talked in more detail about his disturbing and violent childhood, in which there was no one to help him with his feelings. He recalled learning to manage relationships in his hostile family by being tough and independent, and keeping vulnerable feelings in himself and others out of awareness. The therapist wondered if he expected the same from baby Dwaine, as a way of protecting Dwaine from painful feelings. In fact the therapist noted that Russell felt better getting 'these things off his chest'.

At the same time the therapist noticed that Russell was also behaving differently towards baby Dwaine. When the baby toppled backwards from a sitting position, and landed on a toy, Russell responded to him with an empathic tone of voice. This time Russell saw baby Dwaine's distress as appropriate in terms of Dwaine's age. Dwaine cried for a minute or so, but – helped by Russell's contingent response to his distress – quickly regained his composure. Dwaine and Russell then 'chatted' in a warm, involved way, each responding to the other's utterances. The therapist brought out some of the meaning of these events, commenting that instead of behaving as he might have done in the past by suppressing feelings, Russell had been able to respond to Dwaine and think about what his experience might have been. The therapist spoke to baby Dwaine about his daddy being able to understand what it felt like to fall over, now that daddy had someone (the therapist) to help him remember and understand his own feelings.

The therapist will respond not only to what the parent talks about but also to what she observes in the room, making links between the thoughts and feelings of each partner and the relationship between them. This is by necessity a slow process, mirroring the process of mother and baby getting to know and understand each other. It includes observing, remembering, 'holding in mind' and wondering aloud, trying to make sense, recognising mistakes and rectifying misunderstandings. In the process the therapist may feel more keenly for the mother/father for a while, and at other times may identify with the infant. As long as the therapist's identifications are moving between the two she will be able to understand the needs of both (see Winnicott, 1960). However, if the therapist becomes 'stuck' in her identification with either the mother or the baby, the usefulness of the therapy for both, in their relationship with each other, will be disrupted.

From the very beginning the therapist's attention is focused on the relationship between the parent and the infant. At referral the relationship is often quite difficult, for different reasons. For example, early sessions may be filled by the mother's preoccupation with her own current mental state, or filled with a driven anxiety about the infant such that the baby becomes her 'pathological preoccupation' (Winnicott, 1965). The baby may be very small, very passive, or protectively asleep for most of the time.

In focusing on the relationship, the therapist will also address aspects of the parent's make-up, such as experiences from the parent's past, unprocessed feelings of loss, helplessness and rage, or erroneous attributions or projections onto the baby. The therapist does this primarily through empathising with the parent's feelings, and by jointly constructing a narrative that makes sense of the parent's life and creates meaning for him or her. Equally, the therapist also works with the elements that infants bring to the relationship – their innate propensity for attachment, their particular temperament, the primitive, raw feelings in response to situations and precocious attempts to adapt, which result from over-stimulating impingements from the outside world. In her interactions with the baby, the therapist will pick up on the 'language' of the baby – tone of voice and rhythm and intonation, facial expressions, body positioning and gesture. These interactions with the baby also model for the parent alternative ways of thinking about, and being with, her baby.

Four-week-old Jack was in his carrycot, deeply asleep for the duration of the first session. His mother talked almost without stopping about her abandonment by her partner, which repeated an earlier abandonment by her biological parents. As the therapist listened and responded to Chloe, she kept an eye also on the quality of Jack's rhythm, breathing, and movements. In the second session Jack again slept through. As the end of the session approached, the therapist crouched in front of Jack-asleep-in-his-cot, and spoke very softly to him. 'You are sleeping so deeply Jack, while your mummy talks about her strong feelings. Maybe you are giving her space so I can help her feel better? But you need some space here, too, don't you? How can you have a space? We need to help you to be able to be awake?' Chloe stood next to the therapist and Jack during this exchange. She looked interested and puzzled. When the therapist leaned back on her haunches, indicating a break in her talking to Jack, Chloe asked: 'Do you think he needs help too? Maybe next week he will wake up.'

The mother thus responded to the therapist's ability to keep both her and her baby in mind and to her attribution of meaning to Jack's behaviour. Chloe then joined with the therapist in a desire to open up a space in the session to include her baby.

Sometimes the therapist will see a family who have got 'stuck' in a dysregulated state and who cannot find their way back to a state of equilibrium. These ruptures can come about in relation to the therapist too, and then there is the potential for a lived experience of repair if the parent can tolerate it. This is what happened with Russell and Dwaine. Russell was in the habit of making official complaints about professionals with whom he had worked. His therapist was then not surprised when he was upset by something she said and threatened to make a complaint against her. She remained open to and reflective about his complaints, and was ready to acknowledge the reasonableness of some of his criticisms. This 'interactive repair' enabled him to slowly let go of his hostility, and no official complaint was made. Gradually he came to see his therapist as someone who was concerned about his own and his baby's welfare, and who delighted in his growing understanding and pleasure in Dwaine.

The therapeutic setting can also help parents tolerate hostile feelings in relationships. One of the most difficult areas to acknowledge for parents is having unloving feelings towards their baby, although in the normal ambivalence parents have towards their babies this is very common (Hoffman, 2003; Parker, 1996). Often parents who struggle with such feelings will describe their baby in negative terms, or express the view that their baby's behaviour demonstrates hostility to them: for example, they might believe that their baby is intentionally vomiting his milk, or intentionally dirtying his nappy immediately after being changed. Whether the antagonism to the baby is expressed overtly, or covertly – such as when the parent tries to hide it with grimacing smiles (i.e. false positive affect – see Crittenden, 1999) – the baby will pick up the parent's feelings towards them. Such feelings are very frightening to a baby. Often they can evoke a strong sense of guilt, or at times even a sense of 'madness', in the parent. These feelings of course are firmly excluded from the parent's consciousness.

In relationships where there is latent unacknowledged resentment or covert or hidden hostility towards the baby, the baby may express his own reactions through arching away when held by mother, or avoiding eye contact with mother, or through extreme passivity. Such behaviour suggests that this baby experiences mother not as comforting (at least at that moment), but as dangerous and needing to be avoided as her hostility is a threat to his well-being.

Claire had a small-for-dates, premature baby who spent many months on the special care baby unit and required several operations. She felt a sense of shame that she had not managed to give her baby a better start in life. She found herself 'holding back' from truly bonding with baby

Thomas, fearing that he still might die. In addition she was angry with him for not having been able to suck strongly enough to breastfeed, so she had to spend many hours each day expressing milk using a breast-pump. When she finally got Thomas home she worried continually that he was not taking enough milk from his bottle, and that she couldn't soothe him adequately when he cried. She began to have nightmares about Thomas suffocating.

At this point, she reluctantly agreed to a visit from a parent–infant psychotherapist (arranged because the baby was too small and vulnerable to go out of the house). The therapist's first impression was that baby Thomas had a rather wizened, sad-looking face, and looked as though he was clinging on for dear life as he held a piece of his mother's T-shirt in his tiny fist.

Claire's relationship with her own mother had been a troubled one and it was clear from the beginning of the therapeutic encounter that she expected the relationship with the therapist to be just as difficult. But a therapeutic alliance slowly developed and, with support and empathic understanding from the therapist about what she had been through, Claire became able to talk about her ambivalence towards Thomas, and her occasional thoughts that if he were to die of a cot death it would solve her problems. Once she was able to articulate these semi-conscious thoughts, her nightmares ceased. Slowly she allowed herself to open up to loving her baby, and feeling for him.

However, she then felt 'very bad' for having said so many negative things, and questioned the value of the therapeutic sessions.

There are many such moments in the therapeutic process, when it may feel stuck or unproductive. It is not always gratifying or positive. Change is achieved through a complex and often slow process of repeated experiences of getting it wrong and putting it right, of a therapeutic relationship that models consistent attentiveness to feelings and jointly creating meaning out of shared experience.

The therapist reminded Claire that expressing negative feelings had enabled her to be more in touch with her positive feelings. As Claire began to integrate her conflicting feelings, a transformation gradually took place in her relationship with Thomas, and he developed more of an appetite - not just for milk, but for life, it seemed. He began to gain weight steadily and became much more contented with his mother, on one occasion lying peacefully with his feet touching his mother's leg. On another occasion Thomas was sleepy and Claire modulated her voice to match his mood and mirrored him when he wrinkled up his face. The therapist commented that she knew instinctively how to respond to him, affirming and building on her growing confidence in her mothering.

The programmes/projects

At present, parent–infant psychotherapy is not routinely available on the NHS or through other statutory bodies. The Oxford Parent Infant Programme (OXPIP) and the Anna Freud Centre Parent Infant Project (PIP) are both charitable organisations offering parent–infant psychotherapy. As charities they are reliant on institutional grants and private donations. Parents contribute financially what they consider they can afford. Both organisations offer a range of services to parents.

OXPIP works with parents and babies up to the age of 2 and offers services such as parent–infant psychotherapy for individual families, community clinics, group work with families and training and consultancy. Many vulnerable parents with young babies are not able or willing to travel very far away from home and OXPIP has developed a number of small satellite clinics around Oxfordshire. Although home visits would often be preferable they are too costly to provide for more than a small proportion of particularly vulnerable clients.

In addition to clinical sessions, OXPIP offers various groups that introduce parents to the service and support their parenting in a more general way. Currently, OXPIP offers a baby massage group, and a baby 'chatting group', because massage supports the physical and emotional development of babies and helps with the bonding process between mother and baby (see Chapter 2), and 'chatting' is the first step in helping babies to communicate (see Chapter 8). Additionally, from time to time OXPIP provides a parent–infant psychotherapy group.

Training is provided by OXPIP therapists for a wide range of professionals, such as health visitors, midwives, nursery nurses, and CAMH services, Sure Start and family centre workers. This includes a three-day training programme for all social workers working with young children in Oxfordshire, focusing particularly on attachment theory and observational skills. We see training as an important part of our remit, and OXPIP are committed to increasing public understanding of the importance of infancy and the need to enhance parent/infant relationships to protect future mental health.

The Anna Freud Centre Parent Infant Project (PIP) supports infants under 12 months and their parents. The activities of the project include clinical and preventive services, training and research. Core parent–infant psychotherapy services are based at the Anna Freud Centre and in community settings frequented by high-risk populations. The provisions include psychotherapy for individual families and postnatal groups.

PIP is also developing and evaluating two pilot services. One is for homeless families with babies, in which a PIP therapist holds a weekly parent–infant group for parents and babies living in a homeless hostel, in tandem with the midwifery baby clinic held on the premises. The other is a learning and experience-based course, developed by PIP, which supports the early attachment relationship between mothers and babies in prison and prepares them for separation when that occurs.

As with OXPIP the Anna Freud Centre Parent Infant Project's training programmes aim to extend expertise in the identification of risk in infancy and enhance effective intervention (see Baradon *et al.*, 2005). Current training includes:

- An annual ten-week module in parent–infant mental health, for professionals working with infants and their families.
- An annual 'Introduction to the Practice of Parent–Infant Psychotherapy' for therapists, psychiatrists and other professionals working clinically in the area of early intervention and attachment disorders.
- Specially commissioned training packages adapted to individual organisations, in the UK and abroad.

The centre is also involved in ongoing research.

Evaluation

Parent–infant psychotherapy has been extensively evaluated over the years and has shown consistent and positive outcomes (Robert-Tissot *et al.*, 1996; Cicchetti *et al.*, 1999; Grubler-Gochman, 1995; Luborsky *et al.*, 2002; Beebe, 2000, 2003; Maldonado-Duran *et al.*, 2002; Palacio and Serpa, 2002).

An evaluation of the Anna Freud Centre PIP service in 2002 followed up a random sample of families who had attended the project. Based on standardised measures of child functioning as well as parent reports, it was found that no children in the follow-up sample scored in the clinical range, and the parents' sense of efficacy was enhanced (Fonagy *et al.*, 2002).

Data were also collected on a sample of infants with the aim of assessing the size of effects observed before and after treatment. The primary outcome measure in this analysis was the Bayley Scales of Infant Development. At the point of referral, on both intellectual and motor development the infants were seven points behind the age average. By six months into treatment, they were indistinguishable from the age average, and this improvement was maintained and slightly improved at follow-up (Fonagy *et al.*, 2002). Similarly, an analysis was conducted of the Bayley scores of infants living in homeless accommodation who received a PIP intervention, with a comparison group of infants in similar living conditions who did not receive support. The results indicated a significant improvement in infants' development on both the mental and motor scales in the intervention group. No significant improvement in development was found in the control group. In fact, in the control group there was a slight decrease in scores on the mental scale at the follow-up (i.e. indicating that development had deteriorated, although this was not significant). Also, in the control group, the motor scale scores did not change at follow-up (indicating no improvement or deterioration) (Fonagy and Newbury, 2007).

Evaluation of data from the pilot phase of the work with mothers in prison showed a statistically significant improvement in the mothers' capacity to think about their babies' needs and sensitively understand their communications (using a standardised measure of maternal 'reflective function' (Baradon *et al.*, 2007)).

During 2003 a small-scale evaluation of OXPIP's clinical work was undertaken. Maternal mental health and maternal self-esteem were measured. There was a statistically significant improvement on both of these standardised measures in the mothers in this evaluation.

A qualitative study of OXPIP (Barlow and Kirkpatrick, 2006) showed that this service is greatly valued by clients. Parents perceived the service to have had positive benefits not only in terms of their infants but also with regard to other children within the family, as well as for themselves.

The evaluations of PIP and OXPIP suggest that parent–infant psychotherapy can contribute to change in maternal mental health and maternal self-esteem, enhance the parent's capacity to think about and understand their baby, and improve the social and emotional functioning of the baby. These findings need verification, however, using a randomised controlled trial, and such a study is currently being carried out at the Anna Freud Centre.

Conclusion

Parent–infant psychotherapy as a therapeutic modality is underpinned by cutting-edge research and clinical knowledge about the crucial role of emotional regulation in development. The therapy works to increase the parents' capacity to think about the baby, to hold the baby in mind, to reflect and understand, and to promote emotional regulation in the baby. Because so many parents who come to parent–infant psychotherapy have significantly disturbed attachment histories themselves, the process of change for them and their babies emerges through their relationship with an empathic therapist, who does not repeat their past experiences of rejection or retaliation. Through these experiences of being responded to by the therapist's mentalising mind, we contend that the parents develop their own capacity to regulate and reflect on their baby's experience which ultimately will be of very great benefit to the developing child.

Note

1 It is our experience that videoing a few minutes of interaction between parent and baby and subsequently showing this to the parent can provide a third eye that helps the parent to become more thoughtful about the way she interacts with her baby. Parents may be helped to 'see' with their conscious mind what their behaviour might be unconsciously conveying to their baby – as well as seeing more clearly what their baby might be signalling to them (see also Chapter 9).

References

Baradon, T., with Broughton, C., Gibbs, I., James, J., Joyce, A. and Woodhead, J. (2005). *The Practice of Psycho-analytic Parent–Infant Psychotherapy: Claiming the Baby.* London: Routledge.

Baradon, T., Fonagy, P., Bland, K., Lenard, K. and Sleed, M. (2007). *New Beginnings – an experience-based program addressing the attachment relationship between mothers and their babies in prisons* (in press).

Barlow, J. and Kirkpatrick, S. (2006). 'Dispelling the ghosts in the nursery': client views about OXPIP (unpublished).

Beebe, B. (2000). Constructing mother–infant distress: the microsynchrony of maternal impingement and infant avoidance in the face-to-face encounter. *Psychoanalytic Inquiry*, 20, 421–440.

Beebe, B. (2003). Brief mother–infant treatment: psychoanalytically informed video feedback. *Infant Mental Health Journal*, 24(1), 24–52.

Bowlby, J. (1977). The making and breaking of affectional bonds. *British Journal of Psychiatry*, 130, 201–210 and 421–431.

Cicchetti, D., Toth, S. L. and Rogosch, F. A. (1999). The efficacy of toddler–parent psychotherapy to increase attachment security in offspring of depressed mothers. *Attachment and Human Development*, 1(1), 34–66.

Cohen, N., Muir, E. *et al.* (1999). Watch, wait, and wonder: testing the effectiveness of a new approach to mother–infant psychotherapy. *Infant Mental Health Journal*, 20(4), 429–451.

Cohen, N. J., Lojkasek, M., Muir, E., Muir, R. and Parker, R. (2002). Six month follow-up of two mother–infant psychotherapies: convergence of therapeutic outcomes. *Infant Mental Health Journal*, 23(4), 361–380.

Crittenden, P. M. (1999). Danger and development: the organisation of self-protective strategies. In J. I. Vondra and D. Barnett (eds), *Atypical Attachment in Infancy and Early Childhood among Children at Developmental Risk* (pp. 145–171). Oxford: Blackwell.

Fonagy, P. (1998). Prevention, the appropriate target of infant psychotherapy. *Infant Mental Health Journal*, 19(2), 124–150.

Fonagy, P. and Newbury, J. (2007). Unpublished research findings.

Fonagy, P., Gergely, G., Jurist, E. and Target, M. (2001). *Affect Regulation, Mentalization and the Development of the Self.* New York: Other Press.

Fonagy, P., Sadie, C. and Allison, L. (2002). *The Parent–Infant Project (PIP) outcome study*. Anna Freud Centre, London (unpublished manuscript).

Gerhardt, S. (2004). *Why Love Matters: How Affection Shapes a Baby's Brain.* Hove: Brunner-Routledge.

Grubler-Gochman, E. (1995). *Psychotherapy for Mothers and Infants: Interventions for Dyads at Risk.* Westport, CT: Praeger Publishers.

Hoffman, L. (2003). Mothers' ambivalence with their babies and toddlers: manifestations of conflicts with aggression. *Journal of the American Psychoanalytic Association*, 51, 1219–1240.

Kenrick, J., Lindsey, C. and Tollemache, L. (2006). *Creating New Families: Therapeutic Approaches to Fostering, Adoption, and Kinship Care*. Tavistock Clinic Series. London: Karnac.

Luborsky, L., Rosenthal, R., Diguer, L., Andrusyna, T. P., Berman, J. S., Levitt, J. T. *et al.* (2002). The Dodo bird verdict is alive and well – mostly. *Clinical Psychology: Science and Practice*, 9(1), 2–12.

Lyons-Ruth, K. and Jacobvitz, D. (1999). Attachment disorganization: unresolved loss, relational violence, and lapses in behavioral and attentional strategies. In J. Cassidy and P. Shaver (eds), *Handbook of Attachment: Theory, Research, and Clinical Applications*. New York: Guilford Press.

Main, M. and Hesse, E. (1992). Disorganised/disoriented infant behavior in the Strange Situation, lapses in the monitoring of reasoning and discourse during the parent's Adult Attachment Interview, and dissociative states. In M. Ammaniti and D. Ster (eds), *Attachment and Psychoanalysis* (pp. 86–140). Rome: Gius, Laterza and Figli.

Maldonado-Duran, J. M. (2002). *Infant and Toddler Mental Health: Models of Clinical Intervention with Infants and Their Families*. Washington, DC: American Psychiatric Publishing.

Maldonado-Duran, J. M., Garcia, J. M. S., Lartigue, T. and Karacostas, V. (2002). Infant mental health, new evidence. *Infant Mental Health Journal*, 25(6), 59–67.

Meins, E. (1999). Sensitivity, security, and internal working models: bridging the transmission gap. *Attachment and Human Development*, 1(3), 325–342.

Palacio, F. and Serpa, S. (2002). Parent–infant psychotherapies in early behaviour problems. Paper presented at the World Association for Infant Mental Health, 8th Congress, Amsterdam.

Parker, R. (1996). *Mother Love, Mother Hate: The Power of Maternal Ambivalence*. New York: Perseus Books.

Robert-Tissot, C., Cramer, B., Stern, D. *et al.* (1996). Outcome evaluation in brief mother–infant psychotherapies: report on 75 cases. *Infant Mental Health Journal*, 17(2) 97–114.

Schore, A. N. (1994). *Affect Regulation and the Origins of the Self*. Hillsdale, NJ: Lawrence Erlbaum Associates.

Schore, A. N. (2001). The effects of a secure attachment relationship on right brain development, affect regulation and infant mental health. *Infant Mental Health Journal*, 22, 7–66.

Schore, A. N. (2004). *Affect Dysregulation and Disorders of the Self*. New York: W. W. Norton.

Sroufe, L. A., Egeland, B., Carlson, E. and Collins, W. A. (2005). *The Development of the Person: The Minnesota Study of Risk and Adaptation from Birth to Adulthood*. New York: Guilford Publications.

Tronick, E. Z. and Weinberg, M. K. (1997). Depressed mothers and infants: failure to establish dyadic states of consciousness. In L. Murray and P. J. Cooper (eds), *Post Partum Depression and Child Development*. London: Guilford Press.

Winnicott, D. M. (1960). The theory of the parent infant relationship. In *The Maturational Process and Facilitating Environment*. London: Hogarth Press and Institute of Psycho-Analysis.

Winnicott, D. M. (1965). The relationship of the mother to her baby at the beginning. In *The Family and Individual Development*. London: Tavistock Publications.

13 Mellow Babies

Mellow Parenting with parents of infants

Christine Puckering

Progress in our understanding of the development of the infant brain has finally clarified a mystery: how can things of which we have no memory have a long-lasting influence on us? Progress in scanning and imaging babies' brains, and evidence of long-term poor brain development in children who have been abused (Chugani *et al.*, 2001; De Bellis *et al.*, 1999; De Bellis, 2001; Teicher *et al.*, 2003; De Bellis and Kuchibhatia, 2006; Perry *et al.*, 1996) and in children who have experienced severe neglect, such as the Romanian orphans (Chugani *et al.*, 2001), have shown that these early experiences become enduring as a result of their influence on the development of the baby's brain. Pathways that are used become strengthened, while those that are not used wither away. These effects shape the structure and function of the brain, which become increasingly difficult to change as the child matures (National Research Council Institute of Medicine, 2000). By age 3, the child's brain has reached almost its full adult size. What happens in the first three years is therefore critical. Evidence about the shaping of the brain by sensory and interactive experiences has clarified, for example, the mechanism by which infant-centred maternal speech at 6 weeks of age can lead to good later social, emotional and educational development, while the children of depressed mothers who are not able to be child-centred in their talk fare less well, years later (Murray *et al.*, 1993). It had always seemed inherently implausible that words spoken before a child could understand them could be so influential, but if the involvement of the mother in understanding the baby's sensations and reactions is a marker of attunement which continues over the following months, then the effects are potentially profound.

This chapter describes the development of a new group-based parenting programme aimed at supporting postnatally depressed mothers and their newborn babies. The Mellow Parenting programme, from which Mellow Babies evolved, has been used to support a wide range of very vulnerable mothers. This chapter describes how the Mellow Babies programme developed from the now widely evaluated Mellow Parenting programme, and what the programme involves. The chapter concludes with a description of a recent waiting-list controlled evaluation of one of the first Mellow Babies groups.

The evidence base for the development of a new programme

Evidence had been accumulating over some decades that the children of depressed mothers fared less well behaviourally, emotionally, socially and intellectually. They showed higher rates of behavioural and emotional disorders (Weissman *et al.*, 1984). Specifically they had higher rates of depression and, in particular, early onset of depression (Weissman *et al.*, 1987), but also higher rates of all types of behavioural problems (Cummings and Davies, 1994). The mechanism by which these long-term adverse effects arose was not clear, however, until technology allowed us to see the way in which these early experiences can influence the baby's developing brain. Specifically, this research showed that the infants of depressed mothers had greatly reduced brain activity and, perhaps most significantly, lower levels of activity in the left frontal cortex which is associated with the expression of strong emotions including joy and anger (Dawson *et al.*, 2001). This evidence suggests that the infants had developed a muted and undemanding interpersonal response.

As well as the emotional and social difficulties these children experienced, there was evidence that children's cognitive development was impaired. Children of depressed mothers had lower IQs than children of mothers without depression, although the effects were more marked for male children and in the presence of other risk factors such as poverty, low birth weight and low parental educational attainment (Cogill *et al.*, 1986; Hay and Kumar, 1995; Sharp *et al.*, 1995).

Perhaps most importantly, evidence also showed that treating the mother's depression after the first year of life did not protect babies from the long-term consequences of maternal depression (Cogill *et al.*, 1986). Furthermore, the research showed that while treating maternal depression could be an effective means of improving maternal mental health, treating the mother alone was insufficient to improve the mother–child relationship and all that hinges on this early foundation (Cooper *et al.*, 2003; Murray *et al.*, 2003).

Development of the Mellow Babies programme

The Mellow Babies programme was developed from the Mellow Parenting programme, which has been described and evaluated elsewhere (Puckering *et al.*, 1994, 1996). The programme was modified to make it specifically applicable to women with postnatal depression and their babies under 1 year of age. The Mellow Babies programme was initially developed and evaluated in Coatbridge in North Lanarkshire in Scotland as part of their Investing in Infancy programme. Women in Lanarkshire are routinely screened by their health visitors at six weeks postnatally using the Edinburgh Postnatal Depression Scale (EPDS; Cox *et al.*, 1987), and those scoring high on this scale are offered non-directive counselling (listening visits) by their health visitors. All women are again screened at around fourteen weeks postnatally, and those still scoring above the threshold of 10 on the EPDS, consistent with possible postnatal depression, are offered referral to adult mental health services. Many women prefer not to be referred to adult mental health services, perhaps because of stigma or because of reluctance to take medication, although many of them feel comfortable about consulting their general practitioner. Since 2001, women with elevated EPDS scores at the second screening have been offered the opportunity to attend a Mellow Babies group.

Mellow Babies

In parallel with the Mellow Parenting programme, Mellow Babies consists of one full day a week for fourteen weeks, but it is directed at mothers with babies under 1 year of age. The morning group session is targeted at women's own experiences of parenting, their self-esteem and also any mental health problems they might be experiencing. During this session the babies are cared for in a crèche. As well as the obvious depression, many of the women show high levels of anxiety. In some cases this has reached a level where it is difficult for them to leave the house, compounded by the demands of looking after a young baby. Broken sleep, tiredness and the logistics of getting babies ready to go out provide reasons for staying at home. In some cases, however, the level of anxiety can reach phobic dimensions, partly social phobia and partly agoraphobia. In addition, many women show high levels of obsessional and compulsive thinking. With the arrival of a new baby, fears for the baby's well-being and an awareness of hygiene and safety may take on new salience, but for some mothers this can reach a disabling intensity. All these issues can and do arise in the group discussions, and simple worksheets and exercises based on cognitive behavioural models are used to help mothers challenge negative automatic thoughts. At first the group is used to challenge the negative thoughts. This is reinforced by 'homework' sheets which help mothers to practise new ways of thinking at home when the mother has a bad day. After doing this, one mother reported feeling down but challenging herself by reflecting, 'What would the group say to me about this?'

It is notable that many of the mothers have great difficulties leaving their babies in the crèche. For some, this is the first time their baby has been left in the care of someone other than immediate family members. The level of their anxiety, often centring around the safety of the baby, is sometimes evident in their difficulty in relaxing while their baby is being cared for, even though the crèche room is just across the corridor from the mothers' room. It is also evident in the babies' behaviour that separation is already an issue for them. As the age of onset of stranger anxiety often coincides with the timing of the group this may reflect a developmental norm. One mother began the process of being able to be separate from her now 1-year-old daughter – leading to her weaning from the breast and sleeping through the night – after feeling trapped and tied down. She reported that she now believed her daughter could survive infancy and so she could relax and enjoy her company. She was also able to celebrate and support her older daughter starting school, a milestone she had dreaded. She took pride in this because prior to the group she had felt that her own fears would hold back her daughter's confidence in starting school.

At lunchtime, mothers, babies and staff get together to share a meal and also to share activities that bring mothers and babies into playful interaction with each other. The content of the lunchtime activities includes baby massage, looking at picture books, singing songs and lap games, interactive coaching, and any activity that will bring mothers and babies face-to-face. These sessions are aimed at developing attuned face-to-face interactions and a repertoire of enjoyable activities. Remarkable changes can be seen quickly in the babies, who initially seem to be a particularly passive group. Research, using the 'still face paradigm', has shown that the babies of undepressed mothers become distressed if their mother makes her face go blank and unresponsive, while the babies of depressed mothers do not react adversely, suggesting that they are already accustomed to diminished interaction (Tronick and Gianino, 1986). It seems likely that some of the babies in the Mellow Babies groups have already accommodated to rather low levels of interaction. Mothers were often able to cuddle and comfort their babies but the level of stimulation and entertainment they were able to provide was low. One mother was able to reflect, at the end of the group, that she realised that lying on the sofa cuddling the baby was comforting for her, but that the child needed more than just passive contact. In another instance, the psychologist who was conducting the pre-group assessments reported that she thought one of the babies could be developmentally delayed because she was so passive. Within three weeks in the group, however, this baby had become more alert and more responsive. It emerged that the mother, although having perfect hearing herself, had been a child of two parents who were both profoundly deaf. She was therefore unused to the idea that babies should be talked to and might be interested in verbal communication because it had not been part of her experience. It was obvious from her videotape, where the loudest noise was the humming of the spin-drier in the kitchen, that the environment of the baby was very low in verbal stimulation. Within three weeks this baby had begun to respond to a more active interactive style, and had become more alert, and thereby more effective in eliciting chat and conversation from her mother.

Babies quickly learn the routine that lunch will be followed by songs and games, and sit expectantly, demonstrating their readiness for these activities. One little boy who particularly enjoyed a bouncing rhyme, which involved being gently tipped backwards at the end of the rhyme, several times almost threw himself off his mother's knee in anticipation of the activity he enjoyed so much! Fraiberg (1987) refers to the baby as the co-therapist. It is evident that the flexibility of the baby in adapting to and making the best of the environment can lead to the development of a maladaptive style if the environment is not optimal. Field *et al.* (1988) showed that the infants of depressed mothers carried over a depressed style of interaction to their communication with non-depressed adults. This led to the striking realisation that while such babies might seem contented, this pattern of relating might carry the seeds of poor later outcomes.

In the afternoon the babies are returned to the crèche while the mothers analyse their own videotapes, looking for instances of success in engaging the child and mutual enjoyment, but also seeking the support of the group in tackling difficulties. Child development, child safety, and child health are covered, following a curriculum about the six dimensions of parenting that is fundamental to Mellow Parenting, but also led by the mothers' own interests and questions. For example, mothers may begin to question whether watching television is a suitable activity for under-ones, and this can be openly discussed. Anecdotal evidence suggests that while there is considerable overlap of appropriate topics between groups run for mothers with postnatal depression and those run for families where there are child protection concerns, the former often focus on the management of the mother's mental health, while the latter may need more basic childcare information on babies' crying, sleeping, or weaning, and recognising and responding effectively to childhood illness. The aim is to make the sessions active and they involve minimal formal didactic content within an overall structured curriculum. Views and discussion are elicited from the mothers themselves, with some input where helpful and where accessible information and audio-visual materials are available. The Baby Cue cards (NCAST, 2006) are a popular and accessible way to engage parents in learning to 'read' and respond to their own baby's signals. The normalising of the intense feelings aroused by new babies, and the opportunity to reveal that they are not the perfect, smiling mother of the glossy magazines, can be therapeutic in itself. Many of the women fear that they lack the natural feelings for their baby that they should have, and that if they speak about depression in the period when they are expected to be 'glowing' they might have their baby removed from their care.

As part of the package, three evening sessions are set up for fathers. These are extremely well attended and welcomed by the fathers who are clearly bemused and bewildered as to why their partners have become depressed and what they might be able to do to improve the situation. The fathers are often the target of the irritability that frequently accompanies the mothers' depression. Psychoeducational material about postnatal depression, feedback from the mothers themselves about what the fathers could do to help, and opportunities for the fathers to try out the same activities with the babies as their wives/partners do in the group, can all be helpful. The majority of fathers are very involved and even if they are working will set aside time as soon as they come home to be with the baby. As one father said, 'even if she is crying and irritable when I get home, that is my time with her'. Some fathers are less eager to be involved, seeing childcare as the responsibility of their partner and being reluctant to participate after their own long day at work. To engage these fathers, a 'Dad's Challenge' can be set up in which the dads have to change the baby's nappy, feed the baby a fromage frais, and make the baby laugh. One mother, whose partner was no longer in the family home, set herself up as the 'referee' and scored the fathers on the categories of time, cleanliness and style! Making the issue of childcare both fun and familiar was very fruitful in terms of engaging previously disengaged dads in interacting with their babies.

Evaluation of Mellow Babies

The very first Mellow Babies group was evaluated using a matched control group, and the results were striking. Mothers showed a significant reduction in their reporting of depressed mood on the Edinburgh Postnatal Depression Scale. Positive interaction, coded by independent psychologists who did not know whether the videos they were watching were 'before' or 'after' videos, showed a dramatic increase on almost all the measures of positive interaction of mothers and babies. In terms of negative interaction, which was comparatively rare, while there was little change in the Mellow Babies group, the negative interaction in the control group had actually increased over the same time period. In other words, Mellow Babies appeared to have prevented the deterioration in mother–child interaction that had occurred without intervention over the course of four to five months. Ten out of twelve measures of interaction changed in a direction that favoured the Mellow Babies group over the waiting-list control group.

Feedback from the mothers was extremely positive, reflecting not only their greater self-esteem and feelings of self-worth, but also their understanding of the importance of interacting with their babies. Some mothers who had babies on the Child Protection Register talked about having strategies to put the baby somewhere safe when they themselves felt out of control. Some mothers who had had problems with agoraphobia reported that they were now able to go out.

At the end of the group several mothers chose to go on to community education classes. Some mothers supported each other to attend parent and toddler groups together. These resources had always been available, but the women had lacked the confidence to walk through the door of a strange building into a group of people they did not know; they were happy to do so, though, when accompanied by another group member. Some group members were able to return to work after lengthy periods of sick leave.

The women who attended the mothers and babies group, although in an area of high social deprivation, were somewhat better placed than previous samples evaluated in Mellow Parenting groups. Most of the families were still intact, although it was easy to see that the corrosive effects of the mother's low mood and irritability would imperil their relationship with their partner over time. In addition, the majority of the fathers were working and, although not well-off, the families were not socially excluded in a wider sense. However, in group discussions, extraordinary levels of adverse childhood events emerged. Three out of seven mothers in one group had experienced the loss of a sibling in early childhood or late teenage years. Several of the mothers reported neglectful and abusive experiences in their own childhood. This is perhaps not unexpected given that research has shown that loss of a significant figure during childhood can lead to later depression (Brown and Harris, 1978).

Previous randomised controlled trials of intervention for postnatal depression (Cooper *et al.*, 2003; Murray *et al.*, 2003) have shown short-term effects on mothers' feelings of depression, although limited effects on the mother–baby relationship. This study has shown specific effects on the mother–baby relationship and also that, without intervention, things do not stand still, they deteriorate. However, this was a very small study, with twelve mothers in total, and did not include long-term follow-up. It is, however, a very promising start in influencing mother–baby interaction in the context of postnatal depression. The long-term effects of Mellow Parenting for preschool children have been demonstrated, with one-year and seven-year follow-ups showing maintenance of beneficial effects.

Mellow Babies and hard-to-reach families

The Mellow Babies programme has also been used in the context of child abuse and neglect with extraordinarily high levels of engagement of these most vulnerable families and positive effects in terms of babies being returned to the care of their parents (i.e. from a care situation), and removal of some babies from child care measures altogether.

Why has Mellow Babies been so effective? Careful preparation of the mothers for engagement is essential. The first contact with the mother is in her own home. The practitioner gives the mother an information sheet but also reads the content aloud as a matter of course. This ensures that no one is exposed by poor literacy, which is a humiliating experience for an adult. By the end of this first visit, it is expected that the mother will be fully informed about the intervention and will have been able to formulate what she wants to get from joining the group. Strong efforts are made to help the mother to decide a goal for her baby, and also for herself. It might be as simple as getting out of the house and meeting other mums, but the dual emphasis on the mother as a person as well as on the parenting is established right from the start. Practical problem solving about transport and childcare is also tackled and, if need be, taxis are arranged to support attendance. Although the aim is generally to avoid coercion, once mothers have indicated a wish to attend, every effort is made to facilitate attendance, including helping the mother to plan her day to meet the needs of older children who might be in nursery or school. Particularly in child protection services, some mothers are mandated to attend as part of child welfare goals. This might seem contrary to good practice, but by being honest and also making the group welcoming with a pleasant ambience, lunch, and time for themselves, in addition to support for good contact with their baby, even mothers under duress to attend begin to relax and enjoy their day. By week 3 it is very unusual for mothers to drop out, except for unavoidable reasons, such as moving house or serious illness.

Conclusion

The Mellow Babies group intervention can improve both the mental health of women with postnatal depression and their interaction with their babies. The combination of support for mothers and well directed intervention in the relationship itself is one that is likely to prove fruitful but requires further exploration, and particularly long-term follow-up. Future research should include the conduct of larger trials but should also focus on testing out the longer-term progress of these babies, for whom the prognosis was poor without intervention. Mellow Babies costs somewhere in the region of £1,000 (at 2007 prices) per family, including staff training, ongoing supervision, staff time, premises, crèche and catering. While this may sound high, the cost of later mental health services for the women and their children, in addition to the savings resulting from keeping children out of statutory childcare or avoiding the costs of youth justice services, would pay for the intervention several times over.

References

Brown, G. and Harris, T. (1978). *The Social Origins of Depression: A Study of Psychiatric Disorder in Children.* New York: Free Press.

Chugani, H. T., Behen, M. E., Muzik, O., Juhasz, C., Nagy, F. and Chugani, D. C. (2001). Local brain functional activity following early deprivation: a study of postinstitutionalized Romanian orphans. *NeuroImage*, 14, 1290–1301.

Cogill, S. R., Caplan, H. L., Alexandra, H., Robson, K. M. and Kumar, R. (1986). Impact of maternal postnatal depression on cognitive development of young children. *British Medical Journal (Clinical Research Edn)*, 292(6529), 1165–1167.

Cooper, P. J., Murray, L., Wilson, A. and Romaniuk, H. (2003). Controlled trial of the short- and long-term effect of psychological treatment of post-partum depression. I. Impact on maternal mood. *British Journal of Psychiatry*, 182, 412–419.

Cox, J. L., Holden, J. M. and Sagovsky, R. (1987). Detection of postnatal depression: development of the 10-item Edinburgh Postnatal Depression Scale. *British Journal of Psychiatry*, 150, 782–786.

Cummings, E. M. and Davies, P. T. (1994). Maternal depression and child development. *Journal of Child Psychology and Psychiatry*, 35, 73–112.

Dawson, G., Osterling, J., Meltzoff, A. N. and Kuhl, P. (2001). Case study of the development of an infant with autism from birth to two years of age. *Journal of Applied Developmental Psychology*, 21(3), 299–313.

De Bellis, M. D. (2001). Developmental traumatology: the psychobiological development of maltreated children and its implications for research, treatment and policy. *Development and Psychopathology*, 13, 539–564.

De Bellis, M. D. and Kuchibhatia, M. (2006). Cerebella volumes in pediatric maltreatment-related post-traumatic stress disorder. *Biological Psychiatry*, 60(7), 697–703.

De Bellis, M. D., Keshavan, M. S., Clark, D. B., Caseey, B. J., Giedd, J. B., Boring, A. M., Furstaci, K. and Ryan, N. D. (1999). Developmental traumatology, part 2: brain development. *Biological Psychiatry*, 45, 1271–1284.

Field, T., Healy, B., Goldstein, S., Perry, S., Bendall, D., Schanberg, S., Zimmerman, E. and Kuhn, C. (1988). Infants of depressed mothers show 'depressed' behavior even with nondepressed adults. *Child Development*, 59, 1569–1579.

Fraiberg, S. H. (1987). *The Magic Years: Understanding and Handling the Problems of Early Childhood.* New York: Scribner Book Company.

Hay, D. F. and Kumar, R. (1995). Interpreting the effects of mother's postnatal depression on children's intelligence: a critique and re-analysis. *Child Psychiatry and Human Development*, 25, 165–181.

Murray, L., Kempton, C., Woolgar, M. and Hooper, R. (1993). Depressed mothers' speech to their infants and its relation to infant gender and cognitive development. *Journal of Child Psychology and Psychiatry and Allied Disciplines*, 34(7), 1083–1101.

Murray, L., Cooper, P. J., Wilson, A. and Romaniuk, H. (2003). Controlled trial of the short- and long-term effect of psychological treatment of post-partum depression: 2. Impact on the mother–child relationship and child outcome. *British Journal of Psychiatry*, 182, 420–427.

National Research Council Institute of Medicine (2000). *From Neurons to Neighborhoods: The Science of Early Childhood Development.* Washington, DC: National Academy Press.

NCAST (2006). Baby Cues: a child's first language. University of Washington, Seattle. www.ncast.org.

Perry, B. D., Pollard, R. A., Blakley, T. L., Baker, W. L. and Vigilante, D. (1996). Childhood trauma, the neurobiology of adaptation and use dependent development of the brain: how states become traits. *Infant Mental Health Journal*, 16(4), 271–291.

Puckering, C., Rogers, J., Mills, M., Cox, A. D. and Mattsson-Graff, M. (1994). Process and evaluation of a group intervention for mothers with parenting difficulties. *Child Abuse Review*, 3(4), 299–310.

Puckering, C., Evans, J., Maddox, H., Mills, M. and Cox, A. D. (1996). Taking control: a single case study of mellow parenting. *Clinical Child Psychology and Psychiatry*, 1(4), 539–550.

Sharp, D., Hay, D. F., Pawlby, S., Schmucker, G., Allan, H. and Kumar, R. (1995). The impact of postnatal depression on boys' intellectual development. *Journal of Child Psychology and Psychiatry*, 36, 1315–1337.

Teicher, M. H., Andersen, S. L., Polcari, A., Anderson, C. M., Navalta, C. P. and Kim, D. M. (2003). The neurobiological consequences of early stress and childhood maltreatment. *Neuroscience and Biobehavioral Reviews*, 27, 33–44.

Tronick, E. Z. and Gianino, A., Jr (1986). The transmission of maternal disturbance to the infant. In E. Z. Tronick and T. Field (eds), *Maternal Depression and Infant Disturbance* (pp. 5–11). San Francisco: Jossey-Bass.

Weissman, M. M., Prusoff, B. A., Gammon, G. D., Merikangas, K. R., Leckman, J. F. and Kidd, K. K. (1984). Psychology in the children (aged 6–18) of depressed and normal parents. *Journal of the American Academy of Child Psychiatry*, 23(1), 78–84.

Weissman, M. M., Gammon, G. D., John, K., Merikangas, K. R., Warner, V., Prusoff, B. A. and Sholomskas, D. (1987). Children of depressed parents. Increased psychopathology and early onset of major depression. *Archives of General Psychiatry*, 44, 847–853.

14 Enhancing the relationship between mothers with severe mental illness and their infants

Susan Pawlby and Charles Fernyhough

Infants are entirely dependent for their health and well-being on those who care for them, and those whose mothers suffer from severe mental illness (SMI) are at risk if the care provided does not meet their developmental needs. In such instances, the long-term implications for the child and the next generation of children are potentially devastating.

One of the challenges of working with mothers with severe mental illness is their psychological unavailability when they are very ill. The symptoms of their disorder may include disorganised speech or behaviour, flat affect, preoccupation with delusions or frequent auditory hallucinations, extreme negativism or mutism, disinhibition, grandiosity, repetitive rituals, irritability or aggression, all of which make it difficult for the mother to engage with others. Furthermore, mothers with SMI often lack insight into their disorder when they are acutely unwell and are unaware that their symptoms may make it difficult for them to give appropriate care to their infant. They are usually, however, totally committed to being a mother and providing for the infant to whom they have just given birth. The threat of being separated from the baby (Kumar *et al.*, 1995) makes the mother particularly anxious to show that she can care for and respond to her baby's needs.

This chapter will examine the role of a specialist mother and baby unit (MBU) in supporting mothers with SMI and their babies, using videotape feedback. The chapter begins by examining the evidence in relation to outcomes for babies of mothers with SMI, prior to a description of the work of the Channi Kumar Mother and Baby Unit at the Bethlem Royal Hospital in London. The chapter concludes by examining recent evidence about the effectiveness of the work of the unit.

Maternal mental illness and child development

There is now a substantial body of research showing the adverse impact of maternal prenatal and postnatal depression on the development and well-being of children and also adolescents. Evidence from longitudinal studies in the community shows that, compared to children of well mothers, the children of mothers suffering from mild-to-moderate depression or anxiety in the perinatal period are more likely to have increased behavioural, emotional and/or cognitive difficulties (Hay and Kumar, 1995; Murray *et al.*, 1999; Hay *et al.*, 2001, 2003; O'Connor *et al.*, 2002; Pawlby *et al.*, in press), which in turn have an adverse impact on the children's peer relationships and school attendance (Egger *et al.*, 2003). The outcomes for babies whose mothers have severe mental illness are, surprisingly, less well studied, possibly as a result of lower fertility rates in this group (Howard *et al.*, 2002) and because many babies of women with SMI are taken into care. Around 50 per cent of mothers with schizophrenia receiving in-patient psychiatric care in the postnatal period do not retain custody of their babies (Kumar *et al.*, 1995). We also know that these babies have a greatly increased risk of developing SMI themselves: in the case of schizophrenia, the risk is increased fifteen times if one parent has schizophrenia, and almost fifty times if both parents have schizophrenia (Corcoran *et al.*, 2005). In spite of the fact that the babies of women with SMI are at the greatest risk of any in society of developing SMI (Cannon *et al.*, 2002), there is very little research on whether the parenting skills of mothers with SMI are compromised as a result of their illness, and no clinical guidelines on the development of their parenting skills.

Maternal mental illness and mother–infant interaction

It is also becoming clear that early mother–infant interaction plays a significant role in terms of the later development of children. Observational studies have shown that women with postnatal depression often have problems in relating to their new babies (Murray *et al.*, 1996). They may appear indifferent and withdrawn, finding it difficult to smile and talk to their babies, or they may be intrusive and over-stimulating and handle their babies roughly. The babies, in turn, may react by protesting and crying excessively or by becoming passive and avoidant (Weinberg and Tronick, 1998). Most observational studies of mother–infant interaction in psychosis have been limited to carer-report (and therefore non-blind) rating scales such as the Bethlem Mother–Infant Rating Scale (BMIS; Kumar and Hipwell, 1996). For example, Snellen *et al.* (1999) found that the BMIS scores of mothers with schizophrenia spectrum disorders admitted to an MBU with their babies improved between admission and discharge. One exception (Riordan *et al.*, 1999) compared the interaction of mothers with schizophrenia and that of mothers with an affective disorder on discharge from an MBU. Mothers with schizophrenia were more remote, insensitive, intrusive and self-absorbed and had babies who were more avoidant. The deficits in mother–infant interaction were not explained by measures of illness severity or factors relating to adverse social circumstances (Wan *et al.*, 2007).

One important feature of mother–infant relationships is the security of the attachment relationship (Ainsworth *et al.*, 1978). A small number of studies have examined the impact of maternal SMI on the baby's later attachment to the mother, with differing results. Naslund *et al.* (1984) and D'Angelo (1986) both found that infants of mothers with schizophrenia were more likely than healthy controls to receive insecure classifications in the Strange Situation (the standard laboratory assessment of attachment security in infancy). Jacobsen and Miller (1999) reported that, in a diagnostically diverse sample of thirty infant–mother pairs, only four demonstrated a secure attachment. Finally, in a study of twenty-five mothers (with a range of diagnoses) who had been in-patients at an MBU, Hipwell *et al.* (2000) found an association between depression, both psychotic and non-psychotic, and insecure attachment at 12 months.

Findings such as these suggest that early experiences with mothers suffering from mental illness may interfere with the infant's regulation of emotion and attention (Hill, 2004; Gerhardt, 2004), with cognitive and memory function (Hay, 1997), and with the ability to make self/other distinctions (Tronick and Weinberg, 1997), and may continue to exert direct effects on children's lives over a decade later (Murray *et al.*, 2002; Hay *et al.*, 2001, 2003).

The Mother and Baby Unit

The Channi Kumar Mother and Baby Unit (MBU) at the Bethlem Royal Hospital in south London is a twelve-bed unit where women suffering the onset or relapse of a severe mental illness (including major depressive disorder, postpartum psychosis, bipolar disorder, and schizophrenia) following childbirth are admitted with their babies, at any time from birth to 12 months. The multi-disciplinary team of psychiatrists, psychologists, nurses, occupational therapists, social workers and nursery nurses not only treat the mothers' mental health problems but at the same time give mothers the opportunity to promote their relationships with their babies and to develop their parenting skills.

One of the formal ways in which we support the mother in getting to know her baby is by inviting them to play together while we make a three-minute video-recording of the play session. This invitation is offered on admission, during the mother's stay on the MBU, and again on discharge. The mother is asked to place her baby in a baby seat or high chair with a mirror placed adjacent to the chair. The mother sits facing the baby on the opposite side to the mirror so that the camera captures a reflection of her face in the mirror and the baby is seen full on. Mothers are asked to play with or talk to their babies (median age 11 weeks, range 1 week to 100 weeks) as they would normally, preferably without the use of toys. On a separate occasion the mother is invited to view the play session. The aim of the feedback session is to make the experience as positive as possible for the mother and to build on the skills and strengths that she already has. The developmental psychologist encourages the mother to identify moments in the play session when she and the baby are engaged with one another. They may be looking at one another, however briefly, smiling at one another, jointly attending to an object, or imitating vocal sounds. Discussion may focus on the mother and baby taking turns. For example, the baby pokes his tongue out and mother imitates the gesture and together the imitative exchange continues. They are attentive to one another and absorbed in their dialogue. Mother begins to see the baby as another human being and learns to observe his/her behaviours and respond to his/her cues. At other times the interaction may have broken down. This can give the mother an opportunity to reflect on what the baby does not like, or on what aspects of her behaviour might be leading to fretful or avoidant responses from the baby. Together the mother and psychologist try to interpret the baby's cues so that the mother can enhance her ability to respond appropriately. The recordings themselves can be used to chart the development of the mother–baby relationship over the period of admission to the MBU (see Chapter 9).

Some of the mothers find the prospect of having a video record of the interactions between themselves and their babies anxiety-provoking, but retrospectively acknowledge the benefits of watching themselves with their babies, and of discussing the ways in which their relationship develops as they begin to recover from their illness. Written consent is obtained from the mothers taking part in this intervention giving permission for us to use the video clips for assessment, teaching or research. They are given a copy of the video on discharge.

For research purposes the mother–infant pattern of interaction is evaluated using the CARE-Index (Crittenden, 2004), whereby both the mother and infant are evaluated on seven aspects of dyadic behaviour. The first four – facial expression, verbal expression, position and body contact, and affection – are assessments of affect within the dyad, while the final three – turn-taking contingencies, control, and choice of activity – refer to temporal contingencies. These ratings for the seven aspects of interactional behaviour contribute to one of seven specific scales, three for the mother – sensitive, controlling, unresponsive – and four for the child – cooperative, difficult, compulsive, passive. The central construct of sensitivity is a dyadic one. 'The adult's sensitivity in play is any pattern of behaviour that pleases the infant and increases the infant's comfort and attentiveness and reduces its distress and disengagement' (Crittenden, 2004: 3).

A case study

Janet had had schizophrenia since the age of 18. She was admitted to the MBU at the age of 42, following a relapse after the birth of her sixth child, Bryony. The eldest three children were cared for by their father and the younger two were in foster care while their mother was in hospital. Janet was suffering from paranoid delusions and had negative features of schizophrenia. She had poor insight into her illness and was at risk of non-compliance with medication and further relapse. She found it extremely difficult to respond to Bryony's emotional needs, although she was able to provide all her physical care. On admission she did not soothe, talk to or smile at Bryony, nor did she respond to her cues, but sat completely impassive, only raising her eyes upwards when the baby made a sound. Bryony was also passive, but on occasions she would turn to her mother for some response. When this was not forthcoming Bryony's facial expression began to crumble, and she became restless, until eventually she let out a cry. This was not a loud, demanding cry, but rather a restrained 'bleat'. It was as though Bryony had already learned that crying, which was her only means of attracting her mother's attention, did not produce the desired effect. She was helpless.

As Janet recovered from the acute phase of her illness, she became aware that she might not be able to look after her baby herself. In one of the play sessions she said to Bryony (aged 14 weeks): 'I don't want you to go into foster care. They won't look after you properly. You need to be at home with your real mother... Do you miss your brother and sister? ... What do you want me to say to you? I love you.'

Janet and Bryony participated in five video feedback sessions during an eleven-week stay on the ward. During these sessions, the mother was encouraged to converse with her baby, by using the baby's name to gain her attention, by asking questions, pausing, repeating the questions, and allowing time for Bryony to respond. In this way Janet and Bryony began to have conversations. At 18 weeks they had begun to make visible improvements in the way in which they communicated with one another. 'Bryony, why are you dribbling?' Bryony looks up at her mother's face and smiles. There is eye contact and mutual smiling. 'Are you having your teeth coming out?' Pause. 'Are you having your teeth?' Pause. 'What is your favourite food?' Bryony vocalises. 'What do you like best?' Bryony vocalises. Janet and Bryony are engrossed in a dialogue with one another. They are communicating. They are learning to understand one another. The process by which they do this is dynamic, reciprocal and important for the development of the child.

Janet and Bryony were discharged together from the ward at 20 weeks.

Measuring the effectiveness of interventions with mothers with SMI and their infants

From a clinical perspective there is an urgent need to support the mother and her infant in their interaction as part of the treatment and management of mothers with different diagnoses of SMI, while from a research perspective we need to ascertain whether there are differences in interaction style between the diagnostic groups, and how these compare with the interaction in a healthy comparison group. Furthermore we need to document the interaction both during the acute phase of the mother's illness and when she becomes well enough to be discharged from hospital, in order to identify possible intervention strategies.

Beginning in 2000, video clips of mothers at play with their infants have been recorded, as described above, on admission to and discharge from the Channi Kumar MBU, and these have provided evidence about the mothers' developing relationships with their infants. Initial results from a pilot study of forty-nine mothers with SMI, playing with their infants, showed that compared to depressed mothers and babies (N=23) and a group of twenty-two well dyads, those with schizophrenia (N=8) or a postpartum psychosis (N=18) were less sensitive and responsive on admission and their babies were more passive and less cooperative as rated by an independent psychologist trained in using the CARE-Index (Crittenden, 2004). At discharge the mothers with SMI were more sensitive and responsive than on admission, while their babies were more cooperative and less passive, and there were no differences when compared with the well mothers and babies (Pawlby *et al.*, 2005).

The decision about discharge from the MBU is made on the basis of the combined information provided by the members of the multi-disciplinary team. Thus the mother's mental health is assessed, along with her ability to cope in the community and the provision of adequate support. The mother's relationship with her baby and her ability to provide the necessary physical and emotional care for her baby also contribute to the decision to recommend discharge. The evidence provided from the videotaped play sessions on admission and discharge helps to inform this decision. It is not clear whether it is the improvement in the mother's mental health symptoms or the feedback sessions between the mother and psychologist that lead to the observed improvement in the interactive skills of both mother and baby over the period of admission to the MBU. However, we do know from most mothers that they welcome the opportunity to discuss their feelings for their baby and explore their relationship.

In line with the clinical summary in the NICE guidelines (NICE, 2007: 193) we feel that providing an intervention that specifically aims to improve mother–infant interactions is an important part of the work done by any mother and baby unit. To our knowledge this is the only study that has examined the interaction between mothers with SMI and their infants through direct observation on both admission and discharge. In circumstances such as this it is difficult, if not unethical, to conduct a trial whereby some mothers are offered video feedback and others are not. However, our findings suggest that mothers with SMI and their babies become more sensitive and responsive to one another over the period of admission.

There has been no formal cost analysis of this intervention, but mothers appear to find it an acceptable form of help and early evidence suggests that it is an effective means of supporting mothers with SMI. If we can identify (possibly diagnosis-specific) aspects of the mother–infant interaction that differentiate dyads where the mother has SMI from well dyads, intervention trials can be carried out. If successful in enhancing the mother–child relationship these interventions can become routine, and possibly reduce the number of mother–infant separations, with the high financial costs of possible foster placement for the child and the untold suffering for families that results.

Conclusion

We know that the long-term impact of a mother's mental illness on her child is often deleterious and thus it is imperative that support is given very early on, following the birth of a baby where the mother has SMI. This chapter shows the way in which the work of a mother and baby unit can improve patient care for women whose needs following the birth of a child frequently go unmet and who are often prevented from parenting their own children. Ongoing data collection on the MBU will give us the opportunity of replicating the findings from the pilot study and of extending the analyses to explore more precisely how mothers with SMI develop their relationships with their babies. This work will focus on mothers' use of mental-state language to comment appropriately on their infants' putative emotions and mental states/processes (Meins *et al.*, 2001), already found to be a better predictor of infant–mother attachment security than maternal sensitivity. This focus on observable mother- and infant-centred interactional behaviours will help to counter the existing emphasis on symptomatology and the severity of the psychiatric disorder, and potentially biased clinician-rated assessments of parenting competence, as predictors of parenting outcomes. Future work should also aim to relate these findings to evidence about the infant–mother attachment relationship in the second year of life, which has been shown to be predictive of the child's subsequent development. The long-term aim of such research should be to identify as early as possible in the first year of life specific parenting problems in women with a psychotic disorder, in order to plan targeted interventions. Currently there is no research in this area.

Findings from this type of research will provide the evidence base for specific intervention programmes aimed at supporting parents experiencing severe mental illness in developing their relationships with their infants and providing 'good-enough' care to ensure the improved mental health and academic performance of the next generation who are already genetically vulnerable. Liaison with community mental health teams in delivering ongoing support following the mother's discharge will further enhance the mother–child relationship, in addition to supporting mothers and babies who do not require hospitalisation but are treated in the community.

Acknowledgements

The authors would like to thank Dr Veronica O'Keane, the Consultant Perinatal Psychiatrist, Vita Shrinarine, the Clinical Nurse Leader and all the staff of the MBU for their parts not only in treating the mothers' illnesses but also in helping the mothers build their relationships with their babies. Thanks also go to the mothers and babies who have so graciously allowed us to watch the development of their relationships through a very stressful period of their lives.

References

Ainsworth, M., Blehar, M., Waters, E. and Wall, S. (1978). *Patterns of Attachment*. Hillsdale, NJ: Lawrence Erlbaum Associates.
Cannon, M., Caspi, A., Moffitt, T. E., Harrington, H.-L., Taylor, A., Murray, R. M. and Poulton, R. (2002). Evidence for early childhood, pan-developmental impairment specific to schizophreniform disorder: results from a longitudinal birth cohort. *Archives of General Psychiatry*, 59, 449–457.

Corcoran, C., Malaspina, D. and Hercher, L. (2005). Prodromal interventions for schizophrenia vulnerability: the risks of being 'at risk'. *Schizophrenia Research*, 73, 173–184.

Crittenden, P. M. (2004). *CARE-Index; Manual*. Miami: Family Relations Institute.

D'Angelo, E. J. (1986). Security of attachment in infants with schizophrenic, depressed, and unaffected mothers. *Journal of Genetic Psychology*, 147, 421–422.

Egger, H., Costello, E. J. and Angold, A. (2003). School refusal and psychiatric disorders: a community study. *Journal of the American Academy of Child and Adolescent Psychiatry*, 42, 797–807.

Gerhardt, S. (2004). *Why Love Matters. How Affection Shapes a Baby's Brain*. Hove: Brunner-Routledge.

Hay, D. F. (1997). Postpartum depression and cognitive development. In L. Murray and P. Cooper (eds), *Postpartum Depression and Child Development* (pp. 85–110). New York: Guilford Press.

Hay, D. F. and Kumar, R. (1995). Interpreting the effects of mothers' postnatal depression on children's intelligence: a critique and reanalysis. *Child Psychiatry and Human Development*, 25, 165–181.

Hay, D. F., Pawlby, S., Sharp, D., Asten, P., Mills, A. and Kumar, R. (2001). Intellectual problems shown by 11-year-old children whose mothers had postnatal depression. *Journal of Child Psychology and Psychiatry*, 42, 871–890.

Hay, D. F., Pawlby, S., Angold, A. Harold, G. and Sharp, D. (2003). Pathways to violence in the children of depressed mothers. *Developmental Psychology*, 39, 1083–1094.

Hill, J. (2004). Parental psychiatric disorder and the attachment relationship. In M. Gopfert, J. Webster and M. V. Seeman (eds), *Parental Psychiatric Disorder: Distressed Parents and their Families* (pp. 50-61). Cambridge: Cambridge University Press.

Hipwell, A. E., Goossens, F. A., Melhuish, E. C. and Kumar, R. (2000). Severe maternal psychopathology and infant–mother attachment. *Development and Psychopathology*, 12, 157–175.

Howard, L. M., Kumar, C., Leese, M. and Thornicroft, G. (2002). The general fertility rate in women with psychotic disorders. *American Journal of Psychiatry*, 159, 991–997.

Jacobsen, T. and Miller, L. J. (1999). Attachment quality in young children of mentally ill mothers. In J. Solomon and C. George (eds), *Attachment Disorganization* (pp. 347–378). New York: Guilford Press.

Kumar, R. and Hipwell, A. E. (1996). Development of a clinical rating scale to assess mother–infant interaction in a psychiatric mother and baby unit. *British Journal of Psychiatry*, 169, 18–26.

Kumar, R., Marks, M., Platz, C. and Yoshida, K. (1995). Clinical survey of a psychiatric mother and baby unit: characteristics of 100 consecutive admissions. *Journal of Affective Disorders*, 33, 11–22.

Meins, E., Fernyhough, C., Fradley, E. and Tuckey, M. (2001). Rethinking maternal sensitivity: mothers' comments on infants' mental processes predict security of attachment at 12 months. *Journal of Child Psychology and Psychiatry*, 42, 637–648.

Murray, L., Fiori-Cowley, A., Hooper, R. and Cooper, P. J. (1996). The impact of postnatal depression and associated adversity on early mother–infant interactions and later infant outcome. *Child Development*, 67, 2512–2526.

Murray, L., Sinclair, D., Cooper, P., Ducournau, P. and Turner, P. (1999). The socioemotional development of 5-year-old children of postnatally depressed mothers. *Journal of Child Psychology and Psychiatry*, 40, 1259–1271.

Murray, L., Cooper, P. and Hipwell, A. (2002). Mental health of parents caring for infants. *Archives of Women's Mental Health*, 6(Suppl. 2.), s71–s77.

Naslund, B., Persson-Blennow, I., McNeil, T., Kaij, L. and Malmquist-Larsson, A. (1984). Offspring of women with non-organic psychosis: infant attachment to the mother at one year of age. *Acta Psychiatrica Scandinavica*, 69, 231–241.

NICE (2007). *Antenatal and Postnatal Mental Health*. NICE Clinical Guideline 45 (p. 193). London: National Institute for Clinical Excellence.

O'Connor, T. G., Heron, J. and Glover, V. (2002). Antenatal anxiety predicts child behavioural/emotional problems independently of postnatal depression. *Journal of the American Academy of Child and Adolescent Psychiatry*, 41, 1470–1477.

Pawlby, S., Marks, M., Clarke, R., Best, E., Weir, D. and O'Keane, V. (2005). Mother-infant interaction in postpartum women with severe mental illness (SMI), before and after treatment. *Archives of Women's Mental Health*, 8, 120.

Pawlby, S., Hay, D. F., Sharp, D., Waters, C. S. and O'Keane, V. (in press) Antenatal depression predicts depression in adolescent offspring: prospective longitudinal community-based study. *Journal of Affective Disorders*.

Riordan, D., Appleby, L. and Faragher, B. (1999). Mother–infant interaction in post-partum women with schizophrenia and affective disorders. *Psychological Medicine*, 29, 991–995.

Snellen, M., Mack, K. and Trauer, T. (1999). Schizophrenia, mental state, and mother–infant interaction: examining the relationship. *Australian and New Zealand Journal of Psychiatry*, 33, 902–911.

Tronick, E. Z. and Weinberg, M. K. (1997). Depressed mothers and infants: failure to form dyadic states of consciousness. In L. Murray and P. Cooper (eds), *Postpartum Depression and Child Development* (pp. 54–81). New York: Guilford Press.

Wan, M. W., Salmon, M. P., Riordan, D. M., Appleby, L., Webb, R. and Abel, K. M. (2007). What predicts poor mother-infant interaction in schizophrenia? *Psychological Medicine*, 37, 537–546.

Weinberg, M. K. and Tronick, E. Z. (1998). The impact of maternal psychiatric illness on infant development. *Journal of Clinical Psychiatry*, 59, 53–61.

15 'Parenting with support'

Supporting parents with learning difficulties to parent

Beth Tarleton

Studies worldwide show that the removal rate of children from parents with learning difficulties who come into contact with services is up to 60 per cent (McConnell *et al.*, 2002). However, it is also becoming increasingly recognised that the outcome of foster care and being 'looked after' can be very negative, leading to social exclusion (HM Government, 2006). From a policy point of view it makes sense therefore to support parents with learning disabilities as much as possible without compromising the needs of the child or children.

However, there is evidence to suggest that the numbers of parents with learning difficulties are increasing and that their support needs are not being adequately met by health or social services (Booth, 2000). A national survey of adults with learning difficulties in England found that one in fifteen of the 2,898 adults interviewed were parents (Emerson *et al.*, 2005) but that 40 per cent of them were not living with their children (Emerson *et al.*, cited in DfES/DoH, 2007). There are no definite figures regarding the number of parents with learning difficulties in the UK, and many parents with mild learning difficulties are not eligible for support services and only come into contact with child protection services when others are concerned about their parenting.

Services in the UK, as well as elsewhere in the world (Llewellyn and McConnell, 2005), are, however, beginning to support adults with learning difficulties with their parenting, recognising that this may often be a better option for the child or children. This chapter discusses the emerging concept of 'parenting with support' in which adults with learning difficulties are provided with the support they need to ensure the well-being of their baby, and subsequently their growing child, to enable them to parent to the best of their abilities (Tarleton *et al.*, 2006).

In this chapter, the term *learning difficulties* is used to represent adults regarded as having a learning disability. These terms are often used interchangeably but generally refer to the 1.5 million adults in the UK who have an IQ of 75 or below (the average IQ in the general population being 100), and have ongoing difficulties with everyday life. This group of parents includes adults with mild or borderline learning difficulties, who may have attended a mainstream school and may only need a small amount of support in their everyday life, but who may need more support to ensure the welfare of a new baby.

Policy context

The literature shows that parents with learning difficulties who access services often have additional life circumstances, such as mental health support needs, poor housing, etc., that are having a negative impact on their parenting (Cleaver and Nicholson, 2007). However, the literature also shows that parents' learning difficulties do not necessarily negatively impact on their ability to parent unless the adult has an IQ of less than 60. When parents with learning difficulties are referred to child protection services, the concerns for the children's welfare are generally related to potential neglect, viewed by many as resulting from the lack of appropriate support, rather than any kind of deliberate abuse (Llewellyn *et al.*, 2003).

Current policy in England asserts that services should support parents with learning disabilities in order 'to ensure their children gain maximum life chance benefits' (DoH, 2001). Similarly, Scotland's review of services for people with learning disabilities, *The Same as You?*, stated that 'local authorities and NHS Trusts should make sure that the needs of parents with learning disabilities and their children are identified and met' (Scottish Executive, 2000).

Other policies concerning children and families, such as *Every Child Matters* (DfES, 2003) and the *National Service Framework for Children, Young People and Maternity Services* (DfES/DoH, 2004), provide a context in which it is presumed that children should be supported to stay with their families, and that parents with additional needs should receive the support they need.

The right of adults with learning difficulties to become parents is upheld by the Human Rights Act (1998: Article 8) and other recent legislation such as the Disability Equality duty under the Disability Discrimination Act, which states that disabled people, including parents with learning disabilities, should have equality of opportunity and that services should ensure appropriate adjustments are made to accommodate their needs. For parents with learning difficulties, this often means accessible information, so that they understand and meet their baby's needs, and access to an advocate, who can support them in their interactions with professionals concerned with the well-being of their child.

The provision of easy information, with pictures, short sentences and clear wording, and access to an advocate are two of the principles underpinning the recently published good practice guidance regarding working with parents with learning difficulties (DfES/DoH, 2007). The good practice guidance also states that adults and children's services and health and social care should develop clear processes and pathways in order to support parents appropriately. Long-term support should be provided to families, if necessary, and should meet the needs of both parents and children. If, however, families are involved with the child protection system, the guidance confirms that babies and children have the right to be protected from harm and that parents should be treated fairly.

Supporting families with learning difficulties

Recent work by Cleaver and Nicholson (2007) suggests that parents with learning difficulties are more likely than other parents to receive ongoing support from services, and that their child protection cases are more likely to remain open. This finding is consistent with recent literature which highlights that parents with learning difficulties can be supported to be 'good enough parents' through proactive, empowering support which is sensitive to the changing needs of the baby or child (McGaw and Newman, 2005; SCARE, 2005; Llewellyn and McConnell, 2005). Parents at the National Gathering of Parents with Learning Disabilities summarised the support they need:

- Accessible information about you and your baby's health, and how to look after your baby
- Self advocacy groups; coming together with other parents
- Getting support before things go wrong and become a crisis
- Being assessed in your own home, not in an unfamiliar residential family centre
- Assessment and support by people who understand learning disabilities
- Advocacy
- Making courts more accessible
- Support for fathers
- Support for women and men experiencing violent relationships

(CHANGE, 2005: 6–7)

This positive position has been welcomed by services and charities supporting adults with learning difficulties as well as by parents with learning difficulties themselves. Many workers in learning difficulty service contexts have already embraced the right of adults with learning difficulties to parent, and are attempting to provide the support they need.

However, these innovative and empowering services are developing in a wider societal context in which funding for family support and social services is limited, and in which social workers are experiencing considerable time pressures and are readily criticised for failing to protect children appropriately. The general public is also relatively ill-informed about the abilities of adults with learning difficulties, many people automatically assuming that they cannot parent and should have their babies/children taken away.

Recent research shows that parents with learning difficulties, and professionals involved in services supporting them to parent, still believe that workers in family support and child protection services do not have experience of working with adults with learning difficulties (Tarleton *et al.*, 2006). Parents with learning difficulties felt that workers presumed that they would be incompetent and 'never be good enough parents', and would not understand their baby's needs or be able to learn the skills they needed quickly enough to meet their baby's needs. They also felt that workers involved in children's services did not understand the impact of their learning difficulties or the support they needed. This lack of understanding frequently resulted in late or crisis referrals to support services.

Parents, and the professionals supporting them within charities or learning difficulties services, also feel that workers in children's or family services assess parents with learning difficulties against very high standards and expect them to be 'perfect parents'. Parents with learning difficulties report that different professionals have different expectations, even regarding the simplest of issues such as whether a baby should have a dummy, and that parents with learning difficulties who are in contact with services are often in contact with ten or more different professionals all offering different advice.

It was also felt that professionals in children's services had 'fixed ideas' about what should happen to the babies of parents with learning difficulties. Even though the Children Act, and the other policy documents discussed above, stress the importance of supporting children in their family, it was felt that child protection social workers wanted a 'concrete outcome' for children through their adoption, often at birth, and did not wish to expose children to any level of risk.

Parents with learning difficulties may feel disempowered and are consequently reticent about working with child protection or mainstream children's services because their support needs are not understood, workers do not communicate in a way they understand, and they feel that they are expected to fail (Tarleton *et al.*, 2006). Parents also felt that unfortunate life events which would result in other families being offered support were seen as additional reasons why they were unable to parent. This lack of engagement further fuels children's workers' concerns about the ability of adults with learning difficulties to parent. This negative cycle of interaction is deepened if parents have previously had children removed or have had their support needs used against them as evidence that they cannot parent. The literature discussing parents with learning difficulties describes this disempowerment of and lack of support for parents with learning difficulties within the child protection system as 'system abuse', with professionals reporting that the 'system' is 'stacked against parents' (Booth, 2000; Tarleton *et al.*, 2006).

'Parenting with support'

The emerging concept of 'parenting with support' is arising out of the positive practice displayed by workers supporting adults with learning difficulties to parent. As part of a mapping study undertaken in 2004–2005, eighty-five services around the UK shared their positive practice regarding the ways in which they were supporting parents with learning difficulties (Tarleton *et al.*, 2006). The concept of parenting with support enables parents to be supported to be 'good enough' through:

- raising awareness of parents with learning difficulties and ensuring their support needs are understood by professionals in children's support and mainstream services;

- developing multi-professional and multi-agency support for parents with learning difficulties;
- empowering parents with learning difficulties.

Awareness of parents with learning difficulties and their support needs is being raised at a variety of levels. Locally, professionals involved with parents with learning difficulties are championing their needs by networking with colleagues and attending or developing relevant forums, such as maternity alliances. They are also providing information and assistance to colleagues (some of whom do not have any experience of or training for working with adults with learning difficulties), to parents themselves, and to professionals in mainstream and children's services, discussing the impact of having learning difficulties on an adult's life, and how support can be provided to empower them to meet their baby's ever-changing needs appropriately.

Nationally, a number of key organisations have formed the 'Working Together with Parents' network which is raising awareness of parents with learning difficulties and the need for a coordinated national policy, as well as enabling professionals in the field to network and share positive practice (www.right-support.org.uk).

Professionals are also working hard to develop coordinated multi-professional and multi-agency support for parents with learning difficulties through networking and focused interactions with colleagues. When a number of professionals and/or agencies are supporting a family, a 'key worker' system is being implemented in some localities, where one worker is responsible for liaising with the parents as well as with the rest of the professionals involved. In order to facilitate this, consent procedures are being developed with parents so that information shared with the key worker can be passed on to colleagues. Clear communication strategies are also being put in place, such as regular meetings of all professionals involved in supporting a family.

Professionals supporting a family are also working to develop a shared concept of 'good enough' or acceptable parenting through discussions involving the parents about the standards that are appropriate for their family. Each of the professionals then uses these shared understandings in their interactions with parents. They are also developing a wider understanding of and respect for each other's roles through shared training. Professionals with a background in working with adults with learning difficulties are undertaking training in child protection, and professionals with a background in child protection are undertaking training in supporting adults with learning difficulties.

More formal organisation of support has in some areas involved the development of protocols clarifying eligibility criteria, roles and responsibilities, how support will be provided, and how professionals will communicate, spelling out the joint training and service development that is required.

The central aim of the concept of 'parenting with support' is that of empowering parents through respecting, supporting and helping parents acquire the skills and knowledge they need. This support must of course be sensitive to the baby's frequently changing needs. As with all new parents, parents with learning difficulties need detailed support across the wide range of complex skills which form 'good enough' parenting. Parents may need help in understanding about feeding, whether bottle or breast feeding, such as the actual mechanics of the activity – how the baby latches on or how bottles are cleaned and sterilised and how milk is made up when the water has boiled and cooled to the appropriate temperature. The instructions on a box of formula milk may often be too complicated for parents to understand. The same holds true for all other aspects of the baby's development, including sleep regulation, the baby's need for play and communication, etc. Furthermore, these skills must be acquired within a developmental framework that keeps pace with the growing infant's changing needs.

All parents with learning difficulties benefit from and are empowered by access to 'easy-to-understand' information about the stage of parenting they are in, and, where relevant, the child protection or court processes. Professionals should ensure that relevant information is provided in a suitable format for parents, whether this is in short, clear, jargon-free sentences with explanatory pictures or on audiotape. In at least one area of the UK, all of the relevant information about the antenatal pathway has been produced in an easier to understand format. Professionals are also using and adapting, for individuals, easy information about the parenting process that is available to purchase, such as the *You and Your Baby* (Affleck and Baker, 2004) and *You and Your Little Child* books (Affleck and Harris, 2007) and the *I Want to be a Good Parent* pack (McGaw, 1995). The *You and Your Baby* book provides step-by-step illustrated instructions about all aspects of baby care from nappy changing to bathing.

Workers need to invest time in developing positive relationships with parents with learning difficulties. They need to spend time listening to them, praising their achievements, and helping them build their confidence and self-esteem. These workers are endeavouring to communicate clearly and honestly with parents and to maintain a non-judgemental attitude in addition to having clear expectations regarding the skills and changes required in their parenting. They are trying to ensure that parents remain in control of their parenting through supporting parents to do things for themselves. They are supporting parents to learn new skills by breaking tasks down into really small steps, and by 'thinking outside the box' to find creative and innovative strategies to support parents' learning. Parents have been supported to follow picture prompts regarding making up bottles, and to use an appropriately sized container to measure milk rather than having to measure the water when making up formula milk.

Through these empowering relationships, parents are being supported to engage with family support services, including the child protection system when appropriate, and to work with the requirements being made of them to improve their parenting. When possible, independent advocates are provided for parents to ensure that they understand and are emotionally supported through the extremely complicated and often 'harrowing' experience of child and judicial proceedings. Parents frequently report not understanding and being frightened by the court process (Tarleton *et al.*, 2006).

The actual practical support to learn and implement new skills provided to a parent or couple should relate to their individual needs, and these should be evaluated using a competency-based assessment such as the *Parent Assessment Manual* (McGaw *et al.*, 1998). This highlights the parent's skills and abilities as well as the areas which they found difficult. The in-home support provided to parents should enable parents to develop the skills they need to meet their baby's current and future needs. It can therefore, as noted above, initially include help with feeding, clothing, purchasing appropriate equipment, and understanding baby care information, as well as support to attend baby groups. However, as professionals are working with parents not only to meet their children's current needs but also to ensure that they are ready for the next stage of their child's development, they need to help parents to understand and learn the skills they will need in the forthcoming months, such as early play activities, placing babies on their front, weaning, and 'baby-proofing' their home when the baby begins to crawl.

Parents also report enjoying and feeling really supported by parenting groups where they can learn from each other or from information shared by visiting 'experts', and can develop new friendships with other parents. Some areas are also providing specific training courses for parents, such as an adapted Webster Stratton Parenting course or cookery courses, which result in accreditation through non-standard assessment via photographs etc. Parents can also be supported to access family support services such as Sure Start Children's Centres or community baby, breastfeeding or parenting groups. Professionals need to start supporting parents as early as possible to ensure the best outcomes for the baby's development, thus reinforcing the importance of raised awareness of parents with learning difficulties in mainstream services, such as midwifery, health visiting and general practitioners.

Parents also need support to overcome issues such as poor housing, harassment, debt or mental health support needs which are detracting from their ability to parent. This timely, pro-active and flexible support tailored to the needs of the family is protective of babies and children. The ongoing involvement of professionals allows them to spot any potential difficulties before they become significant issues. Professionals from learning difficulties backgrounds who are supporting adults in their parenting role are maintaining an awareness of child protection issues and are willing to report any issues to child protection workers. This joint emphasis on protecting children is furthering their positive relationship with child protection professionals and enabling the development of positive multi-agency working.

Two brief case studies illustrate the positive work that is being done with parents with learning difficulties and how this work is 'keeping baby in mind'.

A single mum who had already had four children removed was extremely reluctant to work with child protection services who were concerned for the well-being of her two youngest children aged 9 and 1. Through the persistence of a community nurse, working with the adult learning difficulties service, a positive relationship with the mother was built and she began to receive support to sort out her untidy house to make it safe for her newly mobile baby, to organise her baby's clothing and to cook healthy meals suitable for herself and both of her children. This mum who could not read or write was being targeted by loan sharks and in considerable debt. The community nurse supported her to say 'no' to loan sharks and to manage her money, and also supported her through child protection and court proceedings when the two children were made subjects of a care order. The community nurse explained what was happening and provided emotional support. The children remain with their mother but with care plans in place including day care for her youngest child and with a high level of monitoring from the community nurse who reports on the family's progress to the child protection team.

Another example further illustrates the complex nature of individual families' situations.

A young couple both with learning disabilities with a small baby were supported by a multi-agency team of seven or eight professionals, including a child protection social worker who was considered by the parents to be very supportive. They received weekly support from a family support worker to help with practical issues such as cooking and cleaning. They also received weekly home visiting from a nursery nurse to help with engaging and playing with the baby. In addition they attended the local Sure Start centre regularly. This support was coordinated at a monthly meeting with the parents, which all of the professionals attended. Finally, the parents saw a psychological therapist weekly with a multiple focus, i.e. the couple's ability to negotiate and resolve disagreements, the mum's mental health support needs, particularly her low mood and lack of self-esteem, and the impact of the father's past childhood abuse. This quite comprehensive 'package' enabled the parents to continue to parent their child.

Conclusion

'Parenting with support' is an emerging model of supporting adults with learning difficulties to parent while ensuring that the needs of the baby and later the child are consistently and adequately met. This emerging positive practice is currently being championed by professionals who are in direct contact with parents with learning difficulties. These professionals have often witnessed babies and young children being removed from their parents' care when, with the right support, they could have continued in the care of their parents. These local champions are working tirelessly to raise awareness of the support needs of parents with learning difficulties and to highlight that when services work together, adults with learning difficulties can often be supported to be 'good enough' parents.

This model of long-term pro-active, flexible protective support for families headed by a parent or parents with learning difficulties is strongly supported by legislation promoting the child's right to grow up in their natural family, and by the recent good practice guidance for working with parents with a learning disability (DfES/DoH, 2007). However, this model of supported parenting needs to be promoted through the dissemination and use of the good practice guidance, fundamental changes in the way support services are currently provided by both adults' and children's services, and the inclusion of parents with learning difficulties in mainstream services for parents. A fundamental change in the way services are provided is needed. Services need to develop a model of ongoing support provided through multi-professional and multi-agency teams. The benefits of providing sensitive ongoing support sensitive to the baby's and their parents' changing needs should be set against the extremely high emotional and financial costs of judicial proceedings.

References

Affleck, F. and Baker, S. (2004). *You and Your Baby*. Leeds: CHANGE.

Affleck, F. and Harris, K. (2007). *You and Your Little Child*. Leeds: CHANGE.

Booth, T. (2000). Parents with learning difficulties, child protection and the courts. *Representing Children*, 13(3), 175–188.

CHANGE (2005). *Report of National Gathering of Parents with Learning Disabilities*. Leeds: CHANGE.

Cleaver, H. and Nicholson, D. (2007). *Parental Learning Disability and Children's Needs: Family Experiences and Effective Practice*. London: Jessica Kingsley.

Department for Education and Skills (2003). *Every Child Matters*. London: DfES.

Department for Education and Skills/Department of Health (2004). *National Service Framework for Children, Young People and Maternity Services*. London: DoH.

Department for Education and Skills/Department of Health (2007). *Good Practice Guidance on Working with Parents with a Learning Disability*. London: DoH.

Department of Health (2001). *Valuing People: A New Strategy for Learning Disability for the 21st Century*. London: DoH.

Emerson, E., Malam, S., Davies, I. and Spencer, K. (2005). *Adults with Learning Disabilities in England 2003/4*. www.ic.nhs.uk/pubs/learndiff2004.

HM Government, Cabinet Office (2006). *Reaching Out: An Action Plan on Social Exclusion. www.cabinetoffice.gov.uk/social_exclusion_task_force/publications/ reaching_out.aspx*

Human Rights Act (1998). London: Stationery Office.

Llewellyn, G. and McConnell, D. (2005). You have to prove yourself all the time: people with learning disabilities parenting. In G. Grant, P. Goward, M. Richardson and P. Ramcharan (eds), *Learning Disability: A Life Cycle Approach to Valuing People*. Maidenhead: Open University Press.

Llewellyn, G., McConnell, D. and Ferronato, L. (2003). Prevalence and outcomes for parents with disabilities and their children in an Australian court sample. *Child Abuse and Neglect*, 27, 235–251.

McConnell, D., Llewellyn, G. and Ferronato, L. (2002). Disability and decision making in Australian care proceedings. *International Journal of Law, Policy and the Family*, 16, 270–299.

McGaw, S. (1995). *I Want to be a Good Parent*. Kidderminster: BILD.

McGaw, S. and Newman, T. (2005). *What Works for Parents with Learning Disabilities?* Ilford: Barnardo's.

McGaw, S., Beckley, K., Connolly, N. and Ball, K. (1998). *Parent Assessment Manual*. Truro: Trecare NHS Trust. www.cornwall.nhs.uk/specialparentingservices/ patientassessmentmanual.asp

SCARE (2005). *Helping Parents with Learning Disabilities in Their Role as Parents*. London: Social Care Institute for Excellence.

Scottish Executive (2000). *The Same as You?* Edinburgh: Stationery Office.

Tarleton, B., Ward, L. and Howarth, J. (2006). *Finding the Right Support. A Review of Issues and Positive Practice in Supporting Parents with Learning Difficulties and Their Children*. London: Baring Foundation.

Useful websites

www.bristol.ac.uk/norahfry/right-support/
www.changepeople.co.uk/default.aspx?page=16991
www.dh.gov.uk/en/Publicationsandstatistics/Publications/PublicationsPolicy
   AndGuidance/DH_075119
www.scie.org.uk/publications/briefings/files/scare14.pdf
www.cornwall.nhs.uk/specialparentingservices/patientassessmentmanual.asp

Part IV

Postscript

16 Developing infant-centred services

The way forward

P. O. Svanberg and Jane Barlow

Introduction

The focus of this book has been on early interventions that can be provided during the perinatal period to support the parenting of babies. The chapters describe a variety of approaches, all of which share the goal of improving the life chances of infants and their families, and some of which have potentially significant economic benefits (Sinclair, 2007), alongside the many other benefits that have been highlighted. This field, which straddles public health, developmental psychology, antenatal and postnatal maternal mental health, and infant mental health, has seen an explosion in research over the last twenty-five to thirty years, and some of the diversity of this new-found knowledge has been reflected throughout this volume. While all of the programmes and projects described have been developed and implemented in the UK, we very much hope that they will be useful in other contexts and countries.

The emphasis of this book has been on supporting parenting, but the development of infants is influenced by a host of factors and it has been observed that:

> a significant proportion of some of the most difficult and costly problems faced by young children and parents today, are a direct consequence of adverse maternal health related behaviours during pregnancy, dysfunctional infant care-giving, and *stressful environmental conditions* [our emphasis] that interfere with parental and family functioning.
>
> (Olds and Kitzman, 1993)

This quotation acknowledges that the development of children is influenced both by the parenting that a child receives, and by the environment in which parents undertake this difficult role. Bronfenbrenner (1979) referred to a number of systems where interactive influences operate, extending from the family to a range of broader social and cultural levels. The policy debate in the UK has tended to be polarised into arguments about 'poverty' versus 'parenting', but the picture is considerably more complex than this, and poverty and parenting are interrelated. In order to produce effective outcomes for children we therefore need to tackle a broad range of factors and particularly those that make the task of parenting much harder and sometimes even completely overwhelming. It is hoped that some of the methods of supporting parents that have been discussed in this book will enable practitioners to work in accordance with this type of 'ecological' or multisystemic model or framework.

We now have in the UK, for the first time since the great Victorian reformers, a government that has made the health and well-being of children a priority. This was partly reflected in its commitment to reduce child poverty, and the development of Sure Start and later Children's Centres. These reforms have continued apace and offer a 'once in a generation' opportunity to develop and implement sensitively responsive and evidence-based programmes such as those outlined in this volume. This final chapter will focus on the further changes that are necessary if we are to effectively utilise what is now known about how to optimise outcomes for infants. It will be suggested that there is a need for a shift in the philosophy of both service planners and providers to enable the provision of more *infant-centred* services. It will also be suggested that while midwives and health visitors have many of the key skills that are necessary to develop such an infant-centred service, recent advances in research and knowledge about 'what works' require that practitioners are now given the opportunity to acquire new skills based on the type of evidence-based and innovative methods of supporting new parents and caregivers that have been examined throughout this book.

Infant-centred services – toward a new conceptualisation

The way in which a society conceptualises things and people tends on the whole to be reflected in how they are then treated within that society. The latter part of the twentieth century in the UK witnessed a radical shift in the way in which children and childhood were conceptualised, which in turn led planners and providers toward the development and provision of more 'child-centred' services. This move followed on the heels of a revolution in the education system in which our understanding about the nature of children and their needs led to a radical restructuring of the process of educating children. For the first time, children were no longer viewed as being miniature adults, and childhood was recognised to be a unique developmental phase with distinctive requirements. Children thereby ceased to be viewed as passive recipients and instead were seen as active participants, and were recognised for the first time as having rights and entitlements, which culminated in the 1989 United Nations Convention on the Rights of the Child (UNCRC). Collectively, these changes resulted in a gradual re-organisation of children's services, all of which resulted in a greater respect for children, and a better ability of such services to meet their needs more appropriately.

We continue, however, to conceptualise infants as being primarily passive recipients of their parents' and caregivers' love and attention. Society continues to portray them as being primarily physiological beings with a range of physical needs that must be met in order for them to thrive. But mostly we view them by adult standards, and thereby in terms of a deficit model, focusing on the things that they *don't do*. So, they don't yet use language and it is thereby assumed that they do not have the means with which to communicate; the lack of language is also assumed to mean that they cannot reproduce early memories and they are therefore conceived of as being without memories about this period; their stage of cognitive development is assumed to mean that they do not require any special input in terms of stimulation; and the assumption that they do not yet have a sense of 'self' makes them without 'agency, coherence or affectivity' (Stern, 1989), this being most frequently expressed in the use of the pronoun 'it' to refer to babies - a pejorative when applied to children or adults.

Stern similarly observes that

> the prevailing views of clinical developmental theory don't reflect the image of an infant with an integrated sense of self', [despite the fact that by 2 months of age] infants seem to approach interpersonal relatedness with an organizing perspective that makes it feel as if there is now an integrated sense of themselves as distinct and coherent bodies, with control over their own actions, ownership of their own affectivity, a sense of continuity, and a sense of other people as distinct and separate interactants.
>
> (Stern, 1989.: 69)

Indeed, Stern goes on to argue that infants as young as 2 months of age show evidence of cued memory for motor, sensory and also affective experiences, and that although this does not provide evidence of truly 'evocative' or 'recognition' memory, this early use of episodic memory, or what he later refers to as 'Representations of Interactions that have been Generalised (RIGS)', provides the basis for a continuity of self in time, and the building blocks for 'the sense of a core self' (ibid.: 92).

Beebe and Lachmann (2005) have more recently marshalled evidence to support the suggestion that babies as young as 2 months have a rudimentary representational capacity, albeit not yet symbolic (i.e. it does not involve language), and that for the period before this the systems for the emergence of organisation are also already in place (Stern, 1989):

1 Babies are able to discriminate from fifteen hours following their birth between a stranger and their mother.
2 They have been learning *in utero* and show a preference at birth for recordings of their mother's voice over that of others.
3 They are able by day one to recognise their own vocalisations and can discriminate their own from the cries of other babies.
4 Neonates can discriminate among surprise, fear and sadness expressions in caregivers, and produce corresponding facial expressions of their own.
5 Infants are able to detect contingencies between what they do and what the environmental response is to their actions, thereby facilitating an early sense of 'agency'; and are also able to 'develop expectancies about how social interactions will go'. Such expectancies represent 'crucial links to the organization of early representations' (ibid.: 71). Thus, infants as young as 3

months can detect similarities and differences between patterns which enable them to generate rules, which guide their expectancies about things.

6 The affect or emotion that an infant is experiencing influences his capacity for learning, and intense negative affect reduces the capacity of the infant to remember an event.

7 The baby's exposure to affect or emotion from 10 months on influences the lateralization of their brain.

8 Infants seek out affective information from caregivers to help them to interpret what is happening in their environment.

9 During face-to-face social interaction infants use brief visual disengagements to regulate their level of arousal.

10 Cross-modal perception permits them to transmit information obtained from one sensory modality such as taste, to another modality such as vision.

11 They have a capacity for pre-symbolic categorisation which means that they can treat 'discriminable entities as similar' (ibid.: 77). This permits them to begin to form prototypes from the regularities that they detect thereby facilitating 'perception, memory and information processing by reducing variation and supplying organizing principles'. This provides 'the beginning of a framework for language and symbol formation' (ibid.).

Like Stern (1989), Beebe and Lachmann (2005) suggest that these pre-linguistic abilities of the infant, which begin *in utero*, form a significant part of the process by which they begin to construct a sense of 'self' and 'others'.

This evidence about the extraordinary capacities of the infant for agency, co-herence and affectivity (Stern, 1989) requires a radical revision of our current conceptualisation of infants, and a move toward more 'infant-centred' services, and, indeed, infant-centred practitioners.

'Infant-centred' services

Many services may regard themselves as being infant-centred in that what they provide is focused *primarily* on meeting the needs of the infant, maternity and neonatal intensive care units being two such examples. However, in many cases, these services have not moved beyond traditional models of infancy (i.e. which view infants as passive and interaction as being unidirectional), one of the consequences of this being the failure to integrate within their practice recent knowledge about the capabilities and needs of babies, particularly in terms of their emotional development. They are also failing thereby to incorporate what is now known about 'what works' to support the optimal development of babies. Such practice is based on outdated knowledge and does not reflect a truly infant-centred philosophy.

What then are the implications of recent knowledge about babies' emotional needs in terms of the development of truly infant-centred services? The goals of services that are designed to optimise a baby's social and emotional development (in addition to their physical development) should be based on what we now know to be important in terms of the key aspects of the different developmental stages of infancy, which are illustrated in Figure 16.1.

It was the paediatrician and psychoanalyst Donald Winnicott who famously said that there is 'no such thing as a baby', meaning that all babies only exist in so far as they are part of a unit with their primary caretaker, which of course reflects their dependency on primary caretakers. One of the central goals of any infant-centred service then should be to provide effective support for an infant's caretaker/parents, and thereby their parenting. Such support should, of course, be focused on helping primary caregivers to become more attuned to their infants, and this points to the need for both practitioners and services that are better attuned to the needs of parents and caregivers. Thus the fundamental principle for any service that is working with babies is that it must reach out and become

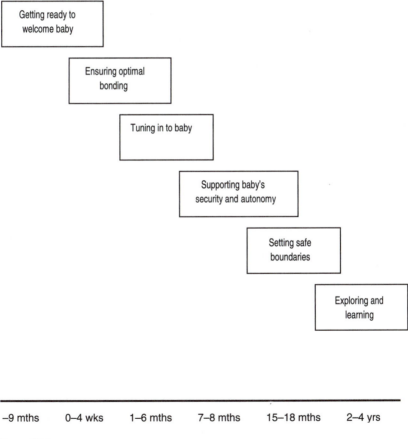

Figure 16.1

sensitively responsive, offering a degree of continuity of support and interventions. The more 'burdened' the parents are, the more significant will be the need to offer intense, consistent and specialist services from small ongoing teams of professionals acting as attachment figures to the parents.

Getting ready to welcome baby

One of the best ways of providing infant-centred care during pregnancy is by supporting parents-to-be, and particularly first-time parents, to make the transition to parenthood. It is now recognised that this transition can be stressful for even the most able of parents, and that parents need more support than is currently provided (Parr, 1997), in order to do what their infant most needs them to do, which is to get ready *emotionally* to welcome them (Barlow and Underdown, 2008). This involves men and women renegotiating their new roles with one another, and with their social group of family and friends, as well as developing an affective relationship with their new infant. This renegotiation often involves 'reworking' relationships and sometimes traumas from the past: 'Pregnancy revives old psychological conflicts, reorganizes a woman's relationship with her own mother and causes her to develop attitudes towards and representations of her developing child' (Huth-Bocks *et al.*, 2004: 81).

Many of the common stresses that are experienced during pregnancy including anxiety and depression not only impact on the adult and his or her family but also on the foetus, where an emerging area of research called 'foetal programming' is creating considerable interest (Glover and O'Connor, 2002). Such stresses are also associated with poorer outcomes for the infant (O'Connor *et al.*, 2003). This evidence about the importance of pregnancy as a period of preparation points to the need for traditional antenatal classes to be supplemented with the type of support that focuses on facilitating the transition to parenthood (see, for example, Chapter 5) for all first-time parents. Attention should also be given specifically to preparing fathers for parenthood, and the changes that will ensue with the birth of the baby (see Chapter 7). A number of methods of working with fathers have been shown to be effective (Magill-Evans *et al.*, 2006).

Evidence about the consequences of more serious problems, such as where the mother is living with domestic violence (Huth-Bocks *et al.*, 2002) or abusing alcohol and drugs (Mardomingo *et al.*, 2003), points to the importance of identifying parents experiencing such problems, who need additional psychological input and help. Often these symptoms are a result of unresolved trauma, loss or neglect in their past. Such experiences are frequently exacerbated by current relationship problems, varying from a volatile relationship with families of origin to domestic violence and sexual exploitation. The consequences of such problems for later child development have been examined throughout this book, and pregnancy is a key time to link pregnant women experiencing such problems into appropriate services.

Brief evidence-based psychological therapy will be helpful to mothers-to-be who are anxious and/or depressed (NCCMH, 2007), and more intensive therapy, which may be ongoing after the baby has been born, may be necessary for parents with more entrenched problems such as alcohol or drug abuse, unresolved abuse experiences or trauma from their past (see, for example, Chapter 14). This demands a range of skills from the psychologists or psychological therapists, which at present are quite rare, including the capacity to work systemically with a family perhaps to resolve conflict or domestic violence issues, and to work with an individual adult through a focus on internal cognitions and beliefs/schemas and 'working models'.

Ensuring optimal bonding

Bonding refers to the possible advantage that is thought to be conferred during the 'quiet-alert state', in which newborn babies initially spend around 10 per cent of their day. Most normal newborns are thought to remain in a quiet-alert state for about forty-three minutes immediately after birth, and this may therefore be a key opportunity for the infant to begin to get to know the mother, and for the mother to begin to revise the 'mental image' that she has had of the baby and adjust to the actual baby (Klaus *et al.*, 1995; Klaus and Kennell, 1982) and thus to bond. While the importance of bonding is now acknowledged worldwide, there is still considerable debate about the long-term benefits or consequences (see, for example, www.birthpsychology.com).

The bonding relationship may be affected if the mother is traumatised by the birth process. Many women experience childbirth as emotionally intense and a significant minority experience it as traumatic, sometimes leading to the development of posttraumatic stress symptoms or even to posttraumatic stress disorder (PTSD) (Olde *et al.*, 2006). In one study 2.1 per cent met criteria for PTSD and 21.4 per cent reported a traumatic childbirth experience (Olde *et al.*, 2005). While there have been few longitudinal studies evaluating the long-term impact of PTSD following childbirth, a number of case studies show poorer mother–infant attachment (Ballard *et al.*, 1995).

Providers of services during this period therefore need to recognise the very small proportion of mothers (1–2 per cent) whose delivery will have been extremely traumatic and who run the risk of developing posttraumatic stress disorder (Olde *et al.*, 2006), and the much broader group of women (one-fifth) who may have experienced the birth as traumatic. Although there is currently little evidence to support the use of debriefing (NCCMH, 2007), women and men should be given the opportunity to talk about their birth experiences during this period.

The immediate postnatal period is also a key opportunity to introduce the parent to the *social baby* and to explore how the relationship between the caregivers and baby is developing (see Chapter 4), which should continue throughout the next few months.

Tuning in to baby

The most crucial aspects of the baby's emotional development between 1 and 6 months are:

1   An increasing capacity to relate to his primary caregivers using turn-taking, and the need for *reciprocal* interaction.
2   The beginning of his ability to experience a range of (sometimes overwhelming) emotional states, and the need to have such states *contained*, and *mirrored* back in a more manageable form.
3   Development of early *internal representations* about self; and self and others; and thereby the need for him to be seen by his carers in terms of his mental states, i.e. *mentalisation*.
4   Cognitive and intellectual growth and the consequent need for sensory and motor stimulation.

One of the most important aspects of caregiving during the first six months of life is the parents' ability to be *sensitively responsive* to the baby's emerging communications. The majority of parents will be able to *tune in to* their baby, and the first section of this book examined a range of innovative and evidence-based interventions that can help parents to do this.

The mental health problems encountered in early parenthood are as diverse as at other times although the main focus has traditionally been on postnatal depression. Having a new baby is a very significant life transition, and the impact of such dynamic changes can be stressful. Stress generates distress and if the parent is unable to cope with this it is quite possible that a vicious spiral of crisis can develop, which rapidly impacts on the baby, the parents, and the wider family. One of the aims of infant-centred services should therefore be to identify the 20–30 per cent of new parents who will struggle with tuning in to the baby. These difficulties are mostly due to the parent's lack of readiness and a degree of preoccupation with their own concerns, which may range from financial problems to partner problems. Families that have been identified as being in need of extra support could be offered up to four visits primarily to support the caregiver–infant relationship (see Chapter 3), with videotape feedback focusing on reducing intrusiveness and increasing sensitive responsiveness (see Chapter 9). Families with more extensive needs can be supported using home visiting (Chapter 10). This period is also a key opportunity to ask the three questions that have been recommended to identify whether the mother is suffering from anxiety and/or depression (NCCMH, 2007), and to link her into appropriate sources of support (see, for example, Chapter 13).

Finally the group of infants who are most at risk will have parents with abuse that include domestic violence, drug and alcohol histories, severe postnatal depression, and overt psychiatric symptoms. The group-based 'Mellow Parenting' programme (Chapter 13) is accumulating impressive evidence for its effectiveness in supporting parents who fall into this group and could be offered as part of a range of infant-centred therapeutic interventions including parent–infant psychotherapy (Chapter 12) and video feedback (Chapter 14), alongside individual, couple (Chapter 7) or family therapy as defined in the NICE antenatal and perinatal mental health guidelines (NCCMH, 2007).

Supporting baby's security and autonomy

One of the key tasks for a baby during the first months is the development of secure attachment. During the second half of the first year the infant begins to develop independence and to explore and experiment. The separation anxieties of some mothers may emerge at this time, and whilst they were sensitively attuned to the young baby, they may now become intrusive and controlling, setting up a conflict which can develop into a serious control struggle, often seen, for example, with mealtime conflicts.

Infant-centred services would as such be focused on helping parents to recognise the corollaries of this developmental stage, and promoting the sort of parenting that will optimise the infant's development. Universal support that is provided at this time could include the provision of information, using a variety of media (e.g. leaflets and DVDs), aimed at increasing parents' awareness of this developmental milestone and the best way to deal with it. Further support could also be provided at this time to fathers, including encouraging them to attend father and toddler groups (Magill-Evans *et al.*, 2006).

Routine interaction with parents provides the opportunity to do this. It also provides the opportunity for infant-centred practitioners to identify parents who may be in need of additional support. Videotape feedback could be used at this point to help identify strengths, and address problem areas (see Chapter 9). There may be a very small minority for whom the baby's emerging autonomy has created significant problems and who may welcome additional psychological help.

There is of course also the truism that 'life happens'. Parents may break up, accidents and bereavements happen, illness and disability occur, all of which impact on parents, and their ability to parent (i.e. the traumas and losses of everyday life). If the health visitor, family support worker or psychologist have been able to establish and maintain a helping alliance with the parents, it will be much easier for the parents to contact them again to try to resolve such issues through brief crisis intervention, thereby ensuring that the impact on the infant is only temporary.

Setting safe boundaries

The development of mobility during the second year of life brings a new set of challenges as parents have to balance 'scaffolding' the infant's natural desire to explore and discover, with ensuring safety. A securely attached toddler will by definition want to explore but is of course not able to recognise dangers or threats. Conflict is then almost inevitable and it is this conflict which lies behind the stereotypical 'terrible twos'.

Having spent the first 15–18 months becoming attuned to the growing infant the parent will now need to learn to become firm, fair and very consistent. The principles of this process of ensuring secure, safe, and loving boundaries are extremely well documented, and underpin parenting training programmes such as Webster-Stratton's 'Incredible Years'. (Webster-Stratton and Hammond, 1997).

Infant-centred practitioners could use routine interactions to assess the family's ability to cope with this transition and to offer the parents either individual or group-based programmes, such as 'Incredible Years', to help them develop the appropriate skills to support their infant's development. This is also a key time at which to make an assessment of the child's social, emotional and behavioural functioning in order to identify toddlers showing early signs of problems, and to provide the appropriate parenting support to ensure that such problems do not become entrenched.

Exploring and learning

One of the key developmental needs of the older infant and toddler is to explore and learn. Infant-centred services should be designed to optimise this aspect of an infant/toddler's development by helping parents to optimise their child's learning environment. This can be done universally through the use of leaflets and DVDs. Families living in areas of deprivation should be supported through the use of early learning programmes such as the one described in Chapter 10. The provision of infant-centred father and toddler groups could be used to help fathers to become involved in their toddler's development through the use of infant-led play. Infant-centred practitioners will also be alert to the need to refer children on to more specialist sources of support such as speech and language services and perinatal and infant mental health services (NCCMH, 2007).

Developing the 'infant-centred' practitioner

Infant-centred services cannot be developed or facilitated without practitioners whose interventions and practices are underpinned by an infant-centred philosophy. Two things have become increasingly clear as key professional groups such as midwives and health visitors have taken on more specialist roles (such as in the Family Nurse Partnership (Chapter 10) and the Sunderland Infant Programme (Chapter 9)). The first is that services cannot offer infant-centred support to parents unless practitioners have the skills and sensitivity to develop a trusting relationship with caregivers that is based on a partnership (see Chapter 6). This is absolutely fundamental, and there are a range of models that provide such 'relationship skills', some of which have been discussed in the first section of this book (see Chapters 3 and 6). Such skill training should be a core part of professional training (see also Wampold, 2001).

The second point is that not everyone has the skills or desire to work more intensively or therapeutically with families. The more intensive parenting support should be provided by staff who not only have a range of different levels of expertise but who are also committed to working 'therapeutically'.

The development of an infant-centred primary care and early years workforce would involve two things. First, an improved capacity of practitioners to work on a universal basis with parents to ensure that they are able to use routine exchanges to promote infant well-being. Second, practitioners need the necessary observational and intervention skills, some of which have been explored in this book, to be able to identify where things are not going well, and to either intervene effectively or refer families on to more specialised services, including infant mental health specialists (Barlow and Underdown, 2008).

Only when services are provided by practitioners with such skills will we be able to say that they are truly infant-centred, and only when the primary care and early years workforce is provided with the necessary opportunities to acquire such knowledge and skills will this happen.

Conclusion

The many and varied intervention approaches in this volume have one thing in common. They all point to the value of services that are underpinned by an infant-centred philosophy, in which the support that is provided (both in terms of parents and parenting during the perinatal period) is underpinned by an accurate conceptualisation of infants and infancy. They also illustrate the way in which such infant-centred approaches to supporting parenting can optimise both infant development and later well-being.

The move toward more infant-centred services and practitioners is inevitable, given the sort of changes that have taken place in our understanding about infants. The current political and public recognition of the importance of supporting families to help their children achieve a healthy and secure life would seem to indicate that *now* is the right time to begin this transition.

References

Ballard, C. G., Stanley, A. K. and Brockington, I. F. (1995). Posttraumatic stress disorder (PTSD) after childbirth. *British Journal of Psychiatry*, 166, 525–528.

Barlow, J. and Underdown, A. (2008). Supporting parenting during infancy. In C. Jackson, K. Hill and P. Lavis (eds), *Child and Adolescent Mental Health Today: A Handbook*. Brighton: Pavilion.

Beebe, B. and Lachmann, F. M. (2005). *Infant Research and Adult Treatment: Co-constructing Interactions*. 2nd edn. Hilldale, NJ: Analytic Press.

Bronfenbrenner, U. (1979). Ecological systems theory. In R. Vasta (ed.), *Annals of Child Development* (Vol. 6, pp. 187–251). Greenwich, CT: JAI Press.

de Chateau, P. (1976). The influence of early contact on maternal and infant behaviour in primiparae. *Birth and the Family Journal*, 3(4), 149–155.

Glover, V. and O'Connor, T. (2002). Effects of antenatal stress and anxiety. *British Journal of Psychiatry*, 180, 389–391.

H M Government, Cabinet Office (2006). *Reaching Out: An Action Plan for Social Exclusion*. www.cabinetoffice.gov.uk/social_exclusion_task_force/publications/reaching_out.aspx.

Huth-Bocks, A. C., Levendosky, A. A. and Bogat, G. A. (2002). The effects of violence during pregnancy on maternal and infant health. *Violence and Victims*, 17(2), 169–185.

Huth-Bocks, A. C., Alytia, A., Levendosky, A. A., Bogat, G. A. and von Eye, A. (2004). The impact of maternal characteristics and contextual variables on infant–mother attachment. *Child Development*, 75(2), 480–496.

Klauss, M. H. and Kennell, J. H. (1982). *Parent–Infant Bonding*, 2nd edn. St Louis: Mosby.

Klaus, M. H. and Robertson, M. O. (1982). *Birth, Interaction and Attachment: Exploring the Foundations for Modern Perinatal Care*. Skillman, NJ: Johnson and Johnson.

Klaus, M. H., Kennell, J. H. and Klaus, P. H. (1995). *Bonding: Building the Foundations of Secure Attachment and Independence*. Harlow: Addison-Wesley.

Magill-Evans, J., Harrison, M. J., Rempel, G. and Slater, L. (2006). Interventions with fathers of young children: systematic literature review. *Journal of Advanced Nursing*, 55(2), 248–264.

Mardomingo, M. A., Solís Sánchez, G., Málaga Guerrero, S., Cuadrillero Quesada, C., Pérez Méndez, C. and Matesanz Pérez, J. L. (2003). Drug abuse in pregnancy and neonatal morbidity: epidemiologic changes in the last ten years. *Anales de Pediatria*, 58(6), 519–522.

NCCMH (National Collaborating Centre for Mental Health) (2007). *Antenatal and Postnatal Mental Health: Clinical Management and Service Guidance*. Leicester: British Psychological Society.

O'Connor, T. G., Heron, J., Golding, J., Glover, V. and ALSPAC Study Team (2003). Maternal antenatal anxiety and behavioural/emotional problems in children: a test of a programming hypothesis. *Journal of Child Psychology and Psychiatry*, 44(7), 1025–1036.

Olde, E., van der Harta, O., Klebera, R. and van Sona, M. (2005). Posttraumatic stress following childbirth: a review. *Clinical Psychology Review*, 26(1), 1–16.

Olde, E., van der Hart, O., Klebera, R. J., van Son, M., Wijnen, H. and Pop, V. (2006). Peritraumatic dissociation and emotions as predictors of PTSD symptoms following childbirth. *Journal of Trauma and Dissociation*, 6(3), 125–142.

Olds, D. (1997). The prenatal/early infancy project: fifteen years later. In G. W. Albee and T. P. Gullotta (eds), *Primary Prevention Works*. London: Sage.

Olds, D. L. and Kitzman, H. (1993). Review of research on home visiting for pregnant women and parents of young children. *The Future of Children*, 3(3), 53–92.

Parr, M. (1997). A new approach to parent education. *British Journal of Midwifery*, 6, 160–165.

Sinclair, A. (2007). *0-5 How Small Children Make a Big Difference*. www.theworkfoundation.com/Assets/PDFs/early_years1.pdf.

Stern, D. (1989). *The Interpersonal World of the Infant.* London: Karnac Books.

Wampold, B. E. (2001). *The Great Psychotherapy Debate: Models, Methods and Findings.* Mahwah, NJ: Lawrence Erlbaum Associates.

Webster-Stratton, C. and Hammond, M. (1997). Treating children with early-onset conduct problems: a comparison of child and parent training interventions. *Journal of Consulting and Clinical Psychology*, 65, 93–109.

Index

Abouchaar, A. 90
Adult Attachment Interview 5
AIMH-UK (Association for Infant
    Mental Health – UK) xvi
'Aiming High for Children: Supporting the
    Family' 2
Ainsworth, M.D.S. *et al.* 4, 100
Anderson, C.J. 46
Anna Freud Centre Parent Infant Project
    (PIP) 141, 149–51
antenatal classes 52, 53, 59, 190; *see also*
    First Steps in Parenting
Armstrong, D. 124
attachment 3, 53, 193; in severe
    maternal mental illness 165–6; Strange
    Situation 4–5, 10, 100, 108–9, 109*t*
attachment: a partnership approach
    100–10; research context 101;
    Sunderland Infant Programme 8, 101–2;
    mother–infant interactions 102–4;
    reflective video feedback 100, 104–7:
    (developing mindfulness 105–6;
    acknowledging ambivalence 106;
    links to mother's own childhood 106–7;
    separation 107); training of health
    visitors 107–8; evaluation 108–9, 109*t*
attunement 3, 18, 29, 30, 53, 155, 191–2
autonomic system 43

Baby Cue cards 159
Baker, F. 94
Ballard, C.G. *et al.* 20
Bandura, A. 115
Bangladeshi community *see* black and
    minority ethnic groups
Baradon, T. *et al.* 144, 151
Barlow, J. 151, 190
Beal, J.A. 46
Beebe, B. 18, 145, 187–8

behaviour management 7, 31, 32
belief systems 134–5
Bennett, David 128
Berrington, A. *et al.* 118
Berthoud, R. *et al.* 118
Besnard, S. *et al.* 29
Bethlem Mother–Infant Rating Scale
    (BMIS) 165
Bick, E. 2–3, 78
Bion, W.R. 32
Birth to School Study (BTSS) 94–5, 96
black and minority ethnic groups 8,
    128–37; belief systems 134–5; clinical
    practice 132–4; facilitating access 129;
    family life 136–7; family support workers
    130, 132; language issues 131–2;
    psychological education groups 129–31
Blackwell, P. 17
Blake, W. xv
BMIS (Bethlem Mother–Infant Rating
    Scale) 165
bonding 48, 191
Booth, T. 176
Bowlby, J. 3, 4, 5, 9, 19, 53, 100
Bowlby, R. 9
brain development 30, 40, 91, 155, 156
Brazelton Centres 42
Brazelton, T.B. *et al.* 32, 40, 46
Brennan, A. 35–6
Britton, R. 79, 80
Bronfenbrenner, U. 115, 185
Browne, G.B. *et al.* 109
Bruschweiler-Stern, N. 46, 47
BTSS (Birth to School Study) 94–5, 96
Buchanan, A. 90

Cabinet Office 115, 117
Cardone, I.A. 47, 54
CARE-Index 102–4, 107–8, 167

CHANGE 175
Chiland, C. 79
Child and Adolescent Mental Health
  Services (CAMHS) 35
child and infant psychotherapy 3
child protection 161, 174, 177, 178, 179–80
Children's Centres 2, 19–20, 128, 129, 186
Cleaver, H. 174, 175
Cohn, J.F. 3
communication 93–4, 105, 149, 158, 168;
  see also attunement; infant massage;
  parent–infant interactions
containment 6–7, 31, 32, 105, 122, 124, 192
Cooper, P. 43, 46
Corboz-Warnery, A. *et al.* 77, 84
Cowan, C.P. 80
Cowan, P. 80
Cox, J.L. *et al.* 156
Cramer, B.G. 40, 78
Crittenden, P.M. 4, 5, 101, 103, 108, 167
Crockenberg, S. 18
cultural issues 129–30, 131, 132–3, 134, 135

D'Angelo, E.J. 165
Darmstadt, G. *et al.* 17
Datta, P. 129
Daws, D. 3
De Chateau, P. 19
Department of Health (DoH) 174
depression 131; in fathers 20, 21, 53; *see
  also* postnatal depression
Desforges, C. 90
Dex, S. 90
Disability Discrimination Act 174
Dodds, N. 108
domestic violence 81–3, 121–2, 190, 191
Douglas, H. 32, 34, 35–6
drug and alcohol abuse 190, 191, 192

Edinburgh Postnatal Depression Scale
  (EPDS) 156–7, 160
EEPP *see* European Early Promotion
  Project
Effective Provision of Pre-School
  Education (EPPE) 90
Egeland, B. 101
Elmira project *see* Nurse–Family
  Partnership (USA)
Emerson, E. *et al.* 173
emotional regulation 18, 30, 32, 40, 105–6,
  143–4
emotional support *see* First Steps in
  Parenting; Neonatal Behavioural
  Assessment Scale

emotional well-being 4
empowerment *see* Peers Early Education
  Partnership
Enabling Parents Study 95
EPDS (Edinburgh Postnatal Depression
  Scale) 156–7, 160
EPPE (Effective Provision of Pre-School
  Education) 90
Ericksson, M.F. 101
European Early Promotion Project (EEPP)
  7, 65–8; effects 66–8; *see also* Family
  Partnership Model
Evangelou, M. *et al.* 90, 95, 96

Fakhry Davids, M. 79
Family Administered Neonatal Activities
  (FANA) 47, 54
Family Nurse Partnership (FNP) 8, 117–24;
  selection of target population group
  118; training programme 119; delivery
  119–20; early learning 120–3: (aims and
  theory 120–1; expectations 122; father
  and family involvement 121–2;
  programme ethos 123; supervision
  122–3; therapeutic alliance 121);
  discussion 123–4; *see also* Nurse–
  Family Partnership (USA)
Family Partnership Model 7, 63–72;
  promotional and preventive strategies
  63–4; need for model of process 64–5;
  model 68–71, 68*f*, 69*f*, 70*f*, 71*f*;
  implications 71–2; *see also* European
  Early Promotion Project
FANA (Family Administered Neonatal
  Activities) 47, 54
Farrell-Erickson, M. 101
fathers 56–8, 59; depression 20, 21, 53;
  involvement in parenting 53, 57, 90,
  102, 106, 136, 193; Mellow Babies
  programme 159; preparation for
  parenthood 190; stress 57; *see also*
  Family Nurse Partnership; parental
  couple
Field, T. *et al.* 46, 158
First Steps in Parenting 7, 52–60;
  transition to parenthood 52–3; four-
  stage model 53–5; evaluation 55–60:
  (becoming parents 56–7; group process
  58–9; programme benefits 57–8;
  programme dissemination 59–60)
Fivaz-Depeursinge, E. 83–4
Flouri, E. 90
FNP *see* Family Nurse Partnership
foetal programming 190

Fonagy, P. *et al.* 4, 5, 79, 150, 151
Fraiberg, S. *et al.* 2, 158

Garbarino, G. *et al.* 97
Gianino, A., Jr 158
Gilkerson, L. 47, 54
Ginty, M. 34
Glover, V. 190
Goldstein-Ferber, S. *et al.* 24
Gomby, D. *et al.* 64
Green, R.J. 136
group-based working *see* First Steps in
    Parenting; Mellow Babies; Solihull
    Approach: Parenting Group
Guild of Infant and Child Massage 24n1
Gunnar, M. 19

Hall, D. 118
Hall, S. 118
Hammond, M. 193
Hannon, P. 91
hard-to-reach families 96, 102, 161
Hawthorne, J. 47
health visitors xv, 102; *see also*
    attachment: a partnership approach;
    European Early Promotion Project;
    Mellow Babies; Solihull Approach
Henwood, K.L. 90
Hipwell, A.E. *et al.* 165, 166
HIV-exposed infants 23
Hoagwood, K. 70
home learning environment (HLE) 30, 90
home visiting 2, 8, 54, 64; *see also*
    attachment: a partnership approach;
    European Early Promotion Project;
    Family Nurse Partnership; Mellow
    Babies; Nurse–Family Partnership
Hopkins, J. 18
HPA (hypothalamic-pituitary-
    adrenocortical) system 19
Huffinton, C. 124
Human Rights Act (1998) 174
Huth-Bocks, A.C. *et al.* 190

IAIM (International Association of Infant
    Massage) 17
indicated programmes 8–9; *see also*
    Mellow Babies; parent–infant
    psychotherapy; parenting with
    support; severe maternal mental illness
infant behaviour 39–41
infant-centred services 185–95;
    conceptualisation 186–8;
    'infant-centred' practitioners 194–5;

'infant-centred' services 188–94, 189*f*:
    (getting ready to welcome baby 190–1;
    ensuring optimal bonding 191; tuning
    in to baby 191–2; supporting baby's
    security and autonomy 193; setting safe
    boundaries 193–4; exploring and learning
    194); policy context 185–6
infant massage 6, 17–24, 149; case
    studies 21–2; early interactions 18;
    tactile stimulation 19; UK classes
    19–21; findings 23–4
infant mental health 2–4
interaction guidance 8
interactive repair 30, 144
internal working model 5, 53, 141, 192
International Association of Infant
    Massage (IAIM) 17
interventions 6; indicated programmes
    8–9; model of process 64–5; targeted
    programmes 7–8; universal
    programmes 6–7

Jacobsen, T. 165–6
Jennings, T. 107–8
Juffer, F. *et al.* 100, 101

Killen, K. *et al.* 109
Kirkpatrick, S. 151
Kirmayer, L.J. *et al.* 131–2, 135
Kitzman, H. 185
Kumar, R. 165

Lachmann, F.M. 18, 187–8
language issues 131–2
Laungani, P. 129
learning difficulties *see* parenting with
    support
Learning Together *see* Peers Early
    Education Partnership
Leerkes, E. 18
Lintern, J. 35
Llewellyn, G. *et al.* 174
Loshak, R. 132
Lowenhoff, C. 35

McClure, V. 17
McConnell, D. *et al.* 173
McDonough, S.C. 101
McGaw, S. *et al.* 179
McHale, J.P. 83–4
Mackinlay, E. 94
Magill-Evans, J. *et al.* 190
Main, M. 4
Martin, L. *et al.* 19

massage *see* infant massage
maternal attunement *see* attunement
Meins, E. *et al.* 5, 170
Mellow Babies 8–9, 155–62; evidence
    base 156; hard-to-reach families 161;
    programme 156–9; evaluation 159–61
Mellow Parenting 155, 159, 160–1
mental illness *see* severe maternal mental
    illness
mentalisation 5–6, 143, 192
Milford, R. *et al.* 36
Miller, L.J. 165–6
mind-mindedness 5–6, 53
mirroring 192
Moran, P. *et al.* 90
mother–child interactions *see* parent–infant
    interactions
mothers-in-law 84, 122, 136
motor system 43–4
Murray, L. 43, 46
music 93–4

Naslund, B. *et al.* 165
National Health Service (NHS) 19, 59,
    117–18
NBO (Newborn Behavioural
    Observations) 46
NCAST 159
Neonatal Behavioural Assessment Scale
    (NBAS) 7, 39–48; Brazelton Centres
    42; infant behaviour 39–41; NBAS
    scale 40, 42; newborn's developmental
    agenda 42–5; research 45–6; trainees
    46–7; *see also* Family Administered
    Neonatal Activities; Newborn
    Behavioural Observations
neonatal intensive care units (NICUs) 23, 48
neuro-developmental science 3
Newborn Behavioural Observations
    (NBO) 46
newborn's developmental agenda 42–5;
    autonomic system 43; motor system
    43–4; social interactive system 44–5;
    state system 44; stimulation 45
Newbury, J. 151
NHS *see* National Health Service
NICE guidelines 169
Nicholson, D. 174, 175
NICUs (neonatal intensive care units) 23, 48
Nugent, J.K. *et al.* 40, 46, 47
Nurse–Family Partnership (USA):
    background 115–16; evidentiary
    foundations 116–17; programme model
    116; *see also* Family Nurse Partnership

object relations theory 79–80, 132
O'Connor, T. 190
Olde, E. *et al.* 191
Olds, D.L. *et al.* 115, 116, 117, 185
Onozawa, K. *et al.* 24
Open College Network (OCN) 95
ORIM framework 91, 96
OXPIP (Oxford Parent Infant Project) 141,
    149, 151

Palacio-Espasa, F. 78
Parent Infant Project *see* OXPIP; PIP
parental couple 7, 77–85; case study 80–3;
    co-parenting and the
    family 83–4; importance of the couple
    77–83
parent–infant interactions 3, 18, 29, 30,
    102–4
parent–infant psychotherapy 2, 8, 141–51;
    aims 141; Anna Freud Centre Parent
    Infant Project 141, 149–51; clinical
    approach 144–9; Oxford Parent Infant
    Project 141, 149, 151; theoretical model
    142–4; evaluation 150–1; *see also*
    parental couple
parent–infant relationship 6, 39, 191; *see
    also* First Steps in Parenting; Mellow
    Babies; Neonatal Behavioural
    Assessment Scale; parent–infant
    interactions; parent–infant
    psychotherapy
parenting skills *see* First Steps in
    Parenting; Peers Early Education
    Partnership
parenting with support 9, 173–81; child
    protection 174, 177, 178, 179–80;
    concept 176–8; information 178; learning
    difficulties 173; needs awareness 177;
    parenting groups 179; policy context 174;
    practical support 179; supporting families
    175–6
Parents in Partnership–Parent Infant
    Network (PIPPIN) 59, 60
Parke, R.D. 84
Parker, S. *et al.* 46
Parr, M. 54, 55, 56–9
Partners in Parenting Education (PIPE) 118
Parvin, A. *et al.* 131, 134, 136
Pawl, J. 72
Peers Early Education Partnership (PEEP)
    7–8, 89–97; aims 91;
    beginnings 89–90; curriculum 92–3;
    Learning Together 90–1; ORIM
    framework 91, 96; principles 92; use

of music 93–4; evaluation 94–5; future 96–7
perinatal home visiting *see* Family Nurse Partnership; Nurse–Family Partnership
Perry, B.D. 30
Phares, V. 77
PIP (Anna Freud Centre Parent Infant Project) 141, 149–51
PIPE (Partners in Parenting Education) 118
PIPPIN (Parents in Partnership–Parent Infant Network) 59, 60
policy context 1–2, 185–6
postnatal depression: and baby's motor tone 43; and child development 53, 164–5; cultural issues 129–30, 131, 133, 134, 135; and interventions 21, 24, 57, 192; *see also* Mellow Babies; severe maternal mental illness
posttraumatic stress disorder (PTSD) 191
Prechtl, H.F.R. 44
pregnancy 52–3, 190–1; *see also* Family Nurse Partnership
preterm infants 23, 48
Procter, J. 90
psychosocial problems *see* black and minority ethnic groups; Family Partnership Model

Quinton, D. 78

Rauh, V. *et al.* 46
readiness to interact signals 41
reciprocity 7, 31, 32, 34, 192
refugees 132–4
regulatory behaviours 41
Reid, S. 29
representational models 5, 53, 141, 192
representations of interaction (RIG) 18, 187
Riordan, D. *et al.* 165
Roberts, R. 89, 91, 93
Rollnick, S. *et al.* 122
Room to Play 96
Rutter, M. 78

safety 193–4
Sawin, D. 46
Schore, A. 19
Scottish Executive 174
Service Utility Inventory 109
severe maternal mental illness (SMI) 9, 164–70, 192; and child development 164–5; Mother and Baby Unit 166–8; and mother–infant interaction 165–6; effectiveness of interventions 168–9

siblings 84
singing to babies 94
Slade, A. *et al.* 101
sleep deprivation 24
SMI *see* severe maternal mental illness
Snell, E.B. 101
Snellen, M. *et al.* 165
social exclusion *see* Family Nurse Partnership
social interactive system 44–5
Solihull Approach 6–7, 29–36; case studies 33–4; model 31–2; Parenting Group 32, 36; research context 30–1; training 32–3; evaluation 34–6
Solomon, J. 4
Sroufe, L.A. 10
state system 44
Stern, D. 3, 18, 46, 53, 78, 84, 187
stimulation 45
Strange Situation 4–5, 10, 100, 108–9, 109*t*
Street, A. 91, 93, 94
stress 131; fathers 57; infants 19, 24, 42; mothers 52–3, 129–30, 131, 191
Sunderland Infant Programme 8, 101–2
Sure Start 1–2, 19, 20, 42, 59, 186
Svanberg, P.O. 108
Sylva, K. *et al.* 90, 95

Tableman, B. 101
Target, M. 79
targeted programmes 7–8; *see also* attachment: a partnership approach; black and minority ethnic groups; Family Nurse Partnership; parental couple; Peers Early Education Partnership
Tarleton, B. *et al.* 175, 176
Tavistock Clinic 3
tone 43
'too good' mothering 18
touch *see* infant massage
Tower Hamlets *see* black and minority ethnic groups
Trainor, L.J. *et al.* 94
Trehub, S.E. 94
Trevarthen, C. 3, 94
Tronick, E.Z. 3, 30–1, 144, 158
turn taking 3, 192

UN Convention on the Rights of the Child (UNCRC) 186
Underdown, A. *et al.* 20, 24, 190
universal programmes 6–7; *see also* Family Partnership Model; First Steps in

Parenting; infant massage;
Neonatal Behavioural Assessment
Scale; Solihull Approach

Vickers, A. *et al.* 23
video feedback 100, 101, 151n, 158; *see
also* attachment: a partnership approach;
severe maternal mental illness
Vygotsky, L.S. 91

Walters, J. 77, 78–9
Wan, M.W. *et al.* 165
Ward, K. 90

Weatherston, D. 101
Webster-Stratton, C. 193
Weinberg, M.K. 14
Wels, P.M.A. 100
Werner, P.D. 136
Whitehead, R. 35
Widmayer, S. 46
Winnicott, D.M. 146
Winnicott, D.W. 106, 189
withdrawal signals 41
Wittgenstein, L. 29
Wolff, P.H. 42, 44
Working Together with Parents 177